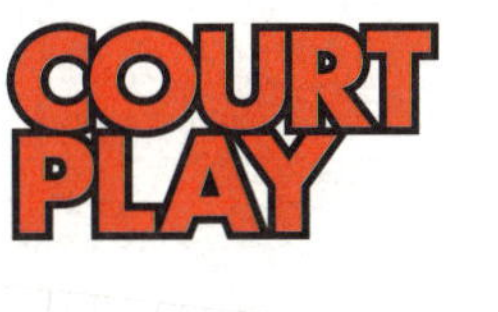

COURT
PLAY

AF371294

This book is published on the occasion of

COURTPLAY
Conceived by Mohamed Almusibli and Ivan Cheng

Presented and realised by Hartwig Art Foundation at the Oude Rechtbank, Parnassusweg 220, Amsterdam, 12 and 13 January 2024.
ALIAS (Turbo Moniker) was a three-act play which included text contributions by Sophia Al-Maria, Josefin Arnell, Ed Atkins, Felix Bernstein, Victoria Colmegna, Claire Fontaine, Robert Glück & Jocelyn Saidenberg, Annie Goodner, Calla Henkel & Max Pitegoff, Shiv Kotecha, Huw Lemmey, Nour Mobarak, Becket MWN, Ariana Reines, Tai Shani, Ryan Trecartin, Angharad Williams. Sequenced and staged by Ivan Cheng and interpreted through the atrium spaces by Soraya Lutangu Bonaventure, Ivan Cheng, Mamı Kang, Geo Wyex, wearing garments by Good & Bad (Marina M. Kolushova, Victor Stuhlmann, Ossi Lehtonen). Arvo Leo accompanied the full performance on video camera, and for a period during each act, Maarten Nauw took photographs, and Aloys Oosterwijk made courtroom sketches, subsequently producing sepia ink drawings for this publication.

Presented through the building were works by Özgür Kar, Brianna Leatherbury, Mire Lee, Sands Murray-Wassink, Jay Tan, aqui Thami, SoiL Thornton, Marina Xenofontos. A courtroom upstairs was transformed into a screening room for a looped video programme of works by Noor Abed, Sophia Al-Maria, Peng Zuqiang, Ryan Trecartin. Food was served from Bakkerij Mater, Comfort Ball, Craft Coffee & Pastry, Sjoerds Cheese, Soup en Zo.

A Conversation between Ivan Cheng and Mohamed Almusibli

Feb 14, 2024 5:40pm

MOHAMED ALMUSIBLI   Hi, how are you?

IVAN CHENG   Hey, how's it going? Um, how's your language school?

MOHAMED ALMUSIBLI   It's good. Third day out of ten.

IVAN CHENG   Okay, wow, the countdown begins to starting the job right?

MOHAMED ALMUSIBLI   Yeah [speaks German]

IVAN CHENG   Oh my god lol. You have such a charming accent.

MOHAMED ALMUSIBLI   [laughs] How are you?

IVAN CHENG   I think I'm okay. Um, yeah, fine. I just gave rehearsal notes for a show I'll host at the new Bologna this Sunday, by Cami Lynch and Inka Hilsenbek. They're trying out a name as a duo. Solution Hierarchy.

MOHAMED ALMUSIBLI   Yeah, I guess it's never easy to find a good name? We could talk about our name.

IVAN CHENG   Sure. Yup. Courtplay.

MOHAMED ALMUSIBLI   Yeah. I mean, it's true that … like, we were both invited to curate this event together, without us really having worked together before or

IVAN CHENG   or barely knowing each other as well.

MOHAMED ALMUSIBLI   Yeah. Barely knowing each other. And I think it was funny, because during the conversations and the research I did with Hartwig I had mentioned you and Bologna. I mentioned you as someone to talk with because you had been running the project space upstairs from where they wanted to have an event, and you were already doing the work that they literally wanted to do – connecting with the local scene through a space. And I think then they reached out to you and came up with this idea of us working together. What was interesting for me was the format that was proposed to us – 24 hours. I was curious how we could also take the core of the space that you've been running – including the performative aspects of it; the event.

IVAN CHENG   Mhm

MOHAMED ALMUSIBLI   And so naturally our research went directly to think about performances and everything. But with our name, it came back to the attitude we quickly agreed on, of centring artistic practice and keeping a sense of lightness within this brutal building. The play on words was with the band Coldplay.

IVAN CHENG   The stadium pop rockers – ubiquitous, reviled, unavoidable? – that we gradually moved away from referencing. But they really were a helpful cornerstone for us – thinking about popular culture or fiction as a way for us to work in this former court, with its ghosts of jurisdiction. The necessity for hooks, scale, universality, but also authenticity. That was related to our coming together.

MOHAMED ALMUSIBLI   The courthouse also had the specificity of being a construction site, including that our event date and spaces got pushed back as well.

IVAN CHENG   With our first timeline, we didn't necessarily have time to start conversations with contributors about site specificity on the level of commissioning work. We turned to practices in the city that we had a continuity with, conversations we could continue. We approached the space by thinking about a courtroom day – within that 'theatre', if you choose or are permitted to enter, you may see sequences of unrelated cases. The hearings generally have two opposing parties presenting evidence or argument. That 'theatre' purports to serve society, but justice doesn't always prevail.

MOHAMED ALMUSIBLI   Yep. Then I remember that during my visit to Amsterdam, we were working on the project at your place and went for a walk in the rain to get a cake and …

IVAN CHENG   Oh to Holtkamp with your precious umbrella.

MOHAMED ALMUSIBLI   Yeah, and on the way back from the shop, or was it on our way there, we were talking about the complications of the festival as a model, and having established we wanted to do an *event* instead, you were questioning 'what makes it special'.

IVAN CHENG   I think I raised the semiotext(e) Chance Event, with rooms of artists' installations and Baudrillard in a gold lamé coat performing a lecture with members of Destroy All Monsters all in a casino in Nevada. The idea of the mythic event and artists' work appearing almost beside their own practices was interesting to both of us.

MOHAMED ALMUSIBLI   Exactly. That's when we started to propose collaborations. Or bringing people together into like one bag, let's say. Yeah. The inventiveness of it or taking a different role as organisers and trying to instead of cut and paste, bring things together to synthesise into something else. A place where we shared a lot of references was in our reading of writers.

IVAN CHENG   Thus our framework for invitations. We were interested in the court and interested in entertainment, and how to frame the function of what the spectator or the witness might be in these spaces. Inviting them to depart from procedural dramas into the lurid and amplified spaces of ethics, beliefs, cruelty brought to account.

MOHAMED ALMUSIBLI   You were insistent from the beginning that you'd organise and stage the contributions. This was somewhat to do with the timeline, right? The contributors had around a month from the moment we made invitations to respond, and then around Christmas you began structuring the pieces. I also saw you asking the contributors for additional things that you wanted. Other texts, music and then permission to break up the texts into parts and performers.

IVAN CHENG   Right. Imagining the performers.

MOHAMED ALMUSIBLI   The ensemble that grew out of conversations for an earlier line-up where we had structured the 24 hours through a series of hosts, giving something like tours within the space.

IVAN CHENG   Yup. I knew the performers besides myself – Mami Kang, Soraya Lutangu Bonaventure, Geo Wyex – as strong makers, with distinct strengths as performers. None of us had worked together like this before; I tried to set a style and dictated many of the tempi by pre-recording all the texts for them to have in their ears. That's how they performed the texts – in-ear relay of my reading, all except for Soraya doing the French bit because what I proposed was a bit too wild as a non-speaker. We had invited stylistic inconsistency from our contributors, which gave good textural variation. I think more than a performance, I was guided by the idea of staging a hearing. The audience was pretty much always hearing my reading of the texts, filtered through the bodies of the performers. Or seeing us read off paper. We had a super short rehearsal period – around two full days and a few prep meetings – so the palette for staging the texts was also reliant on the performers just trusting the structure and running with it.

I wish I had more time to work on the transitions between scenes. They were fragile moments, mostly because the staging was always aiming to move across the levels of the court, connecting things with spotlights and amplification, showing and hiding. We moved up and down stairs a lot, so sometimes we got held up in the wrong place. We also started twice cos of that fire alarm that went on for minutes just after I began the first monologue, presumably triggered by haze … We were performing these special and different bits of text, almost as testimony, in front of an audience, and suddenly almost failing it, pushing through, and maintaining our pattern of adjournments and recesses in the pauses.

MOHAMED ALMUSIBLI   I think the pauses were much less fraught from my position. A priority for me was how to make people feel comfortable in that space, which was so cold in early January. Generous in comfort to the public against or alongside generosity to the artists, and, I don't know, on the second day, some visitors and artists arrived at 7am and left at 6pm when it closed; I was quite happy to see and realise that people really stayed the whole day. I think having food for the visitors helped, but also that there were options of activities present, like going to watch the marathons of videos in the kino room, or having a moment to chat by the bar, or following the performance that was going on, or even going to aqui Thami's room and taking part in the conversation around the zine that she was making. These moments created small bubbles that punctuated viewership of the performance. And I think that was, in that sense it was successful, the space around the texts.

IVAN CHENG Oh good. Haha. In dealing with the language my priority was leaving space for the ambient. Like, incantation in play with the installed works. Then the implied relationships or tensions between the written texts and their presentation. We set up a system that was like a clock, aligned also with Brianna Leatherbury's installation that misted the atrium with the scent of synthetic sweat every hour. It's also interesting, to me at least, that even though readers of this book might assume that the text – the language or the voice might seem to take primacy – the long format and diffuse audience meant selective hearing or partial comprehension dissolved moments, needing patchy conclusion from the outside. Is it that the audience becomes a jury of sorts?

MOHAMED ALMUSIBLI [long pause] No. But for me, the way I perceived it is, um, you know when trials are televised?

IVAN CHENG Mm

MOHAMED ALMUSIBLI It felt as though people were, like, watching a trial, but a trial through a screen, and from their homes. Except that this home was also the place where the trial was.

IVAN CHENG Sure

MOHAMED ALMUSIBLI But there was always a distance. The audience was never a part of the play. They were never meant, to feel like they were …

IVAN CHENG Participating?

MOHAMED ALMUSIBLI   … background. Not participating in any sort of way. So it felt to me that there were two different spaces going on at the same time, almost like two dimensions. They kind of pushed each other, but they never meshed completely. It's quite interesting in a way of thinking about immersiveness. I mean, we've seen a lot of immersive installations, immersive exhibitions, but like this was a sort of immersive performance-play.

IVAN CHENG   Good! Maybe we feigned the objectivity of the audience. During rehearsal and pep talks, I kept trying to emphasise to the performers that we were trying to maintain our network of relations, whether that was between how we were watching each other, listening to each other, manipulating the lights, lighting each other, lighting the space. A kinda closed network vectoring between the levels and floors, trying to avoid the space becoming neutralised or naturalised by the performance into a backdrop. Trying to draw a fourth wall in the space between levels, and continually shatter it through the flickering through characters, the presence of the documenting camera. I think the dimensional difference you describe is apt.

MOHAMED ALMUSIBLI   Yeah, I had been in my head a lot about this idea of navigation and how people navigate in space and what ways to do it. But I think in the end everything seemed to come together quite organically. Some elements and materials that were really successful in that sense were these big theatre lights you put in the space, also functioning like architecture. They were kind of defining spaces and rooms, or redefining them, and they were kind of like giving but influencing a sort of path.

IVAN CHENG   Sure. Yeah, I love follow spotlights. Also cos they can reveal a clumsy technical operation, as you slide the iris focus and change the colour and intensity. Um, in your process of thinking through the program, how interwoven did you want the exhibition, the screenings and the performance to feel with the viewer?

MOHAMED ALMUSIBLI   You know, I think it's funny, but some visitors that I spoke with who came on Friday night and then back on Saturday told me that when they first arrived, it kind of just made more sense to see and to encounter the artworks and installations once they already felt inside the play, you know, once they were invested in following the play and it kind of like just tied things together. We didn't think about artworks or artists through the content of the play either, almost the opposite. But it felt good that once people were invested in the play, they felt they understood our choices of artworks.

IVAN CHENG   Sure.

MOHAMED ALMUSIBLI   Which perhaps I still haven't, but it's good that people did.

IVAN CHENG   Haha. Eep. I felt like it was tacitly agreed between us – that we wanted to give each contribution its own defined space, and then the boundaries of the work would become more interesting. Arvo Leo, who pretty much performed alongside us the whole duration, watching through a handheld camera, asked me why the staging didn't encroach on different rooms with other installations? Like, why it remained persistently in these 'public' spaces of atriums, corridors and balconies, rather than entering some of the courtrooms or some of the side rooms in which we installed work? For me, the answer was first practical: sound amplification and legibility of text, and that I wanted the audience to be able to witness the action from a distance. But the building is also at a transitional stage – we invited people into a building that's about to undergo renovation – it's not yet fit to function as a museum. We revealed all the infrastructure we brought in. Separations are important – we began with the restrictions of where people can and cannot travel. It felt important to imply the maintenance of separation. Former office spaces dictate a certain type of interaction. Former courtrooms dictate another type of interaction. That the play would continuously sprawl and dart through in these foyer and atrium spaces or move onto the stairs …

MOHAMED ALMUSIBLI   The only room you entered was that telephone booth.

IVAN CHENG   Yeah. And the elevators at the end (laughs) where it was not anticipated that the sound would get cut off. But I finished the video edit, by the way!

MOHAMED ALMUSIBLI   Oh you did? I didn't understand that you were going to do it.

IVAN CHENG   Yeah, of course I'm going to do the edit. I know the whole matrix of material and the attempt of the camera.

MOHAMED ALMUSIBLI   Mm. Good. I really don't want this book to be like a sort of documentation per se. Let's transcribe this conversation and edit it.

IVAN CHENG   Yeah, I also want to emphasise the extraordinary contributions of the performers and what they brought to the performance. It really was us meeting for the first time, so I think you saw a conscious listening and occasional edginess of unfamiliarity. We first met as a full group only three days before the performance, coming from different disciplines to face this task. We're a similar generation but all come from different places in the world, now living in these Randstad cities. A lot of the texts that we were interpreting were by authors or voices that were all the different experiences of them, all coming from a different place. So the question of embodiment in performance is an interesting one to trace.

And I also need to mention the costume, or the clothes, which Good & Bad brought and styled on us, all of us going to this little room on the first floor where the garment steamer made the room cosy. They offered the whole performance this kind of visual cohesion and a kind of like, strange collaged-ness of what was going on.

MOHAMED ALMUSIBLI   Yes we can use this space to do that.

IVAN CHENG   Yeah. Great. Is there anything else?

MOHAMED ALMUSIBLI   No. I have to watch half an hour of the news in German and then talk about it with my class.

IVAN CHENG   Oh my god, it starts now?

MOHAMED ALMUSIBLI   Hm in 10 minutes.

IVAN CHENG   How many people in the class?

MOHAMED ALMUSIBLI   Three. It's me, and a father and his son. Teenage son.

IVAN CHENG   Cool, I think. Why are they learning German?

MOHAMED ALMUSIBLI   Because the teenage son loves Germany. He wants to study German at uni and the father is retired and he's like, okay, I'll do it with my son.

IVAN CHENG   That's sweet, I guess. Love is important.

ALIAS (Turbo Moniker)

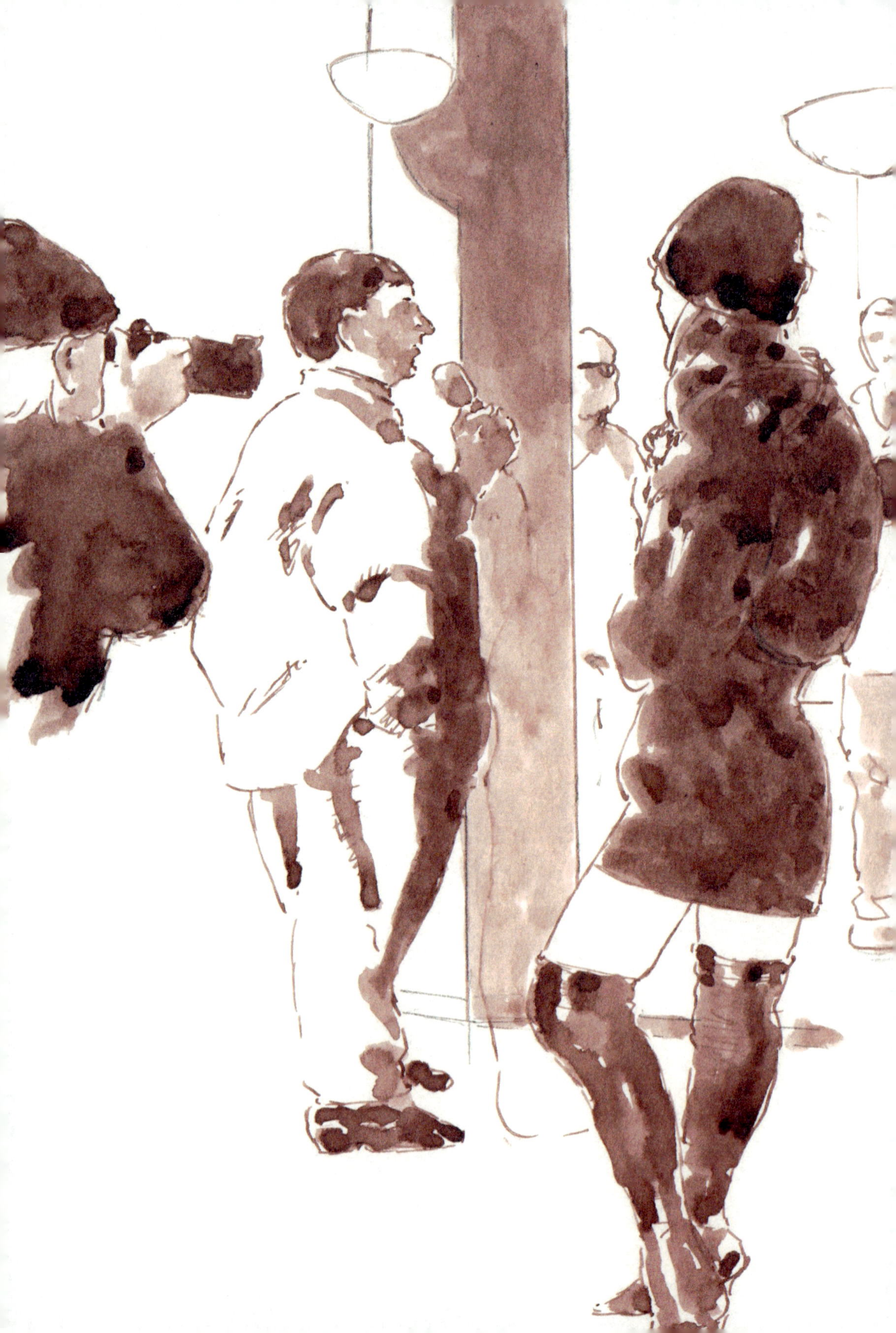

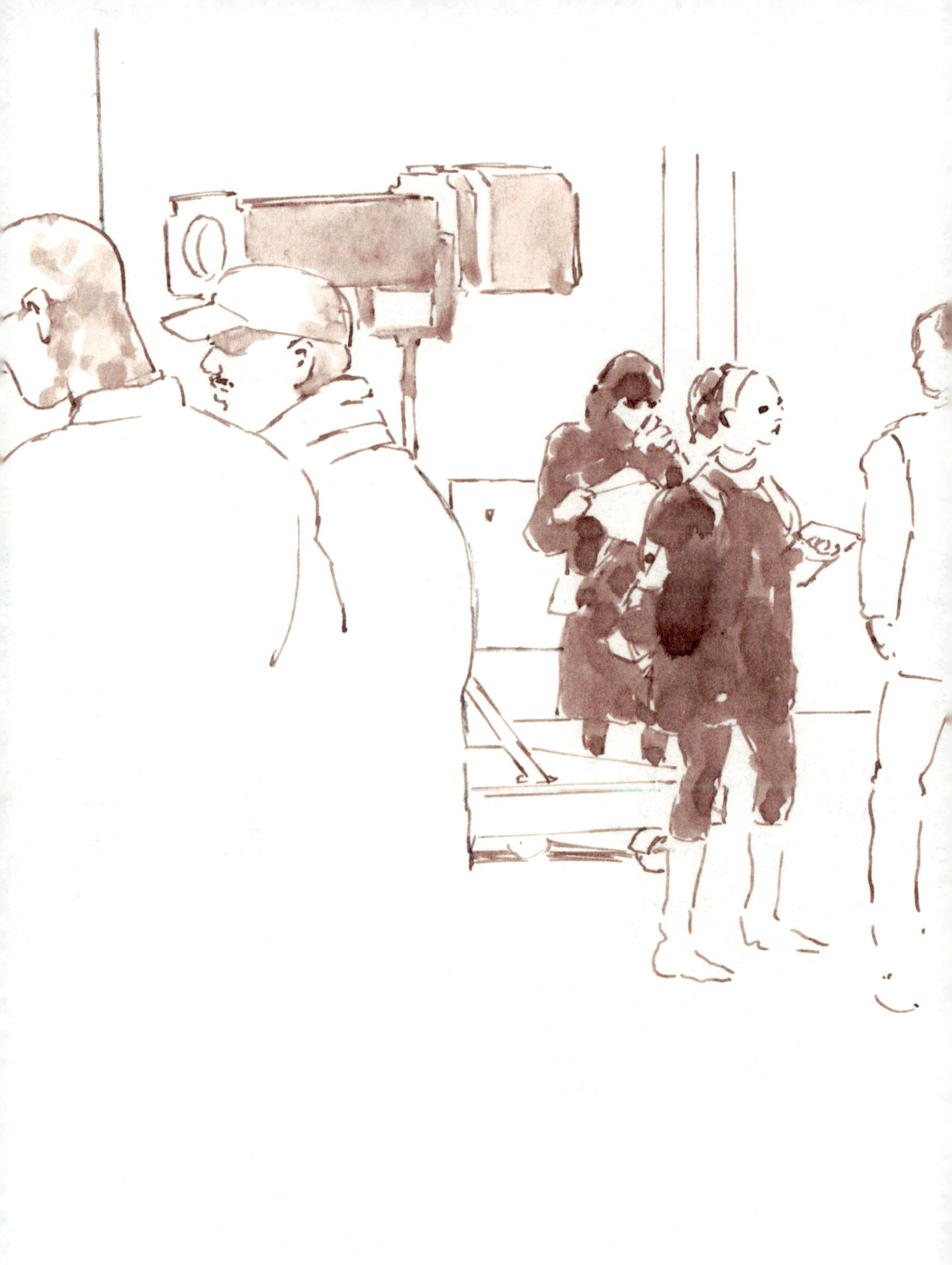

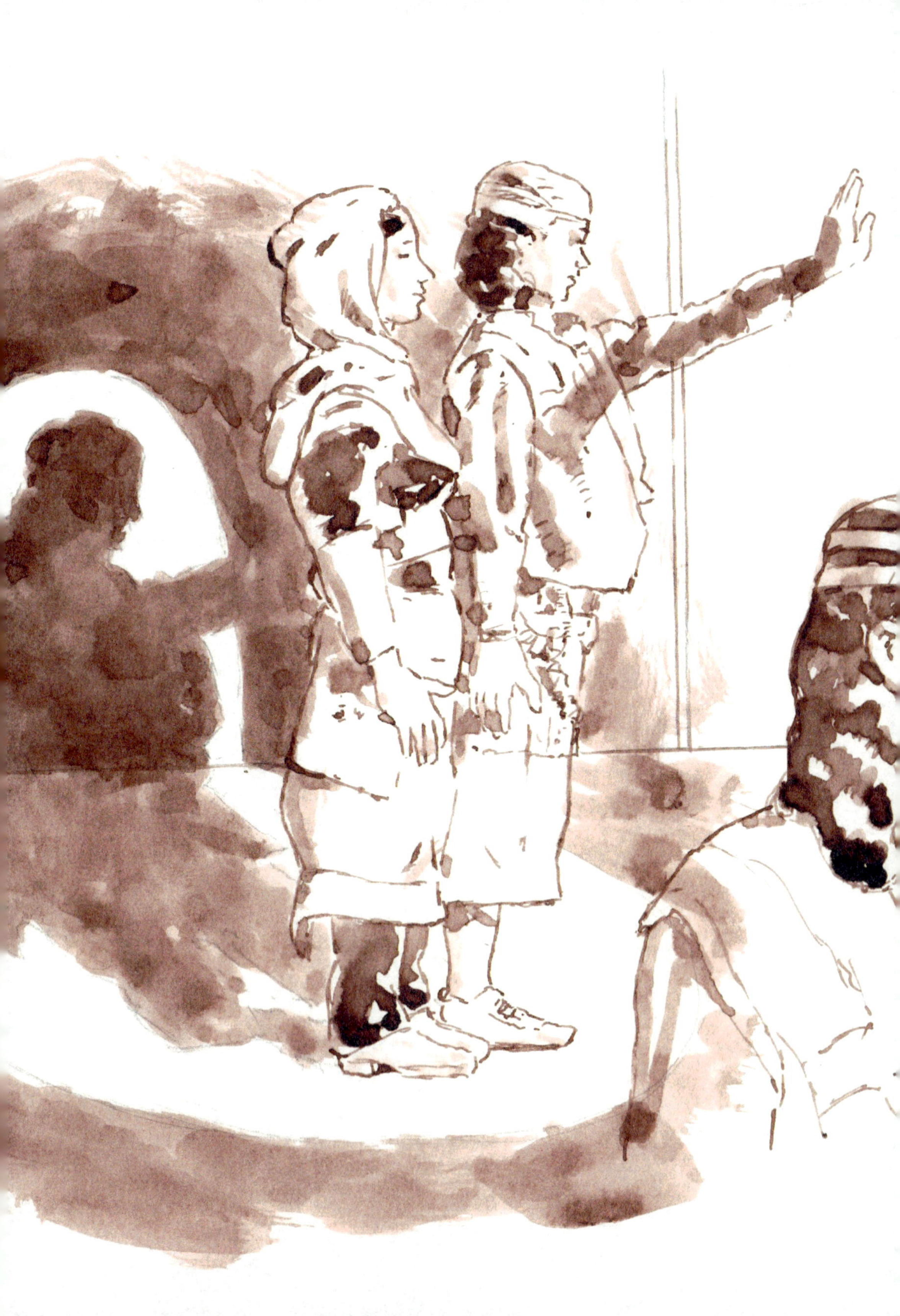

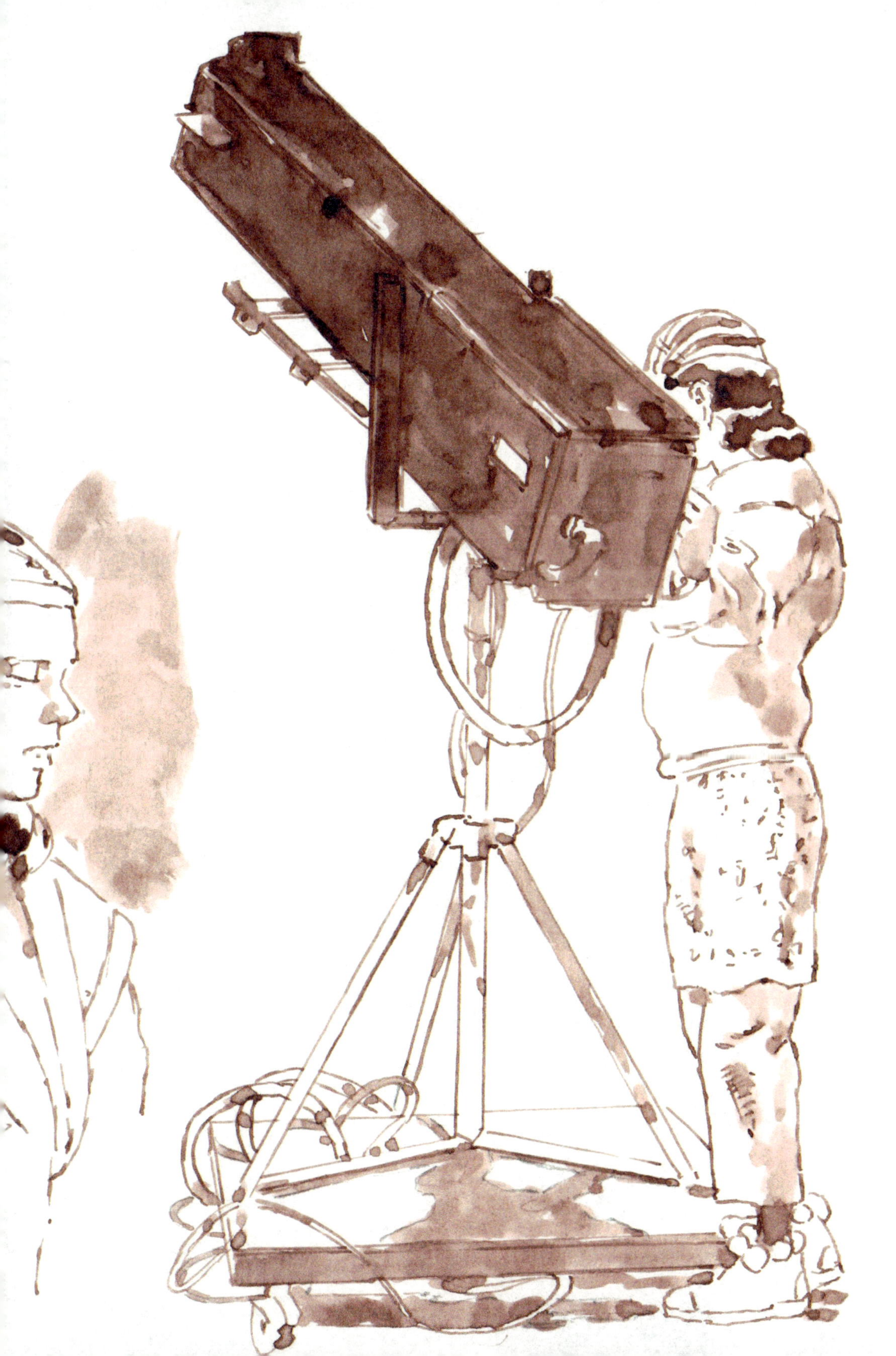

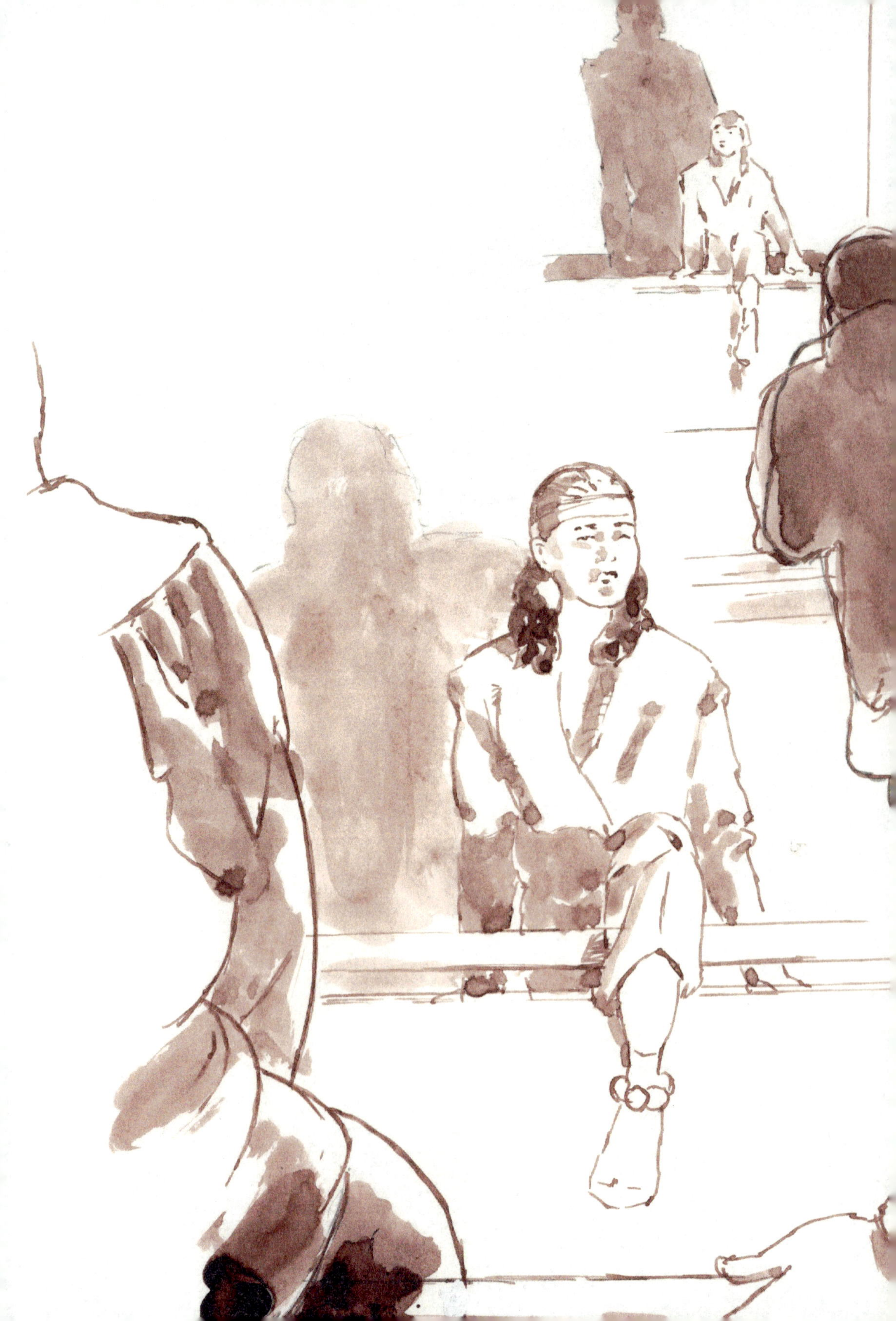

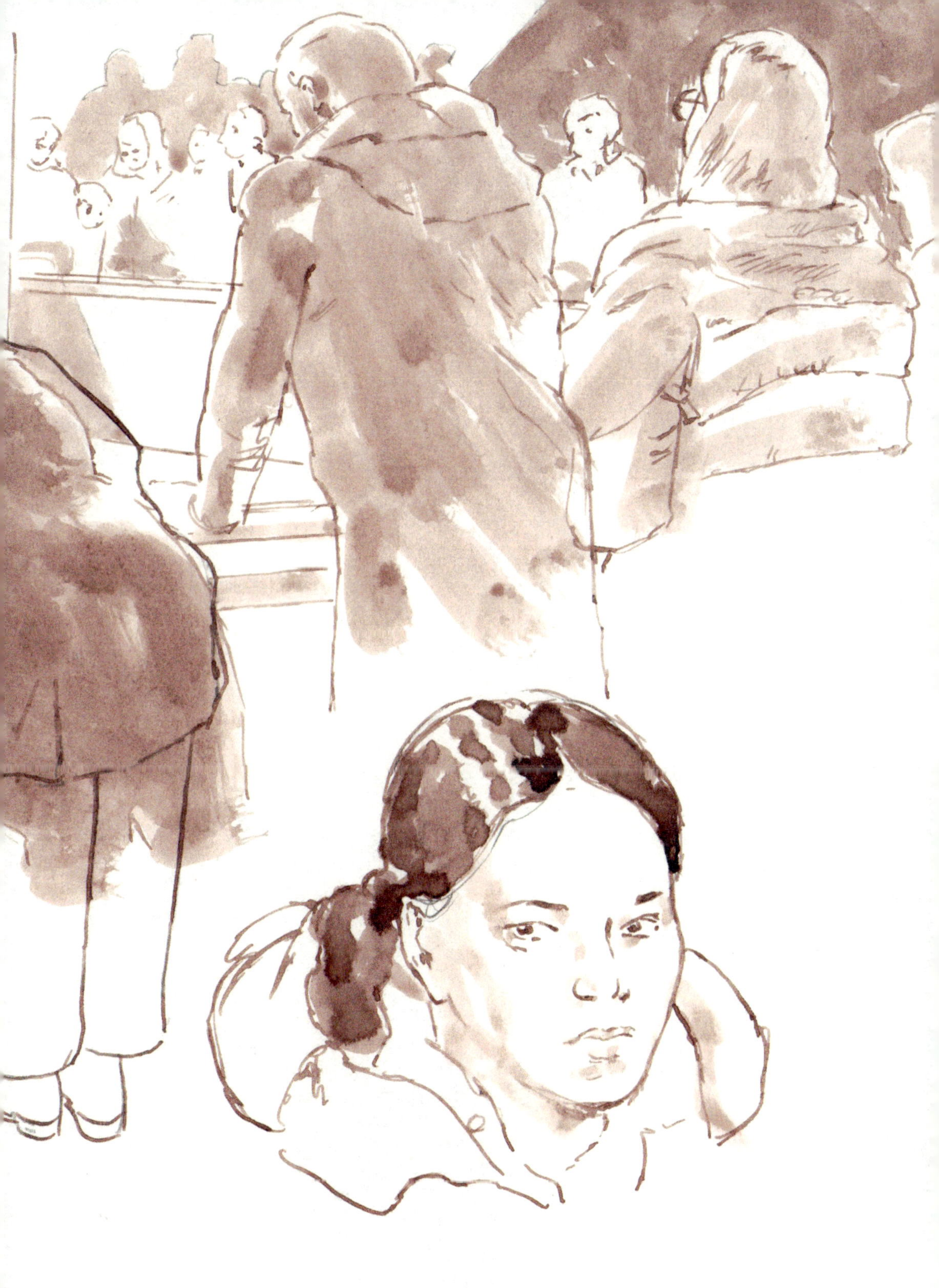
20.30 u Instituting

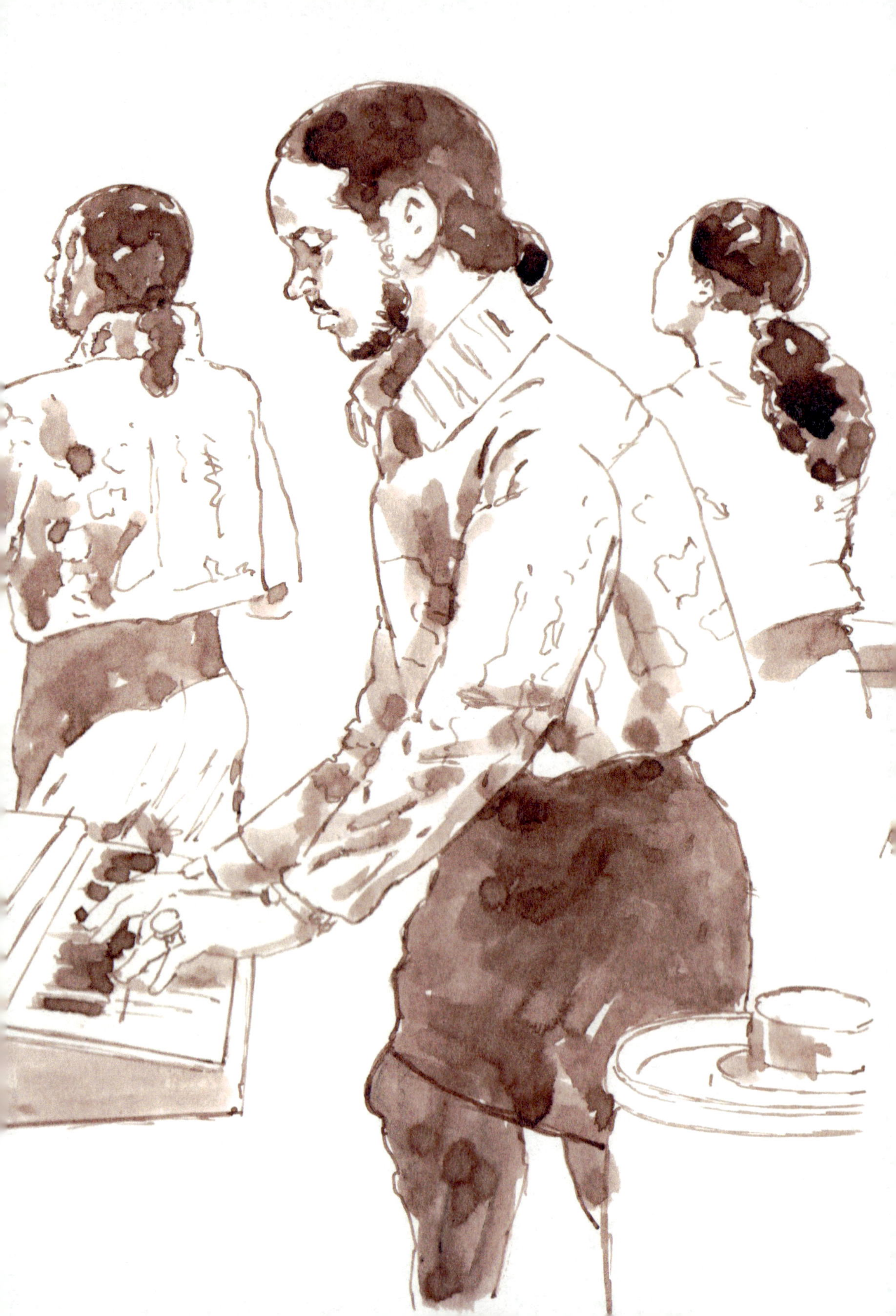

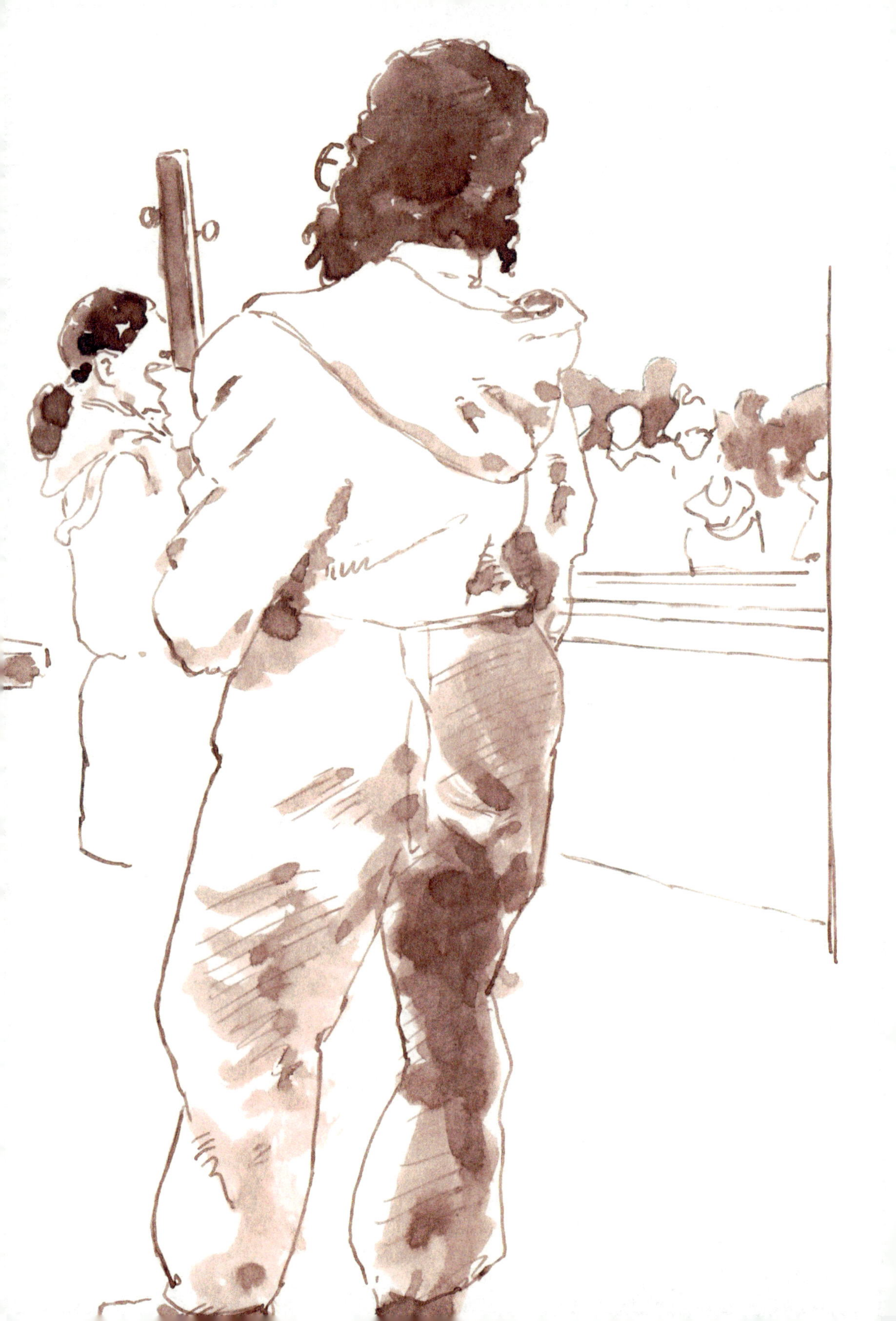

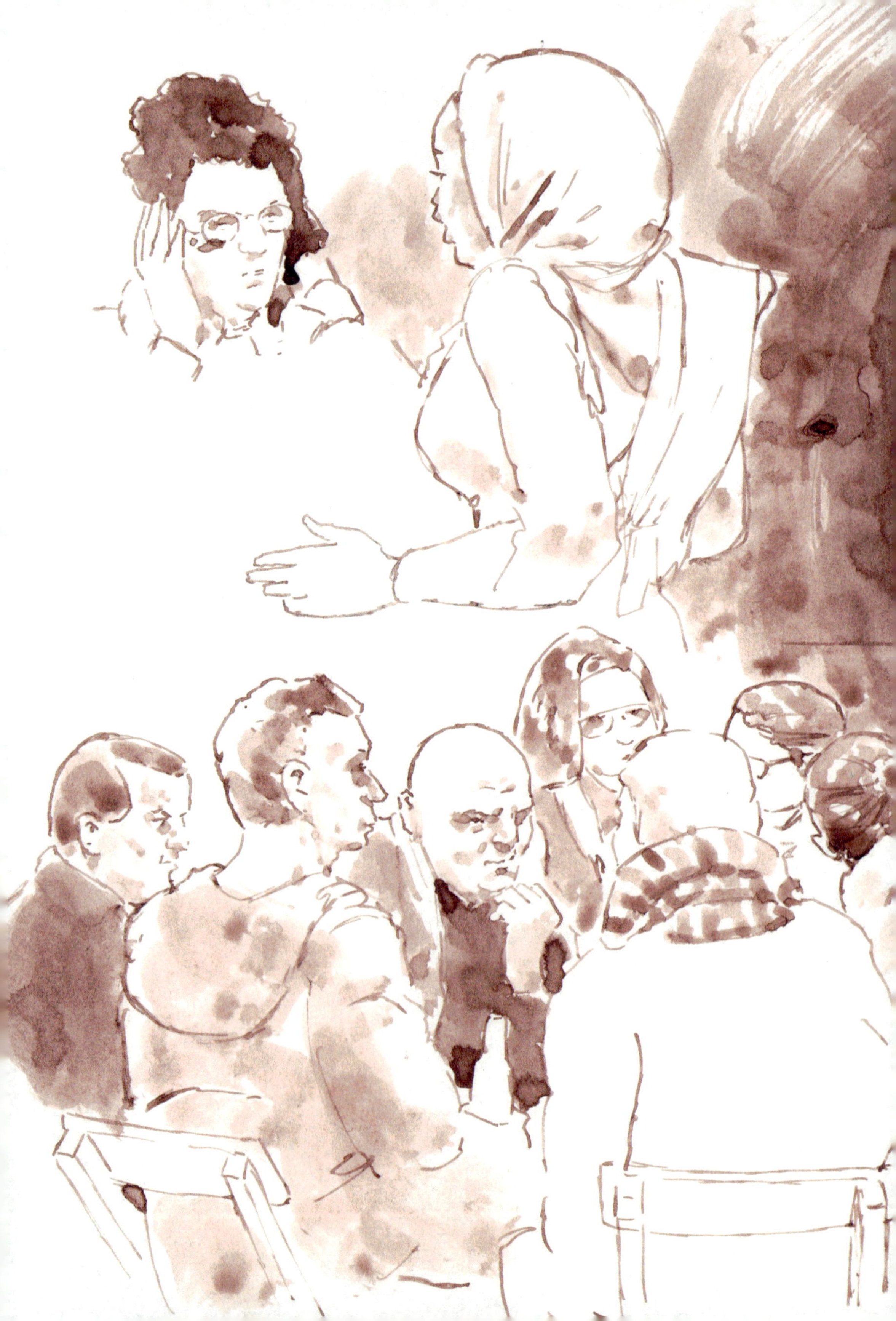

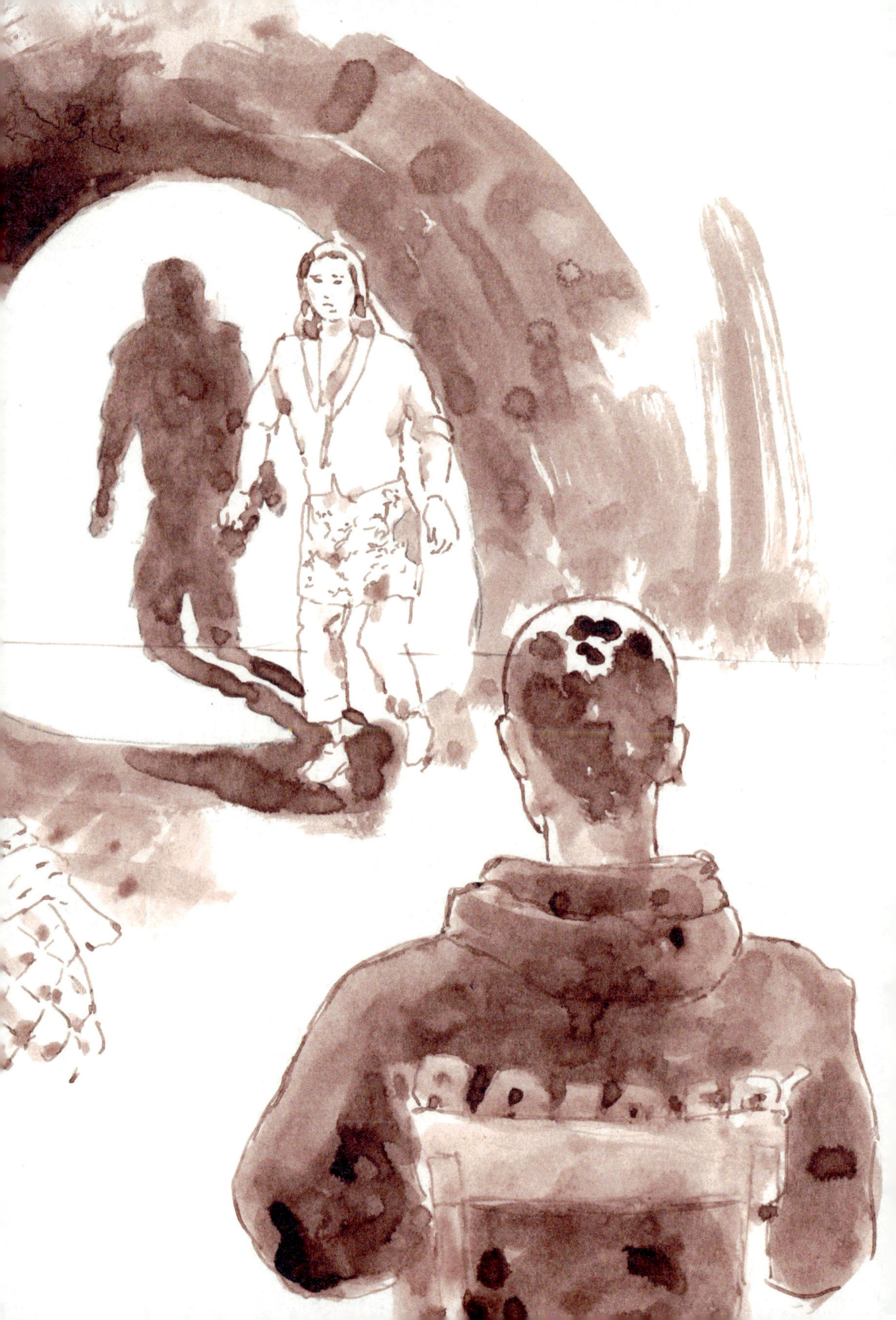

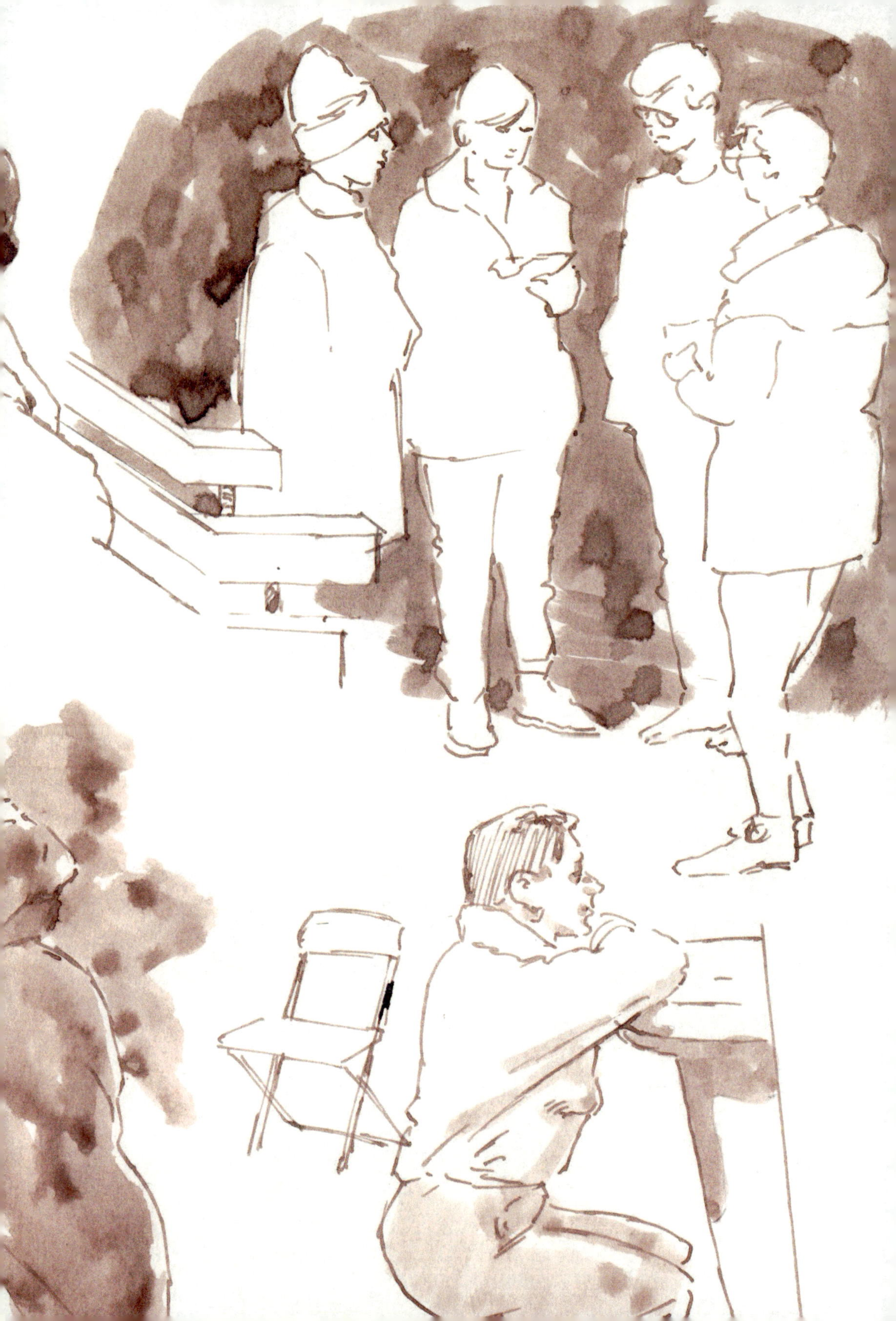

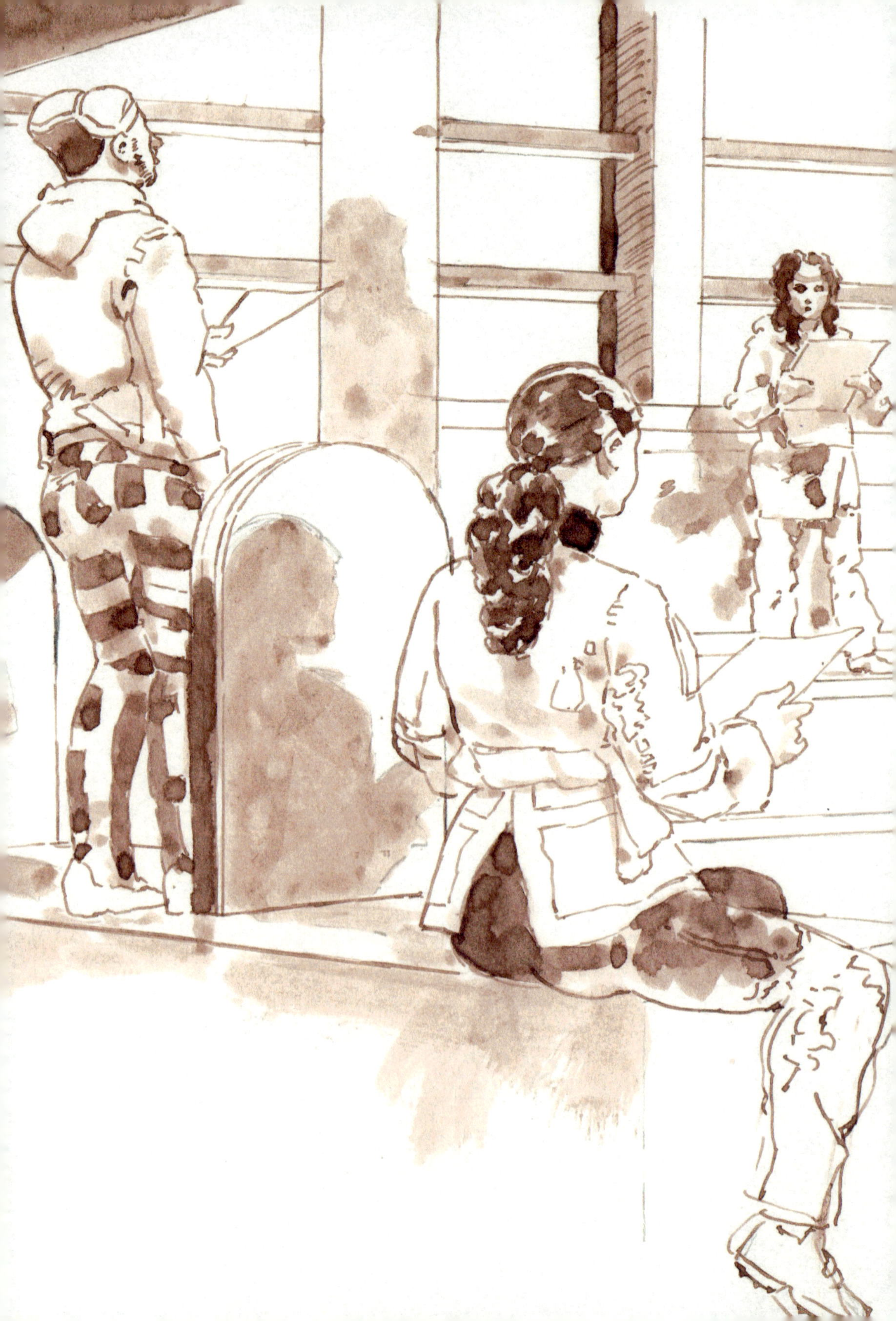

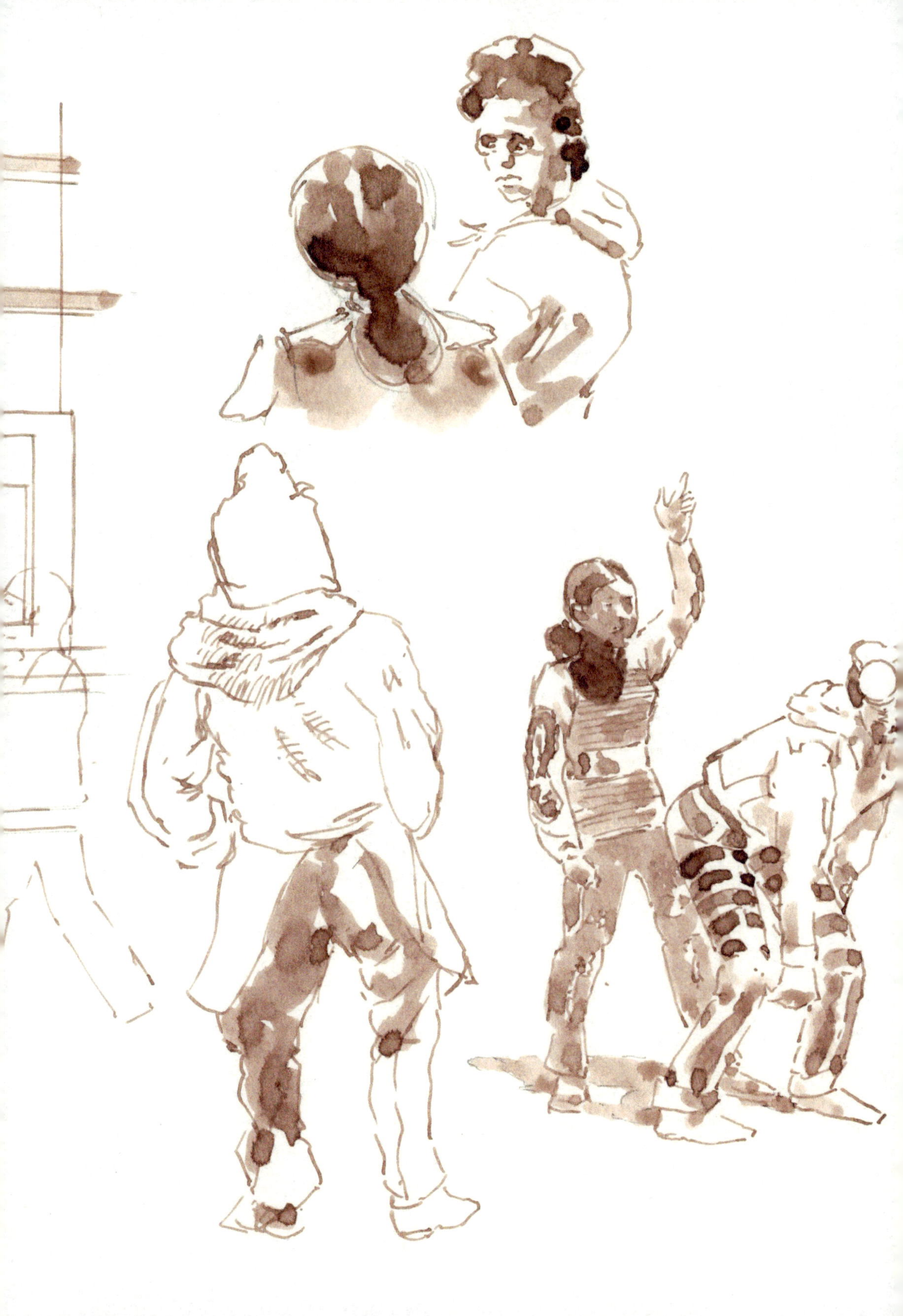

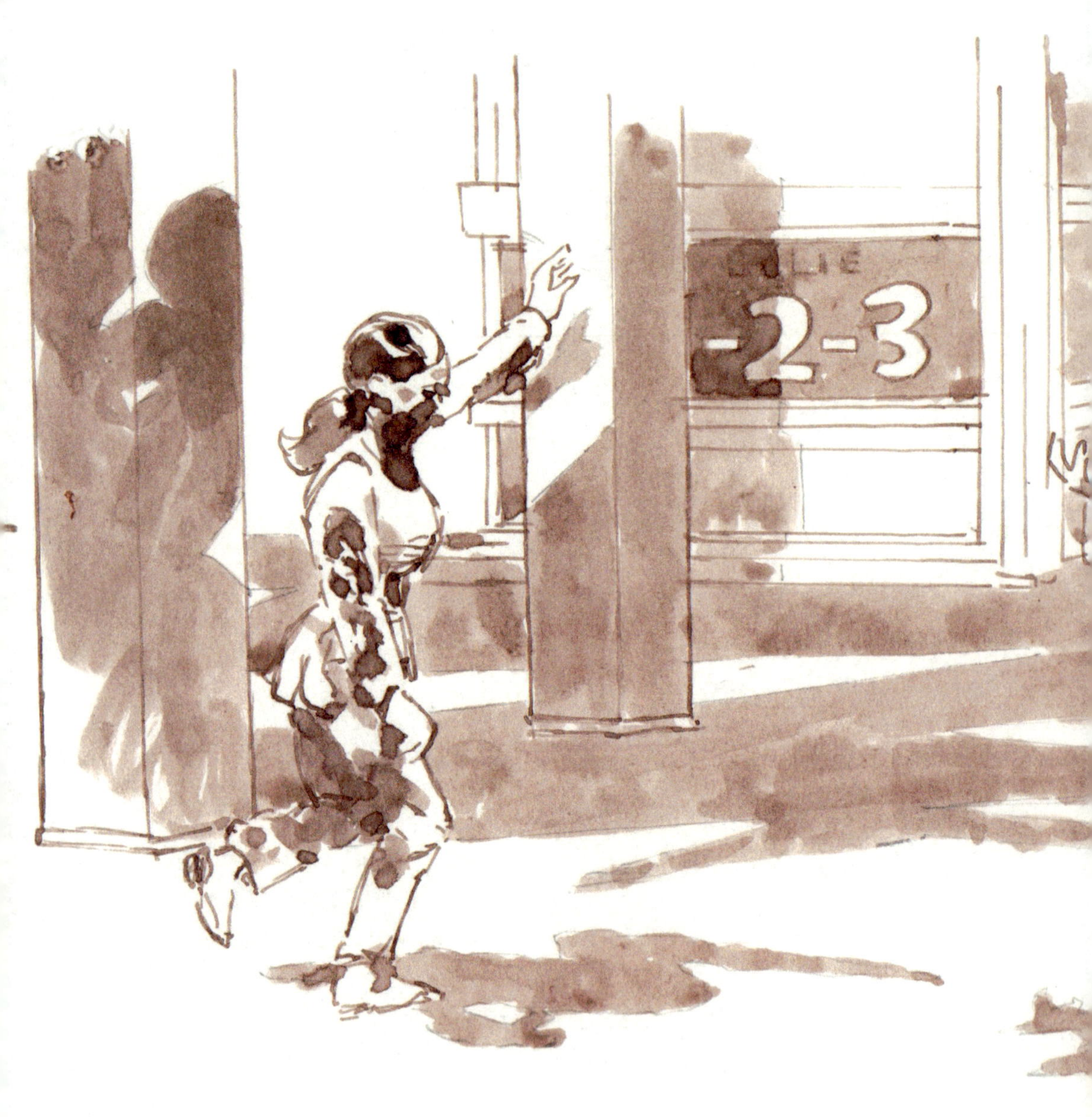
LIE
-2-3

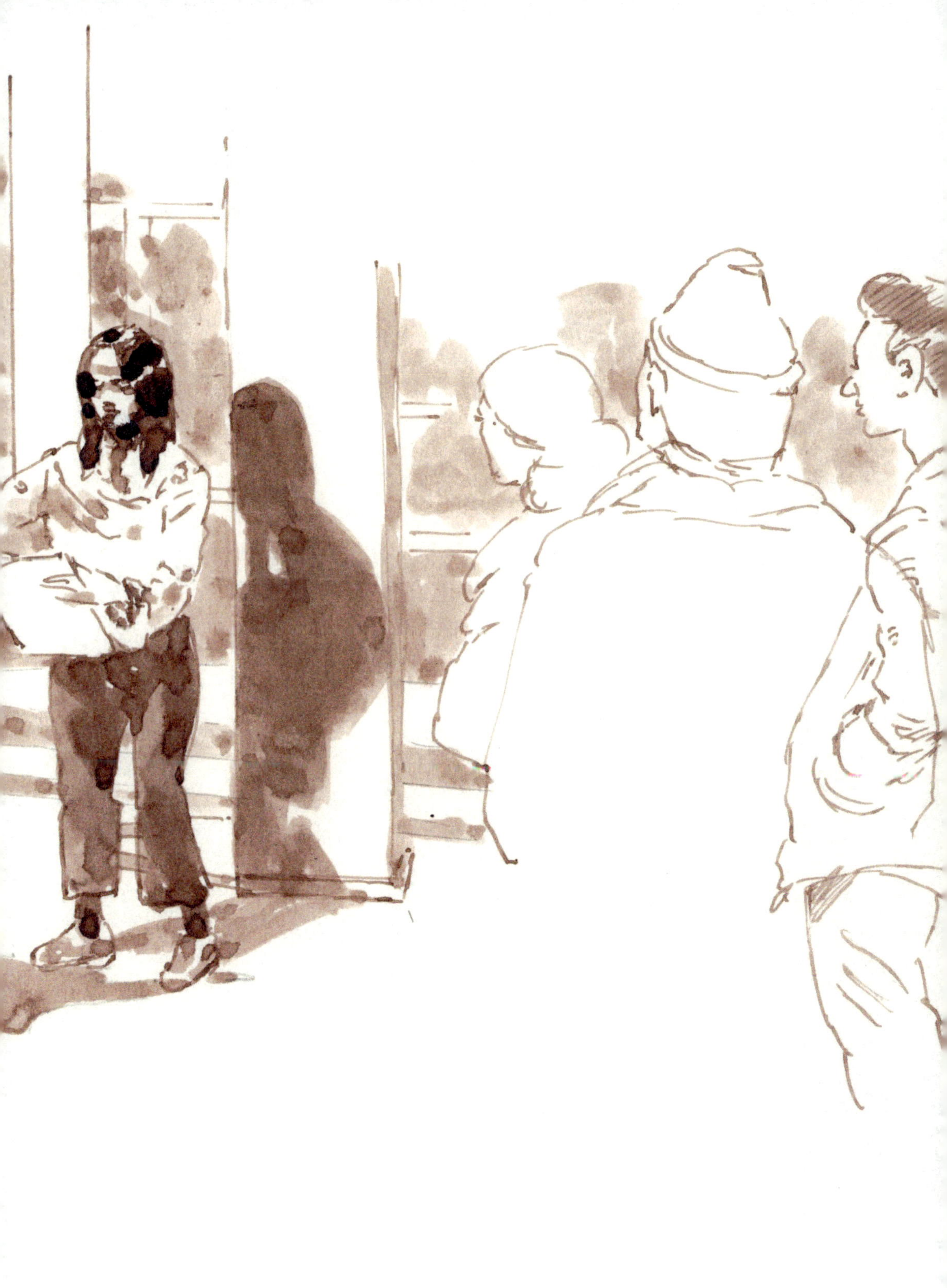

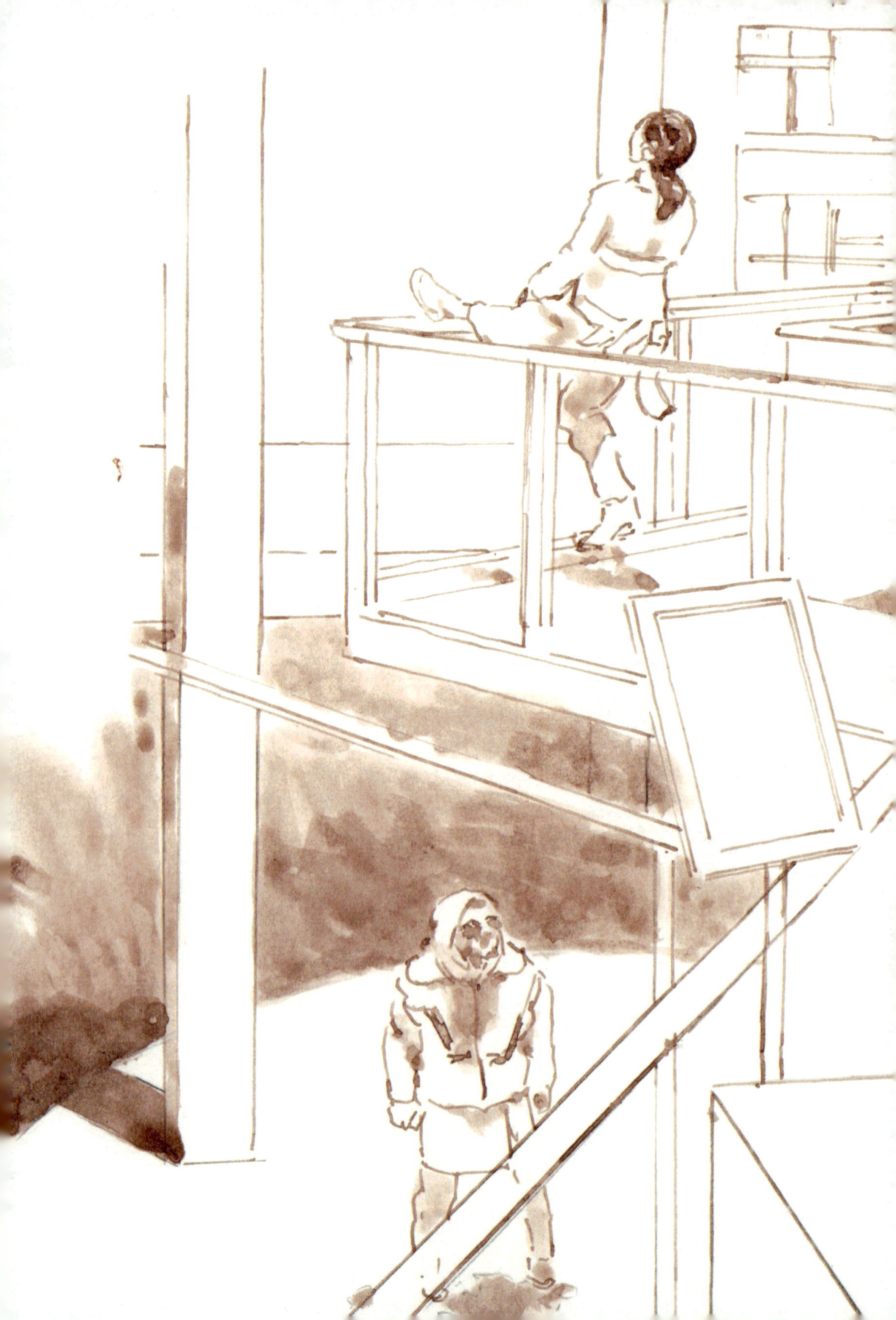

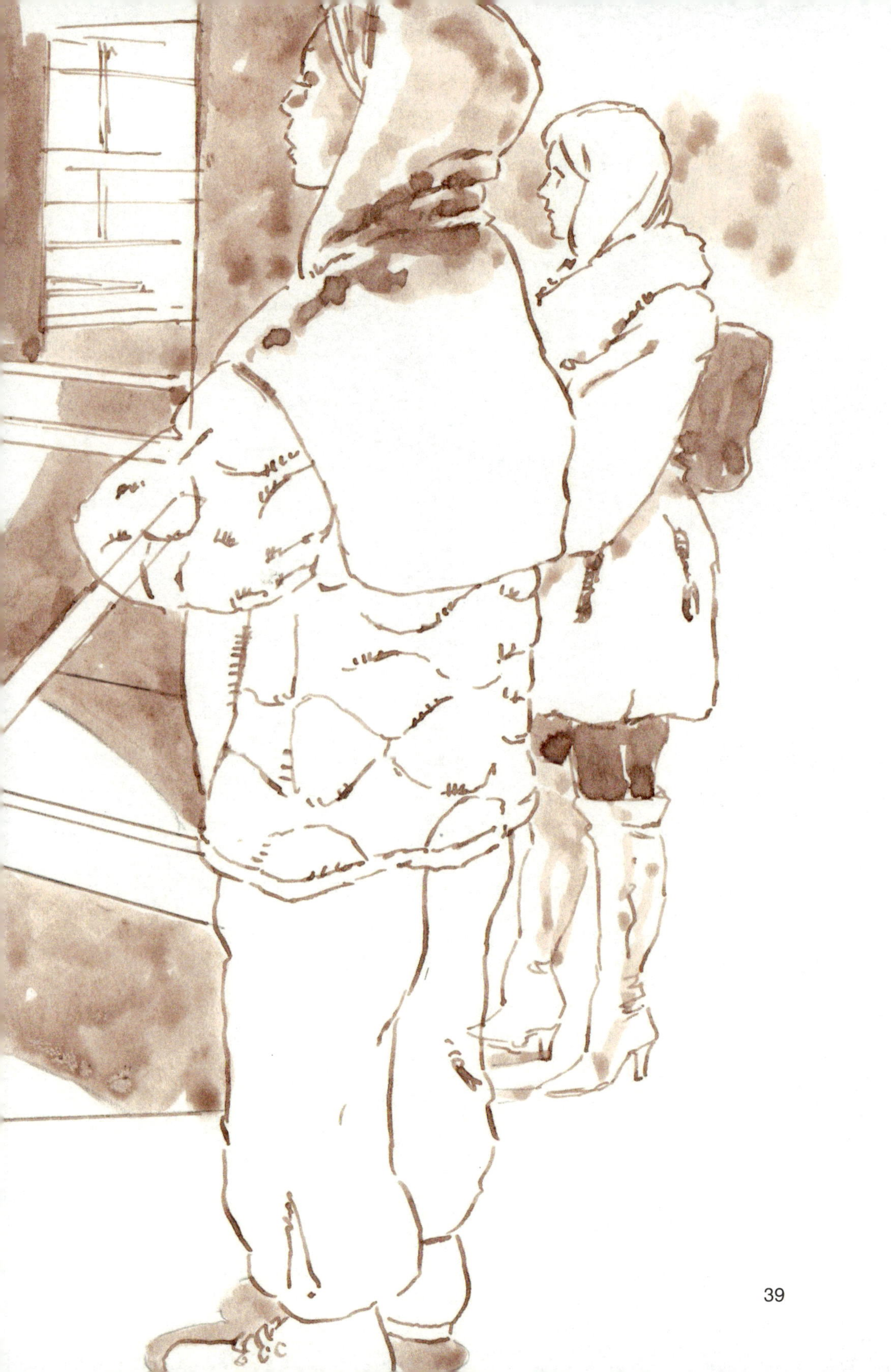

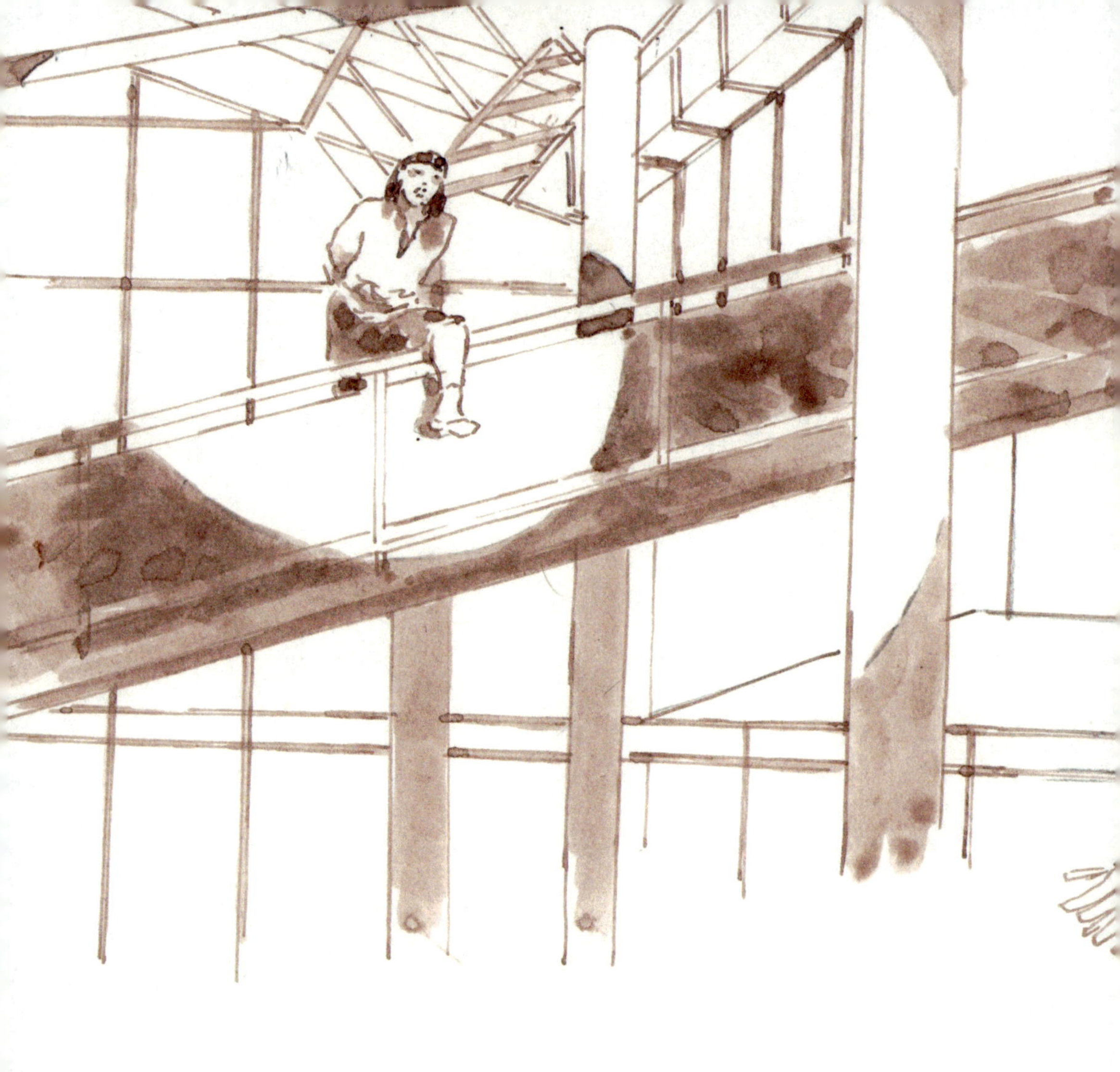

8.30n. interior myth.

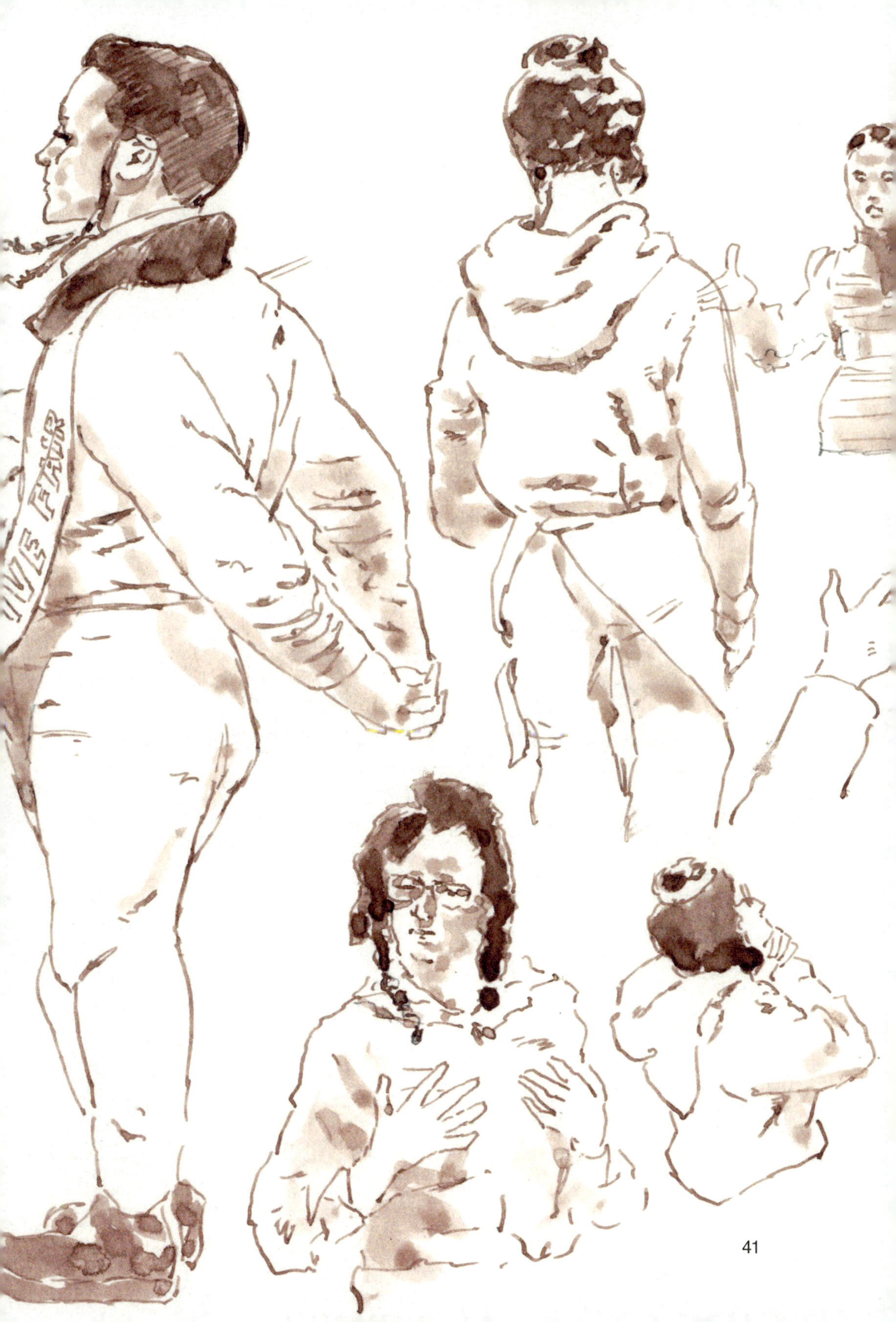

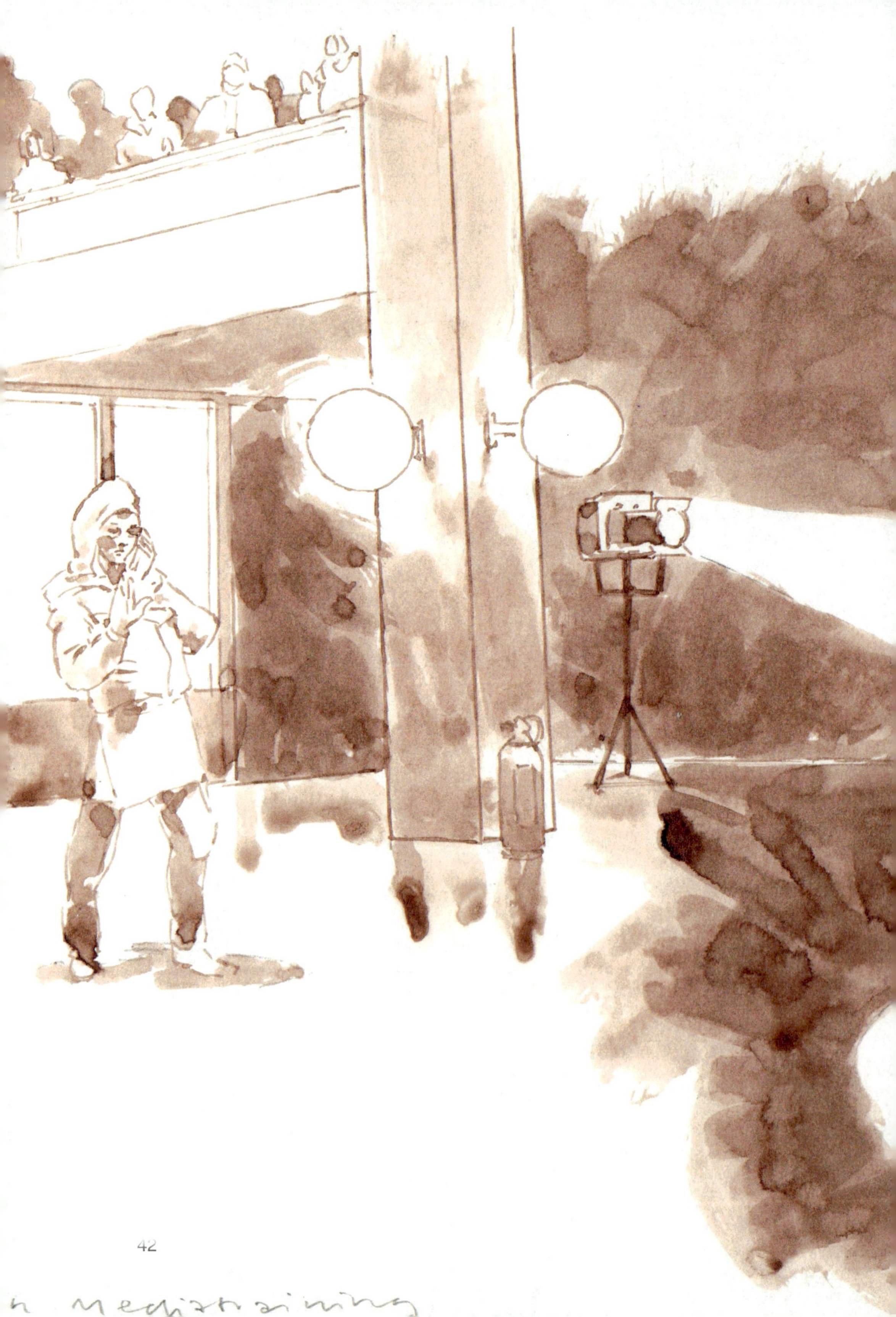
mediatraining

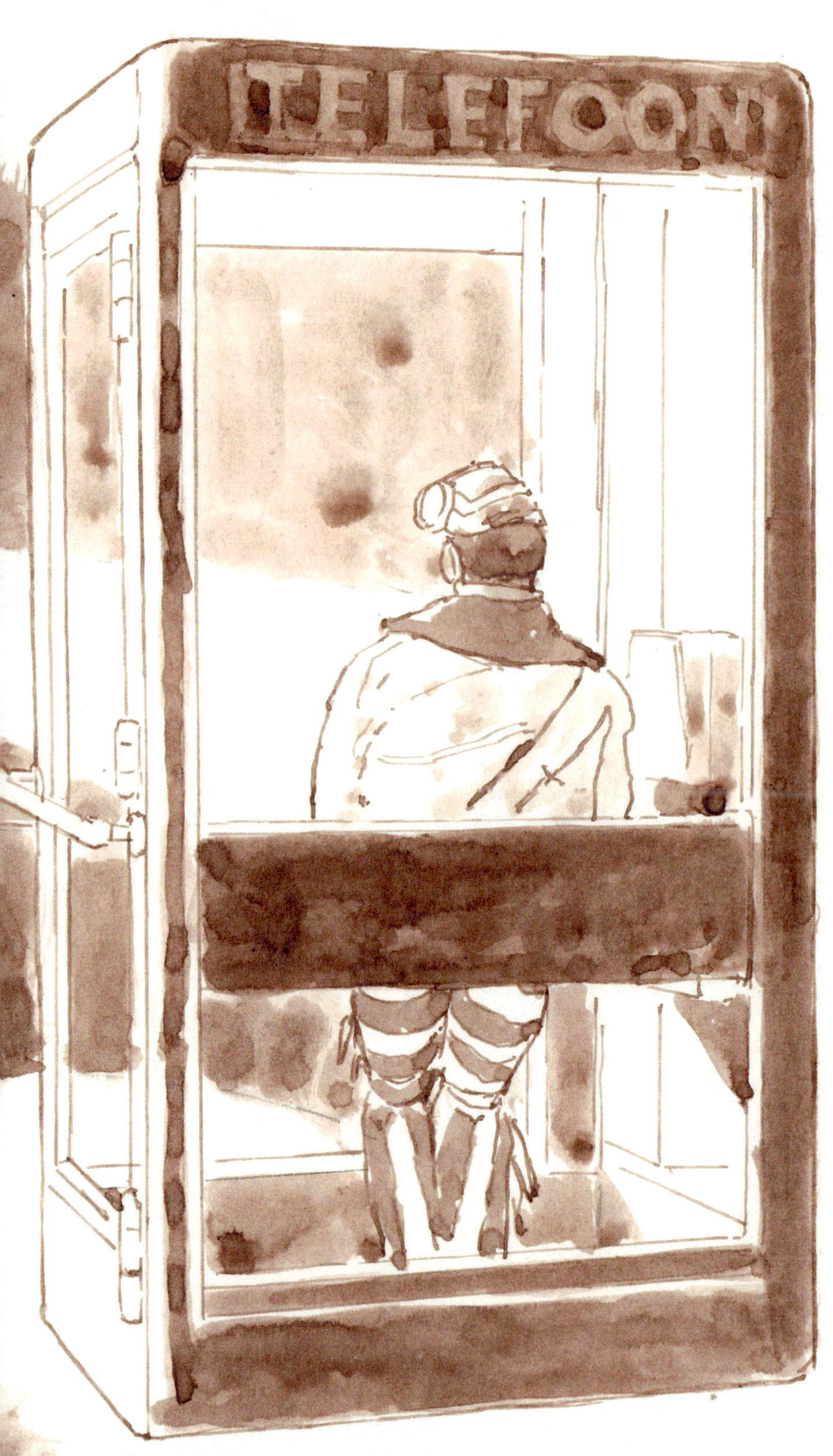
TELEFOON

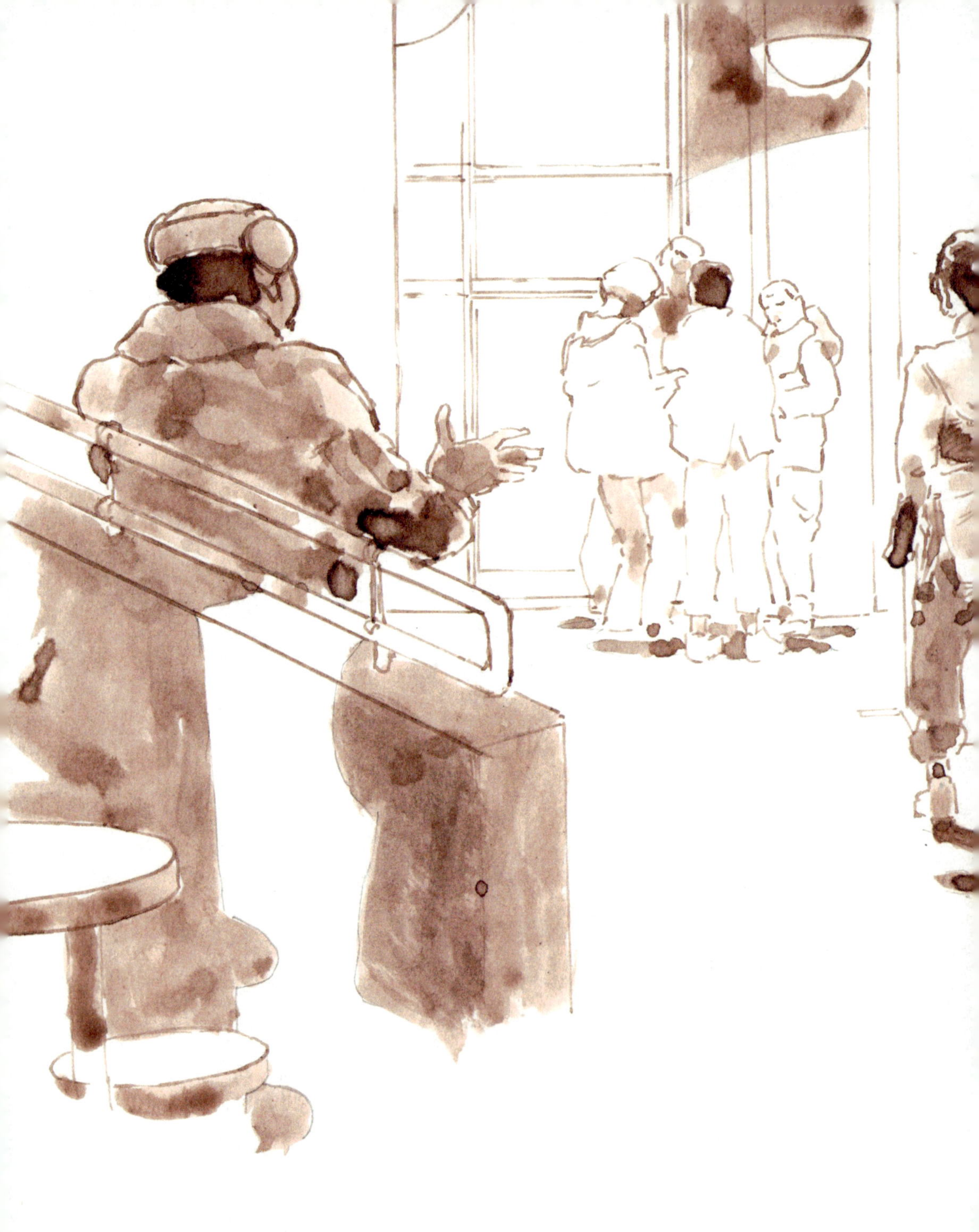
15.00 n Plots.

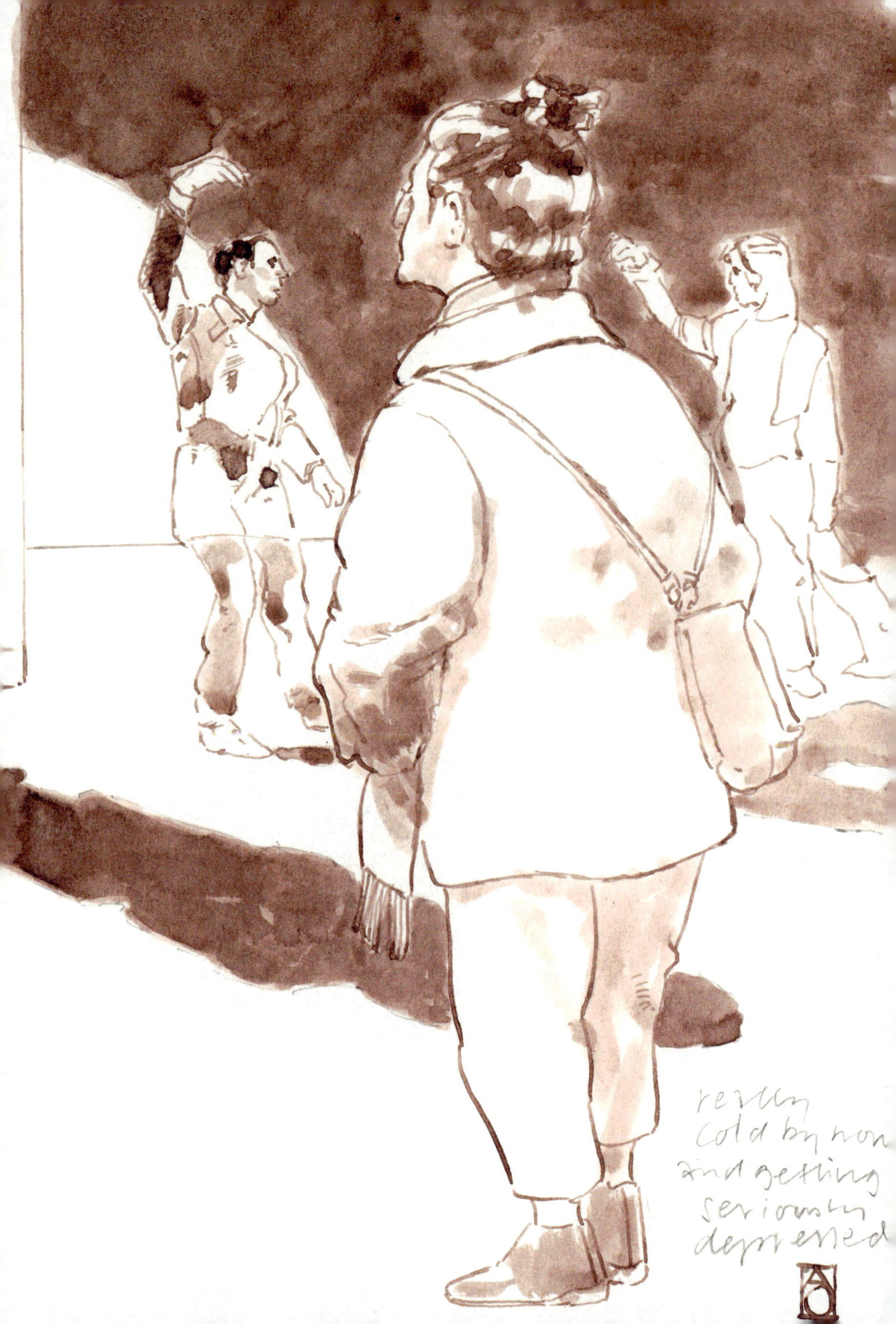

really
cold by now
and getting
seriously
depressed

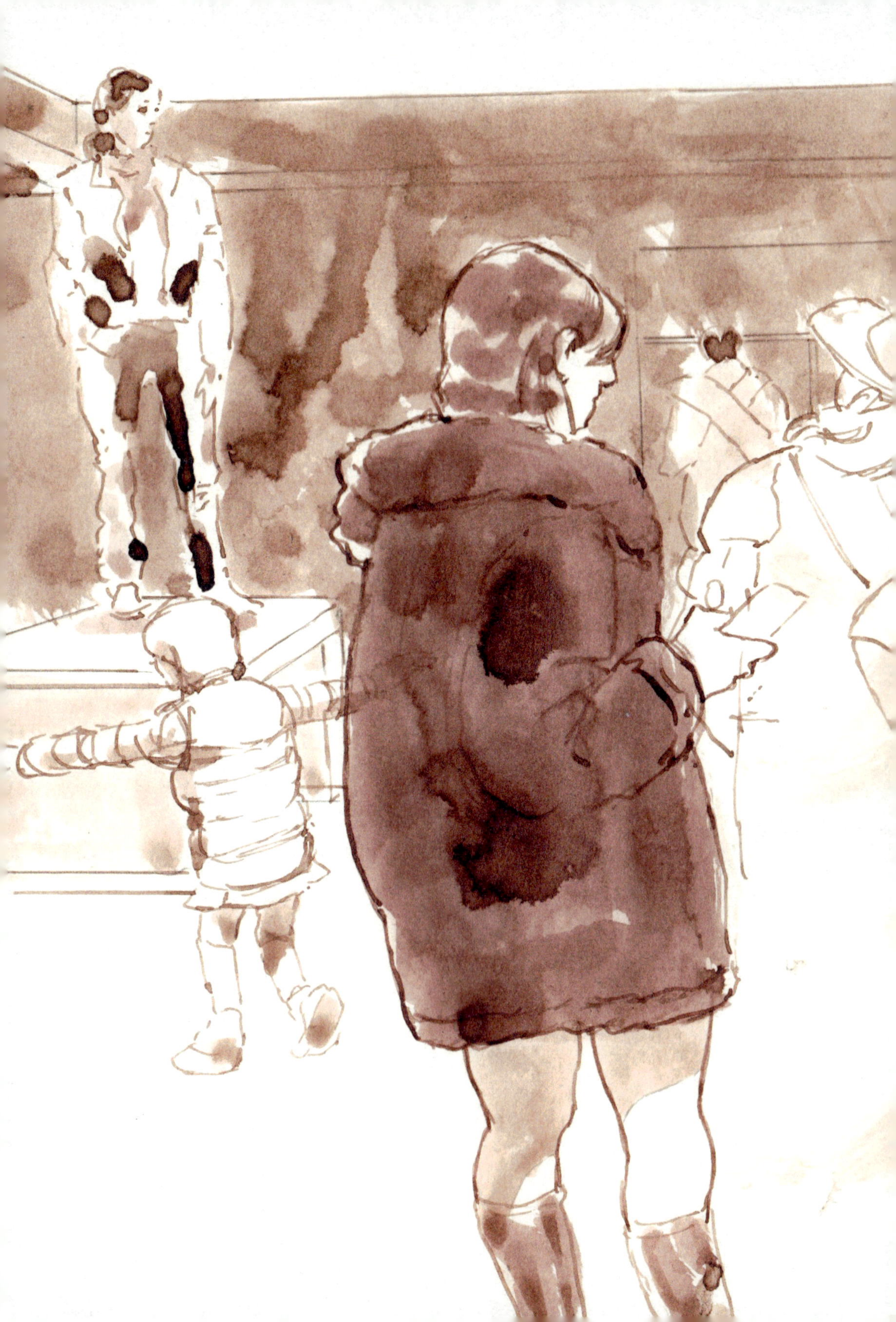

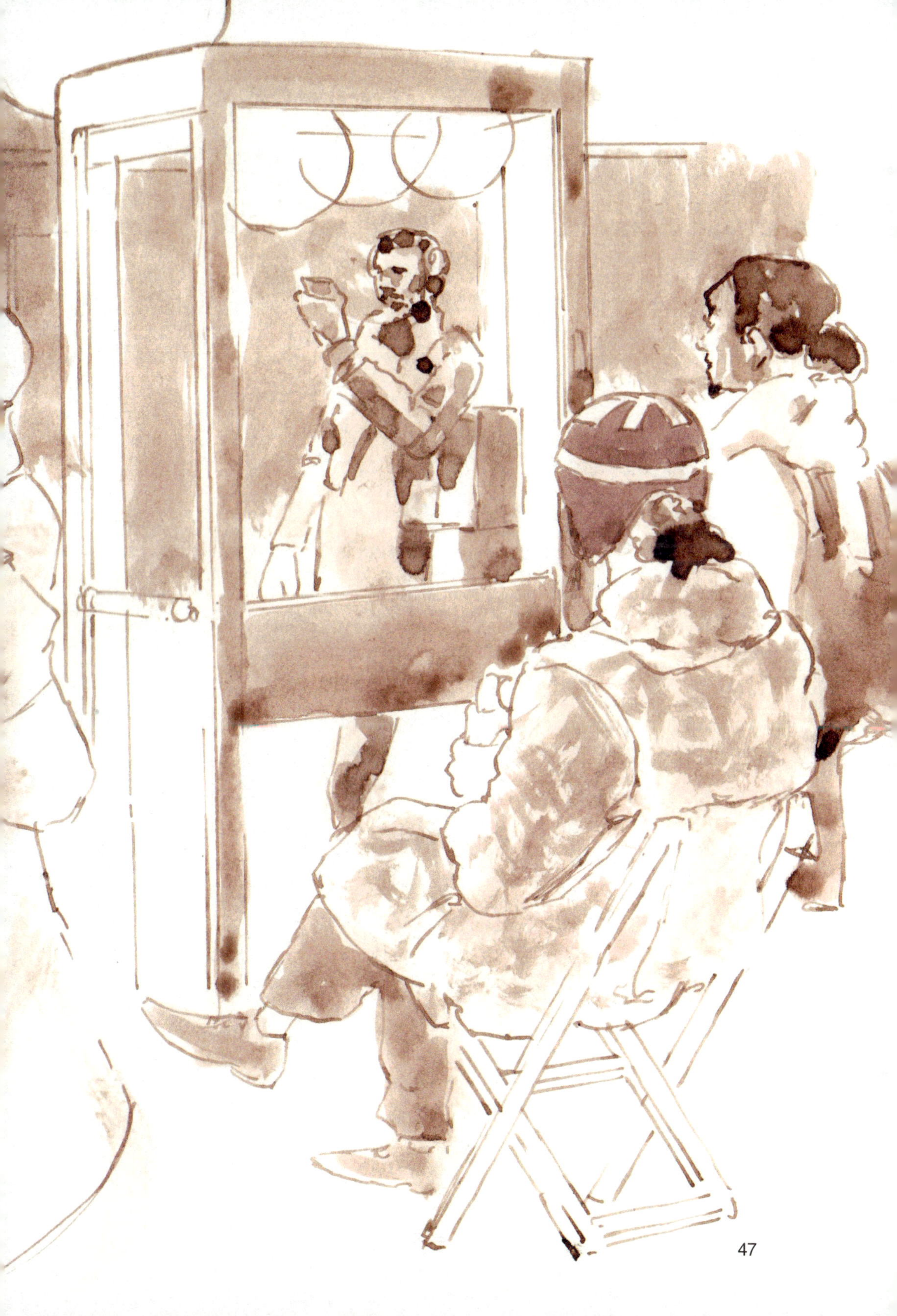

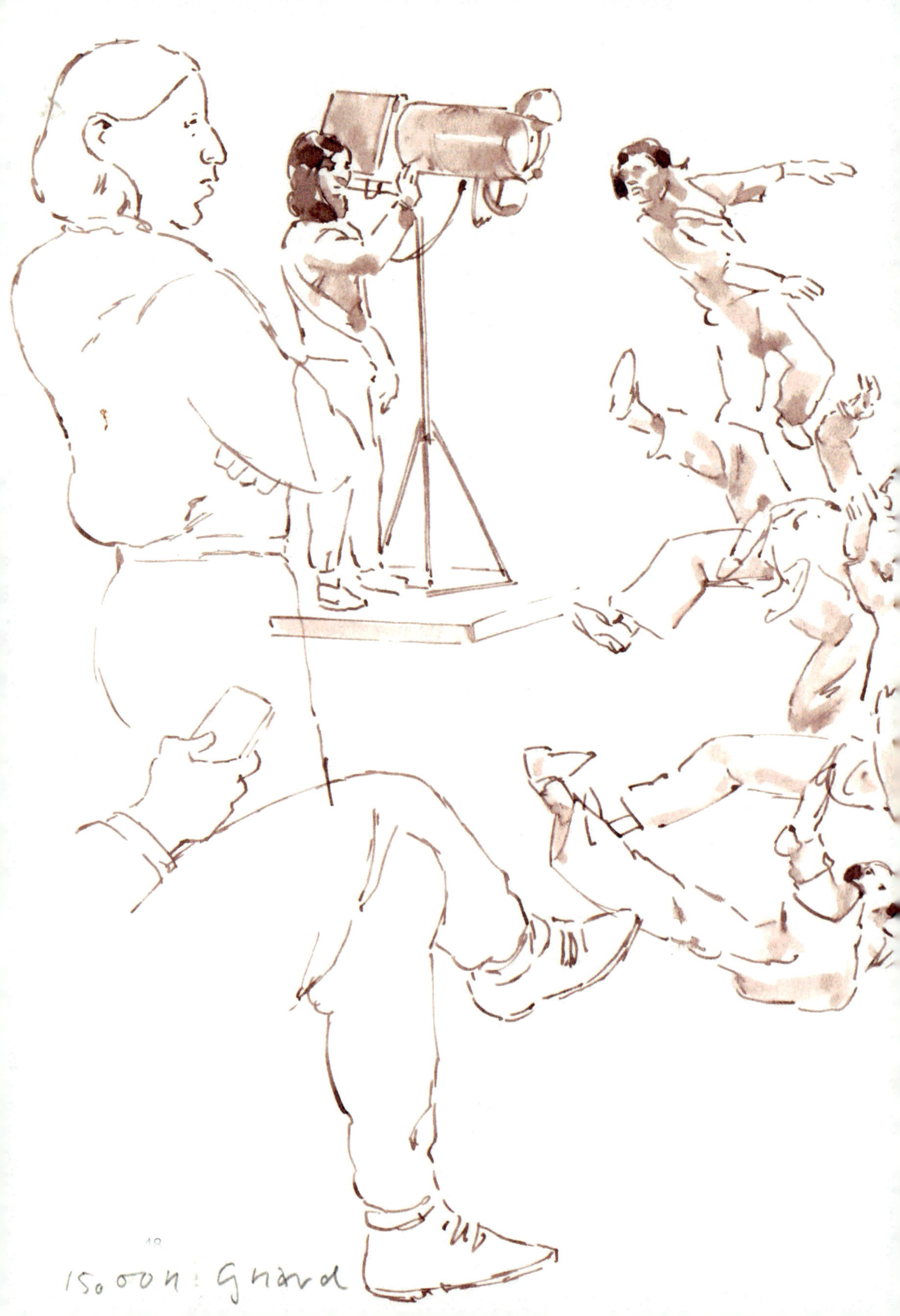
15.00 h Guard

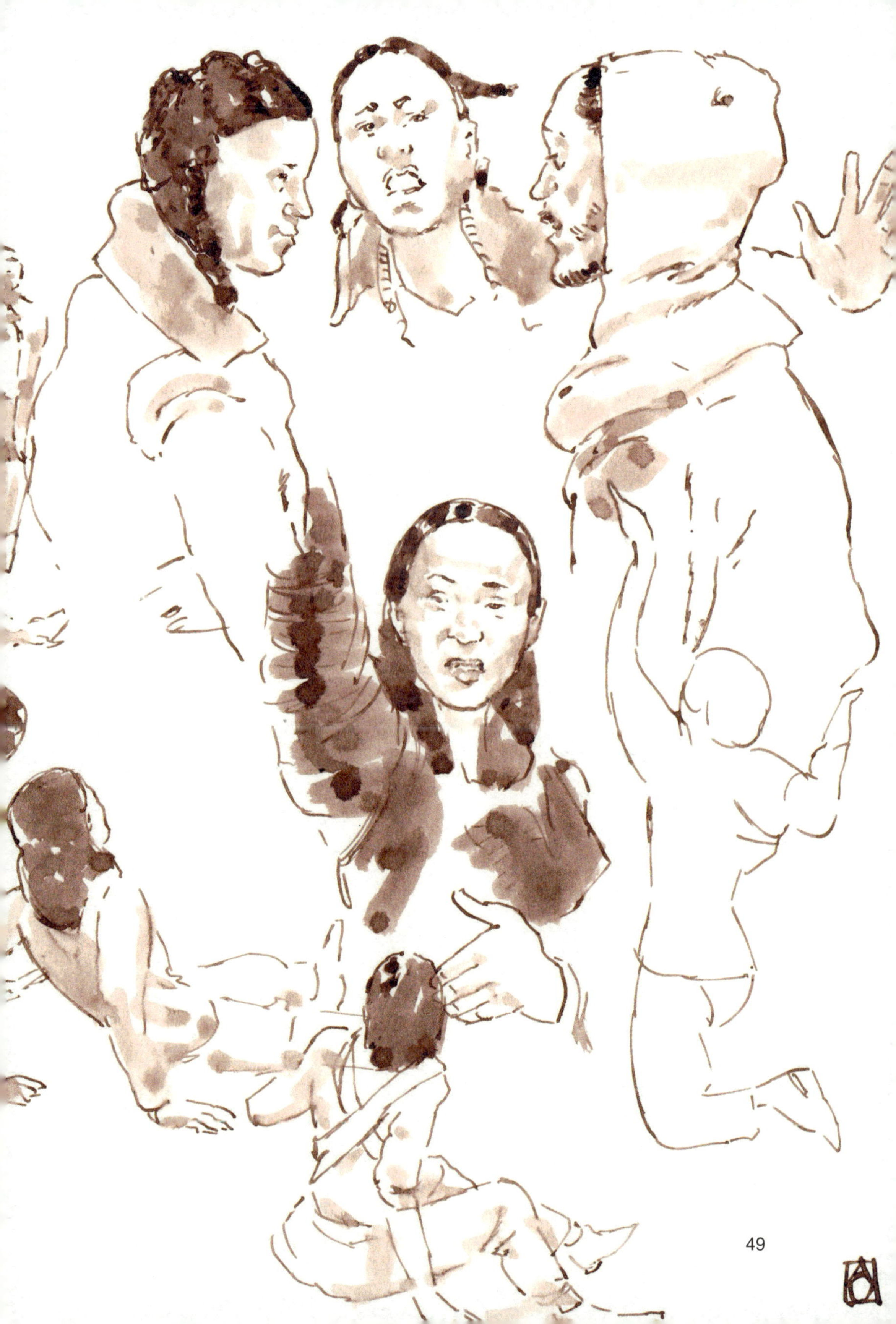

1   Libido   7pm

[Over the building Tannoy, Soraya welcomes the audience, and establishes that they should watch from the first-floor balcony. She establishes the roles that the performers will take, and presents the credits of the coming section 'Libido', from 'City/Mind', pronouncing the / as 'over'.]

1   Tai Shani
      Teenager (*Our Fatal Magic*)

[Central court area. Tripod camera facing down from balcony. Handheld slow tracked shot. Ground floor, Ivan standing, transfixed with gaze up. Mami stands next to him, periodically smiling out at the audience. Gestures are echoed and amplified between them. Geo and Soraya at the follow spotlights on the second floor; one points upwards, the other down at Mami and Ivan. They fiddle only slightly with the lights. Mami and Ivan begin with eyes closed. Ivan speaks as TEENAGER.]

TEENAGER   This is my fatal magic, ok, the first cut is the deepest.

Deep times, in dark ages, end times, much time ago, beyond the burning witch, silicone and engine, settlement and temple, beyond ape, beyond synthetic ape, beyond flesh or smooth fin or scale or feather, before cell after self-generating cell and spangle of mica, then mica, before the white dove rushing into the age of love, then stardust in the lightheaded totality of a bloody dimension ruthlessly cut into the real, to where it grew sticky and sweet like you, past the slick and palpitating glaze, before echoes echo, where, breathless together, we phosphoresce. There, where the black of end times and the pure lux of in the beginning, we gently touch in an immutable, eternal hologrammic kiss.

I have lived a good, good life, we declare in our beautiful telepathic hive mind, and we too kiss, partly formed and spectral, nipples rock hard and dripping wet with peaked sentience in our girlhood beds.

I could never be human to them. Nor was I beautiful enough for them to objectify me. Yes, I knew. Not palatable enough to gain free movement, to be visible, to participate, to elude cruelty, to be essential. Not desirable enough to be deemed powerful, to bear responsibility for the speechless transgressions that this absent beauty and their willingness to use it could compel them to commit. *With great power comes great responsibility,*

I might have been warned, if I had been attractive enough to them. Mythical boys of my late girlhood. [Mami shifts head, gaze down.]

I would be heroic though. I would know Underground Resistance, and R&S, Reinforced and Transmat, and other useful facts with which to transact. Esoteric and committed, I would have taste. I would display a lightness of touch and a soft golden light, the kind that stages a room and invokes the undying knowledge of eternity. I would be spiritual and irrational, feign terminal illness, yearn for my fragility to be recognised. Erotic and available, with undertones of latent violence. Voiceless. I would be feminine. I WAS feminine. I was symbolic, unconfined intensity, with a knowing nod towards (or a rejection of) embodiment. I was curled and coiled and abstracted. I hinged on contrast and tension. At times aggressively jagged, even transgressive. Yes, heroic, yes, mysterious. But maybe also maternal. I would become a woman.

The late-evening navy blue dimmed as though a milk-thirsty, newly born pink-pawed kitten suckled at the day's saturation till exhaustion and all colour had faded into the monochromatic hue of early night. Against the melodramatic backdrop of this dark blue velvet curtain, the branches bowed down. The chalky dark sky was a gothic pitch of spilt ink, where fairy lights burned small pinholes, and the silver light of beyond shone through, signalling from 39 million light years ago.

Inside, the surface quickly marbled. The classic vein swelled, blurred by heart compressing bass, dilating then spreading, blotting darkness till all light was absorbed and it was absolute night. I lost my shadow to the dark. Quicksilver mercury strobe stopped time and momentarily revealed their still, wondrous faces. Suspended angels: Gabriel, Abaddon, Anael and Uriel, their heads flung back, slack-jawed, eyes half closed and holy. Wonderful little pagans.

I love you.

Later, in the neon cradle of light, then the velvet cradle of night, Curly Wurly wrappers twirled in a baroque vision on the passenger seat of a borrowed car. We marvelled in silence at the conquest. Evaporating bone

	Teenager (*Our Fatal Magic*)

and flesh ladder. Slapping sounds erupted, interrupting the concentrated labour of being elsewhere. Films, television and books gave me the blueprint for how to look engaged whilst waiting patiently for it to be over. I spit on your grave.

Beware of the touch.

From a different car window, the past instantaneously formed in front of our very eyes and backdropped the glowing validation of their satisfaction. Both these things fell away from us quickly with the speed of high bpm, and a lightness of carried horizons as we travelled in a neon-hieroglyphic encryption towards the namelessness of psychedelic emancipation.

White doves rushed in with those angels and thrust me into a loving communion. I love you. We will always be this way, we will always know each other, and we will always belong here. This is everything!

Often, in the diminishing echo of pleasure, my face became a sculpture; an undying monument to the contagion of sadness. On the tight weave of my jeans, a plump, milky lagoon whose shores disappeared beneath its spreading reach fed from a viscous waterfall from high above, the mouth of the source smeared reddish, swollen, and softly parted. A strain in my jaw, syrupy saliva gathered and frothed at the corner where the stretch reveals true pink, the slippery threshold of plush mouth interiors, and the glossy, hot-rod, red of my public and painted quiet mouth. That milk that flows against all the laws of nature is galactic and sweet and silky like mulberry wine, like Buckfast.

Diminishing returns. Diminishing horizons.

I was pulled back from the precipice. I answered: Yes, I enjoyed it too. Yes, very much. Yes, just like you, I want to be human. This was very natural. Nature and I ached beautifully for their brutality, where they all systematically refused to.

To dazzle them, I took way more drugs than they could stomach, for their hard-earned respect, and for the repletion and alleviation of their defining gaze on me … boys, boys, boys. I AM looking for a good time.

1   City/Mind
1   Libido
1   Tai Shani

My movements were decelerated and syrupy. I was seeping round, bursting beads, with nectar coming forth from me. I cannot define anything that happens there. Everything is there. Perfect, flawed, endlessly colliding. Like a miracle. In the miracle I felt safer, more unreal than ever, and I came out from the miraculous underworld with miraculous X-ray eyes.

In this time outside of time, I see myself. I do not recognise this terrified me amongst the red splatter that oozes down the mirror. A ruby-red spray of blood, high-drama viscera on my Enter Shikari t-shirt. I didn't clean up my face, didn't hide these provocative wounds. I painted them on with dyed corn syrup that was sticky and sweet, like us. In the red-lit bathroom I bathed in the edifying light of my reflection. In the club I was focal, captivated by their mute attention. A fear of my volatility, and admiration for my willingness to fall through borders of the outer extremities. I was bleeding everywhere. I was setting a difficult standard … Monday, school. I knew hard-core was very sexy to them. I knew sacrifice was very, very sexy to them. Boys. Yes, just like you, I once was epic.

Hi. I got hit by a truck. I broke my hand in two places. My right hand. Just so you know that I am able to be delicate, my body can be broken. I am still masturbating with this hand held tight in a flesh-tone splint, even though it hurts badly. Particularly when I am about to come, and have to move it faster and harder to keep up with my vanishing self. I want to tell you about my masturbation to show you I am free and desirous, that where I maybe lack the looks that you feel so entitled to, I make up for in promiscuity, and a bottomless eagerness to please you all. I want you to know I am extremely tough. Tough enough to endure your violence, not afraid of pain in the search for your pleasure. I obediently extend this invitation of destruction to you all, boys of my late girlhood.

Can we all please agree to protect my precious purity? I can grant you unreserved access to obliterate it. Like everything else, death itself is devastatingly slipping through my fingers. My sister of mercy. Fuck me and marry me young. I'm begging you.

The milk that flows against all the laws of nature is galactic and sweet

                                    Teenager (*Our Fatal Magic*)

and silk, like Buckfast. Monday morning on the way to school, in the passenger seat of a pure white dark-force inverted car-form; an overlay on the elusiveness of the everyday Fiat Lux, with Mum in the overly reclined Olympia driver's seat. She is wearing a finely ribbed, peach-coloured knitted sweater. The ribs are made up of industrial lines, side by side with the reassuring familiarity of parallelism. Lines that extend in certitude beyond horizons, never destined for intersection or transformation. But then, further up above her ribs, corrupted by the chaos of the extended arc of her breasts pushing underneath the weave of yarn, the lines bulge, losing all their modernism; losing the symmetry of civilisation to disruption, the interference of meat. Her feeding flesh is held together in a shocking skin. Her nipple pushes harder against the taut yarn, stretched till the pattern of the weave reveals tiny, tiny loops; and beneath them, the finer, fruit-like flesh, a concentration of pure pigment and affect. Her true pink nipple.

Each tiny peach loop is framed by a halo of fuzzy fibres that bow and rise ceremoniously, like gently swaying anemones in the enigma that is the abyssal ocean. They rise and fall in the ebb and flow of her warm milky breath, which rolls softly from heavy, parted lips of trauma. A string of saliva rests at the threshold of her public and private mouth. Her hand rests carelessly on her lap. I look and learn from the rattlesnake in the paradise of my childhood.

A portrait reflected in the gelatinous glazed arc of my eye: the invisible guest.

I don't care about permission and I don't care that much about disobeying.

[An electronic bed of sound plays. Soraya and Geo are on the overpass of the first-floor mezzanine, near their instruments. Soraya lounges on the edge. Soraya plays THE SERVER, and Geo, THE YOUNG PHILOSOPHER. They come to walk in parallel lines, though they face outwards towards the audience rather than speaking to each other. Ivan has gone upstairs to adjust the follow spotlights, one by one, slowly shifting lighting gels to vary the warmth of light. Mami remains on the floor where she was, reiterating some of the movement vocabulary from the first scene, and presenting the stage directions.]

Mami   On a cruise ship, there is a room with a fake bar and a real bar, and at the real bar, THE SERVER reads Rimbaud's 'Mouvement' to herself. THE HUSBAND, THE DAUGHTER, THE YOUNG PHILOSOPHER and THE ENTERTAINER are at the fake bar. [She gestures to the audience.] THE REPORTER is reading the newspaper at the piano. [She indicates glibly 'off stage'.] THE YOUNG PHILOSOPHER walks slowly with an empty margarita glass from the fake bar to the real bar.

THE SERVER   … Le mouvement de lacet sur la berge des chutes du fleuve, / Le gouffre à l'étambot, / La célérité de la rampe, / L'énorme passade du courant / Mènent par les lumières inouïes / Et la nouveauté chimique / Les voyageurs entourés des trombes du val / Et du strom.

THE YOUNG PHILOSOPHER   I'll have a Margarita. *DING*

THE SERVER   … Ce sont les conquérants du monde / Cherchant la fortune chimique personnelle ; / Le sport et le confort voyagent avec eux …

THE YOUNG PHILOSOPHER   I'll have a Margarita.

THE SERVER   I'm not making you a Margarita.

THE YOUNG PHILOSOPHER   I'm not asking. (*long pause, dings bell*) I WANT A MARGA. RITA.

THE SERVER   … Ils emmènent l'éducation / Des races, des classes et des bêtes, sur ce vaisseau. / Repos et vertige / A la lumière diluvienne, / Aux terribles soirs d'étude.

THE YOUNG PHILOSOPHER   I have no idea what you are saying … I want a salted rim. Five to six ice cubes with lime floaty bits. And a straw.

THE SERVER   (*very enunciated*) So. Make. It. Yourself.

THE YOUNG PHILOSOPHER   Ha! This is my courtroom. Everyone, lazy people, please – join me, as the jury. Finally, polis – here is your purpose. Let's make some order.

Mami   Everyone freezes, watching from the other side of the room.

THE YOUNG PHILOSOPHER   I'd like to bring this court into session. Server, can you please address the room.

THE SERVER   Non.

THE YOUNG PHILOSOPHER   SPEAK ENGLISH.

THE SERVER   Non.

THE YOUNG PHILOSOPHER   You must tell the courtroom why you are here.

THE SERVER   Moi j'existe, tout simplement.

THE YOUNG PHILOSOPHER   This is not a joke. This is a Court of Law. Do you know why you are here? *(ignores him)* Do I need to repeat my question?

THE SERVER   *(very French Non)* Non.

THE YOUNG PHILOSOPHER   You are on trial for being the least entertaining woman in the world. *(pause)* I've prepared my opening remarks –

THE SERVER   Va t' faire foutre

THE YOUNG PHILOSOPHER   No interjections. The Server, has not served – for how long? It's been years, weeks, days. She stands at this bar, reciting those Marxist poems under her breath. And not only does she refuse her service, but she, in all the years, she has never made a joke, nor laughed at one of mine. Or made a nice remark about my clothing, or my hair, or even asked how I was doing.

THE SERVER   I ask you how you are.

THE YOUNG PHILOSOPHER   But you never 'really' ask. Just last week I walked up to the bar – and she never once looked up. I'd like to call The Husband –

Mami   THE HUSBAND slowly walks from the fake bar to the real bar. THE REPORTER notices as he passes, puts down the newspaper, and follows him. She stands close to the organ, watching. THE HUSBAND arrives at the real bar. [She points to an audience member.]

    Scene 4 (News Crime Sports) [part 1]

He says 'Anwesend!', which in German means something like 'present!' – I'm present. THE YOUNG PHILOSOPHER welcomes THE HUSBAND to the stand.

THE YOUNG PHILOSOPHER   Has this woman ever given you the smallest nicety? The smallest compliment. Has she ever laughed at one of your jokes? Has she ever given you a cigarette. Or reminded you what time it is?

Mami   THE HUSBAND says [gesture to the audience] 'Nein. Also sie hat mir mal paar kippen gegeben.' [Mami laughs]

THE YOUNG PHILOSOPHER   That's not enough.

Mami   THE HUSBAND acquiesces. He understands.

THE YOUNG PHILOSOPHER   (to THE SERVER) But she has to do something. She has to fill the vacuum.

Mami   THE HUSBAND reminds the room that THE SERVER plays the flute. THE ENTERTAINER walks across the room and accuses THE PHILOSOPHER of being drunk and lonely. THE ENTERTAINER moos like a cow.

THE YOUNG PHILOSOPHER   Well if she can play flute why doesn't she do it?

Mami   THE ENTERTAINER replies that THE SERVER doesn't do it for 'you'. What she does for herself and what she does for you. These are very different things. THE HUSBAND starts singing 'Meine Freiheit deine Freiheit', jumps down from the stand, grabs THE REPORTER, and pushes her away towards the bar. THE REPORTER

1   City/Mind
1   Libido
2   Calla Henkel & Max Pitegoff

chants 'Flöte!'. There is a chorus of chanted demands for a flute. Flöte! Flöte! Flöte! Flöte! Flöte! Flöte! Flöte! Flöte! Flöte! Flöte! THE SERVER plays the flute.

[Soraya plays the Dvina, an electro-acoustic string instrument, while the bed of sound continues.]

                              Scene 4 (*News Crime Sports*) [part 1]

3   Becket MWN
       The Last Days of Paul VValker

[After three minutes of a Dvina solo, Geo picks up a tin whistle. Across from the musicians' area, and illuminated by reflected light from below, Mami begins a movement sequence as though she is drifting like a driver in a fast car, darting back and forth along the balcony. Ivan joins her, as Soraya and Geo continue to play. Most observers only see them from the torso up. Mami plays VIN DIESEL, Ivan plays MEADOW WALKER, Soraya plays ROGER RODAS, and Geo plays PAUL WALKER.]

VOICEOVER   [prerecorded] The Last Days of Paul VValker: A Tragedy. Scene 1: Huntington Beach, California. Enter VIN DIESEL, Actor, co-star of PAUL WALKER, in the *Fast & Furious* films.

VIN DIESEL   Something is broken inside Paul Walker. Paul Walker, Brian O'Connor, I sometimes get them confused. Paul William Walker IV, born 1973 in Glendale, California. Brian O'Connor, born 1978 in Barstow, California. His mother was a fashion model and his father an amateur boxer. He met his childhood friend Roman in juvenile prison, when they were both boosting cars. His grandfather William went pro, boxing under the moniker "Irish" Billy Walker. When he got his driver's permit, he and his mother got into a five-car pile-up on the I-40, not far outside of Barstow. Raised as a Mormon, Paul was the eldest of four children. Two months after becoming an LAPD officer, his childhood friend Roman was arrested. Paul wanted to become a marine biologist.

See how seamlessly the lives of Paul and Brian intertwine? Is there much to separate the teenager living just outside LA trying to escape his life in the Church of Latter-day Saints, from the kid who wants to leave behind his criminal associations and drive really fast cars? And drive really fast cars? And drive really fast cars? There's something broken in Paul Walker. Probably the fan belt.

VOICEOVER   Enter MEADOW WALKER. PAUL WALKER's daughter, 15 years old.

MEADOW WALKER   Uncle Vin! Or is it Van? Uncle Van, ja?

VIN DIESEL   Meadow! I see your Dutch lessons are coming along well. How's your dad hun?

MEADOW WALKER   He's been acting strange, Uncle V. He speaks in riddles about speed and revolution, acceleration and the coming auto-fascisms.

VIN DIESEL   Huh?

MEADOW WALKER   It all began a couple days ago on Thanksgiving. All of a sudden at dinner he fell quiet. He started to sweat and his face filled with blood. I thought at first he was silently choking, but his breathing was regular. Then I thought it was some kind of new plague, like that full-body rash that went around last year. When I asked if he wanted to see the doctor, he just rose from the table and shut himself in his bedroom.

Mom and I kept vigil the whole evening. Every so often we would go in to check on him, but he never even met our gaze. He just walked around the room in a circle, over and over again, in an endless loop, lopen lopen lopen. I begged him to stop walking, but he could not be stopped, not even by hurling furniture in his path, or clinging to his ankles; he just walked on dragging me with him, until the rug burns on my elbows forced me to let him go. He never spoke; not even a grunt or whimper. This went on well into the night, until around 5am, just as the sun was about to rise, he collapsed onto the floor. He went face-first, which caused a nosebleed that we are still trying to get out of the carpet, but other than that he was OK.

He woke late in the morning, at 10 or 11, and his complexion was back to normal. He had stopped sweating, and even acknowledged our presence in the room. I just wanted him to say something, to break this supernatural silence. He looked me in the eyes, a cold peace settling on him, and he said: dromomaniac.

Godverdomme!!! Dromomaniac, that cruel demon, the new citizen driven to furious perambulation! Dromomaniac, drag racer on the royal road to Hell!

VIN DIESEL   Geeze, Meadow, what's that word even mean?

MEADOW WALKER   Dromo-, from the Greek, *dromos*, to run, like the dromedary, from *dromad*, or runner; and -mania, madness, pathological obsession, a force majeure: it means a compulsive walker!

VIN DIESEL   That sounds pretty bad, Meadow.

MEADOW WALKER   Since then, not a single word has passed his lips that I could not find written in the works of Paul Virilio, the French philosopher of speed. You ask him if he's alright, and he only replies, 'Historical evolution is kept moving literally by a combustion engine'! You beg him to eat something, drink something, but he only opens his mouth to say 'The violence of speed has become both the location and the law, the world's destiny and its destination'!

I want my father back, Paul Walker, Paul *Walker,* not this strange metempsychosis of Pauls. Why must the philosophy of Virilio choose to possess *my* dad? Instead of PW I am talking only to PV's ventriloquised puppet. He has turned PW *(pronounced: pay-vay)* into PVV *(pronounced: pay-fay-fay)*: Paul Virilio's Voice!

VIN DIESEL   I never really got much from reading Virilio, Meadow. He was always a little too macho for me.

MEADOW WALKER   Oh come Vin, there are too many V's in this play: Virilio, ventriloquism, V8 engines, venture capital …

(VIN DIESEL turns to speak directly to audience while MEADOW WALKER continues list of V-words in a semi-trance.) [Mami turns away from the scene with Ivan and heads towards Soraya and Geo.]

VIN DIESEL   Poor Meadow. Maybe something broke in her too. (*pause*) Probably the catalytic convertor.

MEADOW WALKER   … vibe shift, vaccination, vehicular manslaughter, vampire slayer, Verenigde Staten, value meal, vox populi, vermin, vermin, vermin, vermin …

[Like MEADOW WALKER, Ivan continues to shuttle around. Soraya, Geo and Mami begin the next scene together, heading downstairs as the voiceover sets the scene. They stand evenly spaced in a line, faces tilted to be visible from above. They speak without moving. Cut off by the voiceover, Ivan departs to adjust the follow spots onto the area where the other performers speak.]

VOICEOVER   Scene 2: Fundraiser at a convention centre in Santa Clarita, California. PAUL WALKER is at a podium making a speech to an audience. PAUL WALKER is an actor, 40 years old; star of the *Fast & Furious* franchise, and founder of charity organisation Reach Out Worldwide. ROGER RODAS stands just behind him. ROGER RODAS is the co-founder of Reach Out Worldwide, and owner of racing shop Always Evolving. He is also a wealth management director at Merril Lynch, and PAUL WALKER's financial adviser.

PAUL WALKER   … the promotion of a paternalistic and humanitarian comfort civilisation will perfectly replace social aid through the technical assistance of bodies, from the household robot to the company psychiatrist or the latest model of car. In 1921 Marinetti metaphorises about the armoured car: the overman is over-grafted, an inhuman type reduced to a driving – and thus deciding – principle, an animal body that disappears in the superpower of a metallic body able to annihilate time and space through its dynamic performances. No more riots, no need for much repression; to empty the streets, it's enough to promise everyone the highway.

VOICEOVER   Enter VIN DIESEL, speaking as PAUL WALKER continues with speech in background.

VIN DIESEL   Paul Walker, or Paul V-Valker, fully automated droning dromomaniac, has left his audience in mild confusion. They came for a charity event, an update on the good work they are funding in the Philippines, where this NGO has had staff on the ground for a week now. They came to see the signifiers of disaster relief, congratulate each other on their good work, and of course compare sports cars while queuing for the valet.

PAUL WALKER   [simultaneous] On the shores across the way, the perpetual transformation of the barbarous aesthetic of the mass-produced American car, the provocative excess of its body, of its ornaments, manifest the permanence of the social revolution (progress towards the 'American way of life'). But at the same time, this great automobile body has been emasculated, its road holding is defective and its powerful motor is bridled. Just as for the laws on speed limits, we are talking about acts of government, in other words of the political control of the highway, aiming precisely at limiting the 'extraordinary power of assault' that motorisation of the masses creates.

VOICEOVER   PAUL WALKER abruptly leaves the stage; audience sparsely claps. VIN DIESEL pulls him aside, as audience begins to slowly get up and quietly mingle among themselves. ROGER RODAS goes to try and reassure donors in the audience.

VIN DIESEL   Paul! Paul! Snap out of it! It's me, your co-star and dear friend Vin Diesel. We worked together on *The Fast and the Furious*, *2 Fast 2 Furious*, *Tokyo Drift*, *Fast and Furious 4*, *Fast Five* and, currently in production, *Fast and Furious 6*.

PAUL WALKER   The indiscriminate boarding of soulless bodies as metabolic vehicles.

VIN DIESEL   Dammit Paul, you're scaring people!

PAUL WALKER   The masses are not a population, a society, but the multitude of passers-by.

VIN DIESEL   You don't mean that. What about our communities?

PAUL WALKER   To survive in the city one had to stay informed daily, by radio, about the strategic situation of one's own neighbourhood; everyone transformed his car into an assault vehicle, loaded with weapons in order to ensure freedom of movement.

VIN DIESEL   How do you think this ends Paul? What's left of society when citizenship is replaced with survivalism? Once every individual is turned into a projectile, what's next? We become bullets, missiles?

PAUL WALKER   The kamikaze will realise in space the military elite's synergistic dream by voluntarily disintegrating with his vehicle-weapon in a pyrotechnical apotheosis; for the ultimate metaphor of the speed-body is its final disappearance in the flames of explosion.

VIN DIESEL   Paul, you're scaring me. What you're describing is a fascist suicide pact!

PAUL WALKER   Whatever the case: since fascism never died, it doesn't need to be reborn.

VOICEOVER   ROGER RODAS turns to VIN DIESEL. PAUL WALKER continues to speak in the background to himself while ROGER RODAS and VIN DIESEL talk.

ROGER RODAS   Vin, what's going on?

VIN DIESEL   Hey Roger, Paul's in a pretty bad place. I don't think it's a mechanical problem. It's behind the cylinder head, deep in the engine block.

ROGER RODAS   Is it a nomadology? Restless leg syndrome?

VIN DIESEL   'Fraid not Rog. It's in the drive shaft.

ROGER RODAS   Not —

VIN DIESEL   Yes — the death drive.

PAUL WALKER   [simultaneous] The soul neither pre-exists nor survives the disappearance of its body-vehicle or machine; but as potential Reason, and especially scientific Reason, it can act on foreign bodies which are distant in time and space. Animal, territorial, vegetable bodies, bodies without will, bodies not yet born, become technical bodies or technological objects. Here is true social domination, the bestiary of engines. The pure-bred horse no longer acts, he is acted on by his rider thanks to the drive shaft of the bridle and the gas pedals of the spurs. Or else he takes the bit in his teeth, returns to his controllable, wild state … he expresses himself!

ROGER RODAS   What can we do?

VIN DIESEL   There's nothing we can do. It's time to say goodbye. He's not Paul anymore. He's PVV.

VOICEOVER   VIN DIESEL turns to PAUL WALKER.

VIN DIESEL   Paul, you're like family to me, and love for my family is the most important character trait I have as Dom Toretto. But perhaps it's time for you to go your own way. Maybe it's time to say goodbye to familiar institutions and established franchises.

PAUL WALKER   Stasis is death, it really seems to be the general law of the World.

VIN DIESEL   You're right, Paul. Change is the nature of things, and dialectical thought demands we ask not why things change, but why they stubbornly stay the same. What comes next may be worse, but it's not going to get any better by pretending it doesn't exist.

PAUL WALKER   Speed is Time saved in the most absolute sense of the word, since it becomes human Time directly torn from Death.

VIN DIESEL   I wish I could go with you, but my place is here among the living, to build something new atop the ruins of the West.

PAUL WALKER   We must still apply aesthetic, functional and other meanings to this world of giant cars.

VIN DIESEL   Amen, Paul. I have a feeling they're going to re-place you with a computer-generated avatar. Goodbye old friend.

VOICEOVER   PAUL WALKER turns to leave, walking off stage, as ROGER RODAS and VIN DIESEL watch. PAUL WALKER stops before leaving, turns to look back at VIN DIESEL.

PAUL WALKER   It is again an engineer and director of fortifica-tions, of course, who in 1782 will publish one of the first known flow charts.

VOICEOVER   PAUL WALKER exists. Lights fade on ROGER RODAS and VIN DIESEL. Scene over. Intermission.

2   Instituting   8:30pm

[Over the building Tannoy, Geo welcomes the audience, and establishes that they should watch from the first-floor balcony. He establishes the roles that the performers will take, and presents the credits of the coming section 'Instituting', from 'City/Mind', pronouncing the / as 'over'.]

1   Felix Bernstein
     Confusion of Confusions (1688), Joseph de la Vega

[Set in the Amsterdam Stock Exchange, with Mami as THE CURIOUS, and Ivan as SHAREHOLDER. They stand by the follow spotlights on the second-floor balconies, shining them on each other. During the scene, they light each other, but occasionally pan the lights in horizontal lines, away from and returning to the other. Taking little steps and mincing hops while they speak, they move backwards, sideways and in diagonal lines back to the lights.]

THE CURIOUS   And what kind of business is this, about which I have often heard people talk, but which I neither understand nor have over made efforts to comprehend?

SHAREHOLDER   I really must say that you are an ignorant person, if you know nothing of this enigmatic business which is at once the fairest and most deceitful, the noblest and the most infamous, the finest and the most vulgar. It is the quintessence of learning, and a paragon of fraudulence; it is a touchstone for the intelligent and a tombstone for the audacious, a treasury of usefulness and a source of disaster …

THE CURIOUS   Does my curiosity not deserve a short description from you of this deceit, and a succinct explication of its riddles?

[Geo begins to play keyboard in an upbeat manner, and gradually Soraya plays her string instrument with long bows into his repetitive groove.]

SHAREHOLDER   In 1602 a few Dutch merchants founded a company. Gradually the company developed to such an extent that it surpassed all such enterprises. Every year new shipments and new riches arrive, the proceeds from which are distributed as profits, or are utilised in expenditures. The dividends are sometimes paid in cloves, sometimes in promissory notes, at other times in money, just as the directors think fit. Some call the Company the tree of good and evil, such as exists in Paradise, because it is kept informed of everything that happens along all the branches. And those who are satisfied with the fruits do not insist on pulling up the roots …

Here you can become rich without risk – without endangering your capital, and without having anything to do with correspondence, advances of money, warehouses, postage, cashiers, suspensions of payment, and other unforeseen incidents – you have the prospect of gaining wealth if, in the case of bad luck in your transactions, you will only change your name.

THE CURIOUS	I think I have fully grasped the meaning of the Company. But what has this to do with that mysterious business you mentioned, with the tricks you pointed out, with the difficulties you emphasised, with the entire exclusion of risk, with the changing of names, and with other exaggerations and expressions which have filled me with perplexity, rapture and confusion?

SHAREHOLDER	The truth of this paradox becomes comprehensible, when one appreciates that this business has necessarily been converted into a game, and the merchants have become speculators and gamblers who have tried to decide all by themselves about the magnitude of their gains. A new order of life has been created by these double-dealers.

[Pause in the music.]

THE CURIOUS	I cannot deny that, in spite of my natural inclination, I would try my fortune on the exchange. But with my limited capital, I could win … only if I were willing to renounce my reputation frivolously. But to feel degraded … without being compensated by wealth, such a thought is vain and insane.

	Confusion of Confusions (1688), Joseph de la Vega

1   City/Mind
2   Instituting
1   Felix Bernstein

[Geo resumes playing the keyboard, now with dramatic clusters of string samples.]

SHAREHOLDER   Even without going into technicalities I can overcome your doubts. The difficulties and the frightful occurrences in the exchange business … have taught some precepts …

Take every gain without showing remorse about missed profits …

Profits on the exchange are the treasure of goblins. At one time they may be carbuncle stones, then coals, then diamonds, then flint-stones, then morning dew, then tears.

Whoever wishes to win in this game must have patience and money, since the values are so little constant and the rumours so little founded on truth.

It is certain that he who does not give up hope will win, and will secure money adequate for the operations that he envisaged at the start.

THE CURIOUS   And where does this business occur?

SHAREHOLDER   The business is so constant and incessant that hardly a definite place can be named where it goes on. The Dam and the Exchange, however, are the places most frequented. On the Dam, business is done from 10am to 12 noon, at the Exchange from 12 noon to 2pm. The Dam is a square which is faced by The Palace. At this place, once a dyke had been constructed in order to protect the town against the Amstel, the Amstel Dam.

The Exchange is an enclosed building surrounded by columns. Some people lean against these columns of the Exchange, which they find to be like columns of fire, others hide behind them as behind a cloud.

The name 'Exchange' is explained by the fact that it encloses the merchants like a purse, or because here everybody makes eager efforts to fill his purse. As the word 'purse' means skin in Greek, perhaps not surprisingly

Confusion of Confusions (1688), Joseph de la Vega   75

1   City/Mind
2   Instituting
1   Felix Bernstein

many players leave their skins at the Exchange … When the speculators talk, they talk shares; when they run an errand, the shares make them do so; when they stand still, the shares act like a rein; when they look at something, it is shares that they see; if they eat, the shares are their food; if they meditate or study, they think of the shares; and even on their death bed, their last worries are the shares …

THE CURIOUS   These speculators seem to have sacrificed their internal compass to the weathervane of chance. They are guided by a light that shines from a chain of reflections that disorients the seeker of truth until they are altogether snuffed out by the invisible perimeters of fact. Having bumped along the labyrinth without awareness, the final convulsions and concussions will dam up this generation of luminosity, as they are finally hit by their limits.

SHAREHOLDER   Yes, but the chain of reflections is more than just a degenerating impediment to truth: it is an endless source of power to reformulate the human image. When a mirror is broken, each piece of crystal remains a mirror, the only difference being that the small mirrors reflect one's countenance in miniature and the large ones in larger size … Stock shares are similar to mirrors, at least a special sort of mirror, which makes it appear that the reflected object is hanging in mid-air, or the sort that makes the viewers stiffen from amazement because, while they are looking, they see themselves flying by …

[Mami and Ivan move in a counter-clockwise direction around the balcony, swapping their light positions. Geo has been adding Kaoss Pad into the mix of his keyboard, and Soraya begins to pluck her instrument. It is tense and cornily futuristic.]

THE CURIOUS   A mirror that forever preserves us without limit? Never crossed by a limit you cannot gamble away … bargaining against

     Confusion of Confusions (1688), Joseph de la Vega

all that makes this bargaining possible … setting and resetting the wager against being done in … or doing in or is it done away?

SHAREHOLDER   He who says merely, 'I give', does so with an equivocal aim … For his wish is not to sell but to cause the prices to move. If there is someone who expressed a desire to buy, the dealer's prompt answer is, 'I give, but not to you', and he cannot be obligated to anything else because – strictly speaking – he has said only, 'I give.'

THE CURIOUS   I'd like to give but only to you. And I'd like to receive only from you too. Will you give me as I give you? Will I be done away with? Will you do away with me? Will you do me in? Will you do me in for good as I am made into something else for you to do what you will with?

[Geo, moving away from the keyboard, is now manipulating a metal chain, which chimes against itself as he moves it up and down.]

SHAREHOLDER   'The stones speak', says the prophet, and 'the walls have ears', says the proverb; and our conspirators know this truth to be verified by experience. If their secret spreads, their advice seems to have met with approval, and *when* it becomes obvious that they sell blocks of stock, the walls and the stones do *appear* to talk; people seek the secret reasons of the *whispered* assertions; one is grateful for the hint; and, as cheating a close friend is thought impossible, the manoeuvre meets with success, the fish take the bait, the net becomes filled, the victory is celebrated, and the intention of the ring is very advantageously achieved.

THE CURIOUS   What meaning does it have that the bears buy one share, when, protected by their alliance, they sell ten shares?

SHAREHOLDER   The bears are completely ruled by fear, trepidation and nervousness. Rabbits become elephants, brawls in a tavern

1	City/Mind
2	Instituting
1	Felix Bernstein

become rebellions, faint shadows appear to them as signs of chaos. [Geo gradually returns to the original groove, a slow crescendo.] In spite of these difficulties, *however,* I advise you to speculate for a rise and not for a fall. Finally, I should like you to play 'The eye-opener', though I am about to perform 'Give all and give nothing', for, although I teach you carefully all I know, I am convinced that I give you nothing when I want to give you everything.

   Confusion of Confusions (1688), Joseph de la Vega

2   Victoria Colmegna
     Gossip Girl Episode 206 (2008), McNally & Safran

[Audio plays, from the episode of *Gossip Girl*. Beginning with an alarm sound, the scene has upbeat music, fitting for a montage that skips between the mornings of SERENA and BLAIR, former best friends and prep school classmates. They are preparing to visit colleges; this episode involves a visit to Yale University, spoiled by BLAIR's acting out as she feels SERENA is receiving undue attention, and perhaps taking away her dream. BLAIR is in conversation with her family maid, DOROTA, about newspaper coverage of SERENA's recent fashion appearance, and SERENA eventually speaks to her mother. As the sound plays, Mami and Ivan descend from upstairs towards the overpass where the musicians are. Coming to stand in a line, a movement in which weight shifts between feet modifies into a more dynamic movement, as though cantering on the spot. This is a unison. They spend a little while together in this movement. Ivan is the first to depart.]

3   Shiv Kotecha
     Two-Page Interlude for Two Players Experiencing Anxiety
     and Guilt About Forgetting

[With the recording of the television show abruptly cut off, Ivan is now at the first-floor balcony. He will recite the following sequence with two players as a dialogue between an upper and lower voice, differentiating also in pose. PLAYER 1 leans over the railing, fingers braced lightly, while PLAYER 2 has a single leg thrown over the railing. Geo is on the ground floor, watching and lighting Ivan with the spotlight. Mami, leaning on a concrete column, watches Ivan from below, and appears to be listening while stretching – there is some correlation between their gestures. Soraya is at the railing opposite from Ivan, and also puts her leg over the railing when Ivan does.]

PLAYER 1   There's more, but I can't remember … I can't, I can't.

PLAYER 2   You know that you must. It's not as if anyone here knows what you're talking about. Only you know what you've seen, what you've done.

PLAYER 1   What if we tried the movies again?

PLAYER 2   That worked the first time, but it won't work again. Not here!

(Echoes of PLAYER 2's voice ping across the room like an emergency alarm.)

PLAYER 1   Okay. Let me try again.

1   City/Mind
2   Instituting
3   Shiv Kotecha

(PLAYER 1 searches the crowd around them as if looking for a mirror or some version of themselves, then finds what they are looking for.)

PLAYER 1   I'm starting to, I'm starting to rem – Shit, no. I've lost it. What am I going to do, what am I going to do?

[Head gradually turns in the next passage.]

PLAYER 2   Let's try something. You've seen the movies *My Cousin Vinny* and *Anatomy of a Murder*. You've seen *Saint Omer*, when for minutes nothing moves but the light and tears. Beige gets just a little less beige. *Young Mr. Lincoln* and 'all he'd rather not say.' The baby in *Erin Brokovitch*, the clasped arms on the cover of *Liar, Liar*. What about *Inherit the Wind*, *12 Angry Men*, Keanu's bum in *The Devil's Advocate*. C'mon, *Amistad*? Fine, *Paths of Glory*? I was with you. We were both there during *A Civil Action*, both there during *Just Mercy*, both there during *Primal Fear*, both there during *Witness for the Prosecution*. *In the Name of the Father*, *Dark Waters*, *Ace Attorney*, *Mulk*. How about *Runaway Jury*, *Philadelphia*, *The Accused*. *Kramer Versus* motherfucking *Kramer*. Nothing? *Sleepers*? *The Rainmaker*? *Murder in the First*? This stuff is Hollywood baby, you've got to remember. Okay, *Disclosure*. Okay – *High Crimes*. Okay – *The Gingerbread Man*. You've seen *A Few Good Men*, and *Adam's Rib* and *Fury*.

(This list of courtroom dramas and their descriptions can be endless.)

PLAYER 1   A guy escapes a lynch mob, yes, but of course the townspeople deny it. But the footage is played back to them! And they see themselves rioting and trying to murder the guy. They don't need to remember anything because the film is the evidence.

(Player 2 pulls out a cellphone and takes a video of Player 1 'acting'.) [Ivan just picks up a phone and seems to hold it in a position to be speaking to

1   City/Mind
2   Instituting
3   Shiv Kotecha

camera. The phone, however, is not set to camera mode.]

PLAYER 2   Alright, then. Go. Start with the day of the accident.

PLAYER 1   (*remembering, in snatches*) 'I was hungry. And, and … love came to my door … He was dancing … dancing up a river … in the dark … looking for a woman … when something strange happened … he was looking for a woman … and … he read my mind … he saw mistrusting him … acting kind … '

PLAYER 2   What did he say?

PLAYER 1   '"All the guilty people", he said … "they've seen the stain" … his eyes were the colour of the sand … and the sea … and the more he talked to me, you know, the more he reached me …But no – it was no accident … I wanted to shoot him … So I sent the kids to school and I went and bought a gun …'

PLAYER 2   And then?

PLAYER 1   'So then I got very hungry.'

PLAYER 2   Wait, when?

PLAYER 1   'When I bought the gun.'

PLAYER 2   Yeah?

PLAYER 1   'So yeah. I went in this hamburger place and I ate two rare, and one lemon meringue pie.'

1   City/Mind
2   Instituting
3   Shiv Kotecha

PLAYER 2   And then?

PLAYER 1   'And then I was still hungry.'

(*PLAYER 2 stops recording.*) [Ivan resumes the physical indications of the two players.]

PLAYER 2   *(to audience, as if they were a jury)* Think of that.

PLAYER 1   No, shut-up, wait. This is the wrong film. This isn't *Fury*. It's *Adam's Rib*, but it isn't. But it doesn't matter … I'm getting it back, my memory. I'm starting. I'm starting again to remember.

4   Huw Lemmey
       Dutch Play

(The scene opens in an empty courtroom. MATILDA enters, humming the tune of 'Greensleeves' to herself. She has a broom, and a small box of cleaning supplies. She leans the broom against the witness box.)

[Geo leaves the spotlight and heads to the musicians' area. He starts to play a simple harmonisation of 'Greensleeves' on a keyboard. Ivan leaves the first-floor balcony and replaces Geo's position at the spotlight, shifting to a red gel filter. Soraya heads towards the ground-floor spotlight. Mami plays MARGERY, and Ivan plays MATILDA. The exchange here is between the apparatus of the light and the so-called stage. It takes a while to settle into these roles, and the fact that the scene is between early Dutch Anabaptists cleaning a courtroom remains evasive. Mami's movement sequence refers to the scene proposed by Victoria Colmegna in Almodóvar's *La flor de mi secreto*; an abstracted series of gestures. Ivan is by the spotlight on the same floor, and also skirts around it.]

MATILDA   Bear with me a second. The action will soon begin in this room.

(MATILDA puts down the box and starts sweeping. After a few moments, MARGERY enters, also carrying cleaning rags, brushes and supplies.)

MARGERY   Good morning, Mrs Matilda.

MATILDA   And a good morning to you, Miss Margery. Right ho: we have quite the task ahead of us today. I am told the court will reconvene again shortly after noon, and these men made quite the mess yesterday. We shall have our work cut out for us. You take the benches, and I shall take the floor. Don't tarry.

MARGERY   Right you are Mrs Matilda.

(The women start to empty their cleaning supplies and begin their work.)
[Ivan moves backwards from the light in a triangular path of a hop, skip and
trot, as earlier in the section.]

MARGERY   How's your husband, Mrs Matilda? Still crook?

MATILDA   Rough, and getting worse I'm afraid. His leg
has never been the same since returning from the uprisings, and between
the weather and the tumult, he gets sicker each month.

MARGERY   I'm sorry to hear it. I shall pray for him.

MATILDA   Prayers are what he needs, I fear. Neither my
food nor the apothecary has done much more than slow his descent. The
light has gone out of him, and it flickers only in small moments, with a
bird outside the window or our granddaughter at the door. But even their
presence reminds him of his failures. Still, I feel myself lucky: Brother
Beukelszoon still lies as a bag of bones in the cages hanging from the St
Lambert's.

MARGERY   It's wicked.

MATILDA   Aye, 'tis wicked, the whole business. But I never expected him to return, so for me even his demise is blessing. Each
morning I wake up beside him is a gift. Prayers may sustain him a while, but
the Lord is calling for him, I know it.

MARGERY   I admire you, you know, Mrs Matilda. I don't
know if I could have followed my dreams like that, all the way across the land.

MATILDA   I followed my husband, and he followed not his dreams. God's dream, perhaps. Our nightmare. You were too young, thank God, for you could not have kept your head in that city.

MARGERY   I wish you held me in higher esteem Mrs Matilda!

MATILDA   Oh Margery, I hold you in the highest esteem. Your lightness is a compliment, believe me!

MARGERY   I wish I could believe you, Mrs Matilda, but I fear you think me unserious.

MATILDA   I do! But I do! And your unseriousness is a joy. A light! In fact, the only thing I hold higher is your lack of belief in me!

(MARGERY, confused, begins to scrub the woodwork of the courtroom. She begins to sob, gently.) [Mami begins a sequence that involves slamming her thighs with her palms, a modern dance lamentation. Ivan begins to trot in a loop around the light and Mami.]

MATILDA   And you cry? Now you cry? What have you to cry about, girl?

MARGERY   I'm sorry, I don't mean to. But you judge me too harshly.

(Matilda stops cleaning.)

MATILDA   Hush your crying, Margery dear. Yes I judge you, but do I find you wanting? Rather the opposite. I am saying you seem to me light, without guile and hence guilt. Nothing hidden. Open to the Lord.

MARGERY   Perhaps just better at hiding.

MATILDA   Perhaps. There's plenty to hide from in these
last days.

(MATILDA puts her arm around MARGERY, who stops crying.)

MATILDA   Come on, girl. We must clean this place before
the court starts again this morning. [Mami and Ivan both stop moving.]

MARGERY   It's terrible, Mrs Matilda. If I hadn't seen it with
my own eyes, I doubt I could have believed men capable of such brutal
inquisitions. The state of these poor men they bring before them, bones
cracked and broken, little more than a sack of viscera, and in no position to
defend themselves.

MATILDA   I know. And here we clean for them, and feed
them, while they insist upon their falsehoods, dunking their little ones under
the water and shovelling money to their paper god in Rome.

MARGERY   But we help them in our labours. Shouldn't we
present ourselves to them?

[Mami and Ivan both stop moving.]

MATILDA   And what good would we do as just more bundles of human firewood?

MARGERY   What must the Lord think of us, fearful to be
martyrs in his name. Oh Matilda, mother, better to burn in this life than next,
surely?

MATILDA   You hold a light in you, my dear girl. And we mustn't let them extinguish it from us. We have a duty to pass it down, and never let their courts put it out.

MARGERY   But to lie? I know we shall have our rewards in heaven, but it feels like a sin to lie in rebellion against their authority. [Mami brings her arms up.]

MATILDA   The way I see it is this: from where does their right come? The Lord? It's not in scripture, the things they do. Papists or Lutherans, it seems worldly power is what must be maintained. They have more that unite than divide. But in the Book and in Love we have our own authority. That's all I answer to: divine love.

MARGERY   Divine love, that's right.

MATILDA   It's right, but is it enough? I still don't know.

(MATILDA sits, her shoulders slumped.) [Moving further away.]

MARGERY   Between our family, we are enough, for sure, Mrs Matilda. I believe.

MATILDA   After Münster, I am filled with doubt, Margery. Filled with doubt.

MARGERY   Doubt in our Lord?

MATILDA   In our minds. In our worldly justice. In my own ability to know wrong from right. If I don't know, how can they? But no, not in the Lord.

MARGERY   Then we should pray, Mrs Matilda.

MATILDA   Oh I pray, dear girl, but the waters seem muddier
with each new parcel of refugees tracking their weary feet through our yards.

(MARGERY sits with MATILDA, and puts an arm around her shoulders.)

[Unison arm swing, and walking slowly in parallel lines with each other,
arms extended.]

MARGERY   The more hate I see, the more love I believe.

MATILDA   I can't tell if your youth brings foolishness or
hope, girl. In fact, I can't rule on the difference between the two.

(MATILDA rises, shrugging off MARGERY's arm, and begins cleaning again.)

MARGERY   It is against my better judgement to tell you this,
Mrs Matilda. But I have a plan to move, to England, in the near future.
Familists there have work for us, and a place to live. I planned to move this
summer, but should the Good Lord take your husband, well, I should do well
with a mother to accompany me.

MATILDA   To England?

MARGERY   Aye, in the East.

MATILDA   I shouldn't know what to do with myself, outside
of Delft or indeed without dear John.

MARGERY   I shan't demand of you know. But know that it
might be in the way of the Lord.

MATILDA   I'm touched by your offer, Miss Margery.

MARGERY   I think you will make the right judgement, despite your doubts, Mrs Matilda. Or because of them.

MATILDA   Which makes you more afeared, Miss Margery: if justice were in the hands of men, or if it were not?

MARGERY   Oh, if justice belongs to men.

MATILDA   We are few and growing fewer, girl.

(The two women pause and rest a moment.)

MATILDA   Now, you fetch some boiling water, and I shall grab the mops, and let's get down to this as quick as we can. The magistrates shall be here within the hour, and it's fair difficult to get blood out of wood.

5   Ariana Reines
      WATSON+BELL (*Telephone*)

[Geo switches from the keyboard to small percussion instruments, also
speaking the text from this position. Soraya picks up the Dvina but does not
play immediately. Geo plays BELL, and Ivan plays WATSON. Mami takes
the position that Ivan had at the follow spotlight, and Ivan moves in the
space of the stage, continuously tracking back and forth in a triangular pattern that dives towards the large table, set in the ground floor of the space.
He speaks upwards to the audience, invisible to Geo, and vice versa. Geo
plays into his speech and even the silences.]

W   Yes?

B   Yes yes!

W   Yes yes yes! Oh Bell! Do you remember June
2, 1875, when we proved that different tones vary the strength of an electric
current in a wire, just as they vary the movement of the air?

B   Yes indeed! My harmonic telegraph! Yes!

W   My twanging spring! Your harmonic telegraph!
Yes! And now?

B   Electric speech! The method of, and apparatus
for, transmitting vocal or other sounds telegraphically! By reproducing – elec-
trically – the vibrations in the air as caused by human speech! The trans-
portation of sound via electrical undulations, the form of which match the
vibrations upon the air, the vibrations caused by vocal – or other – sound!!!

W   Yes yes!!!!

B   Once a voice spoke to Moses through a burning bush!

W   And now! Any home or office can have a burning bush of its own! Any voice can be freed from the encumbrance of its
body! Free to travel miles and miles, over land and sea!

B   Yes yes! But – but wait! Watson. What did you
hear!

W   Oh!

B   What did you hear! Over the electromagnetic receiver! What did it sound like! On the electromagnetic receiver!

W   Well. *(silence)* Complicated. Complex.

B   Watson. Just say what I said. Just tell me what
you heard.

W   I heard *(silence)* a lot of things. A great many
things.

B   Such as.

W   I don't know where to start.

B   What about my voice.

W   Yes.

B   Yes what?

W   Yes, I heard your voice.

B   You're sure you heard it.

W   Yes Alec.

B   What did it sound like?

W   Like. Well. It sounded. Like. *(silence—silence—*
silence)

B   Like?

[Soraya begins to play, and the musical texture escalates.]

W   A. *(silence)* A small man. Calling forth from deep.
In a. In a. Barrel. Of brine. Like. A thrush. In a metal can on, ah, upon the
foaming sea. *(silence)* Uh. Like. The darkness. Being divided. From the light.

B   Like what?

W   Like the darkness being divided from the light.

B   Really?

W   And. Like. Like the insides of the throats of, of, of
hornets. If hornets had throats. And reverberating. As though inside a single
metal teat. Metal teat. You know, like a rubber teat, but metal. Like a bell.

B   Please Watson.

W   Yes Bell.

B   Did you even hear what I said.

W   I'm here aren't I.

B   Watson. Tell me what I said.

W   Watson. You said Watson. Come here I want
you. Ah. Wait. Actually, what you said was. Um. Watson come here I need
you. Uh — Bell. What did you call me for?

B   I was in a state of excitement and distress.

W   Over what.

B   Well as you saw I spilled the battery acid.

W   But what about before you called. What about
right before.

B   I don't know. I just. I just did what I do. I do
something. About something. We do.
                        (silence) Watson. *(silence)*

W   Alright, alright, excellent. And this. This does
something about something.

B   It has many uses.

W   What about friendship?

B   Certainly, if one friend is far away from another.

                                          WATSON+BELL (*Telephone*)

W   Is a friend a friend if that friend is a distant friend?

B   Now Watson. It's a small world, after all.

W   Bell. What would you say we are doing right now.

B   We are talking to one another in a friendly way.

W   Right. *(silence)*

B   And our device is an extension of this. But I
don't see how this solves –

W   Just hang on, Bell. You say our device is an
extension. Of talking in a friendly. Way.

B   An amplification. Of fellow feeling. Our device.
The telephone, it seems to me, Watson, should make bigotry impossible. It
shall. And render war unlikely, if not impossible. *(silence)* People will understand one another.

W   Right, Bell, right! We're really getting somewhere now!

B   Where? Where are we getting?

W   Wait – wait, just wait Bell. Bell. Pretend I am
Socrates. Alright?

B   *(sighs)*

W   Alright. Suppose you are a lonely man. Who does not own a telephone.

B   What are you saying.

W   Suppose you are a lonely man who does not
own a telephone.

B   Alright.

W   Then you are a lonely man.

B   Tautology.

W   Nevertheless. Suppose you are a lonely man.
Who owns a telephone

B   Yes?

W   And nobody ever calls.

B   Oh.

W   Or if somebody ever calls. Something interferes. Bell. Perhaps one person cannot hear or understand the other or
both people cannot understand each other, or the one says things in such
a way that the other cannot understand either because of himself, something in himself, in his – his Essential Being! – or because of the way the
one has said what he has said, and perhaps some of what one says makes
sense and perhaps it makes so much sense that the other one cannot bear
it, or both begin to panic and behave as though they hate one another but
perhaps really it is the frustration of failing to reach some concord, something both can partake of, each thing the one proposes the other says.

                                    WATSON+BELL (*Telephone*)

But no it is not like that it is like this, perhaps some people argue and this expresses love and some people agree and this expresses morbid resignation, all those nights I waited for you making ready my singing repertory, and wouldn't you say Alec that there could be more required to cause one person to agree – to agree in a – in a – a spiritual way – with another, more required for this than having set up a proper machine and – and. And.

B   And what?

W   And pronouncing all the words correctly.

B   Of course. Tone. Timbre.

W   I'm talking about COMMUNICATION. What we made.

B   We did not make communication. We made 'COMMUNICATIONS'.

W   We did not make COMMUNICATIONS. Sam Morse made that. *(pulls a voice)* WHAT HATH GOD WROUGHT.

B   Morse did not make COMMUNICATIONS. Gutenberg did.

W   Hieroglyphics.

B   Cuneiform.

W   Shakespeare.

B   Mother Goose.

W   Paul Revere.

B   *(strikes tuning fork)* I don't know. Watson. Are we old or young?

W   *(silence)* I think we're somewhere in the middle.

B   What if we're dead. *(silence silence silence)* Though I suppose in that case we should be with the others. Should we not?

W   If you say so. It doesn't make much difference to me really. You know. At least I have a mouth. I could put a song in it. Hey Bell? The air's in my mouth. My tongue is.

B   Mmmm. Mine too. Perhaps we are somewhat more electric now than before. Sort of electronically preserved, or –

W   Yes, electric is possible. Why not, somewhat?

B   Air is inconstant, but it is where we are.

W   Right. *(silence silence)* But *(silence)* we are not smoke. We are not light. Are we? We are not, not music or. Or wind! But then again – now and again – I feel – you know? On occasion I must admit that I DO feel myself to be a. A beam of light. On occasion. Or like a. A! Wind! As though I am translated! Into something! You know? Something. Overtakes me. On my Sundays in the woods. It's like nature. But – extra. A second. Nature. I mean. I slip into a kind of.

B   I know.

W   Just wait. I'm saying. A kind of dreamy bliss.

The contents of which I feel powerless to put into words. If I had a friend who was disposed to understanding my way of expressing things, perhaps in time I could learn to express some of them by extraverbal means. I tried to learn the piano but I could not master it. I bought myself a horse but it did not like me. I can't – I can't – TRANSMIT myself.

B	Well. You are now.

W	No, I'm not. I'm failing.

B	You are expressing your failure. In English.

W	I'm trying.

B	Yes.

W	But. If nobody knows what I'm saying. Then I
might as well be mute.

B	I'm right in front of you. I can hear you. I'm not
deaf.

W	Not hear. Understand.

B	I understand.

W	You understand the words. There's – there's
more than that.

B	I taught elocution for years. I know.

W	No I mean – something obscure. Something

vast! Oceanic!

B   What?

W   *(wretched silence silence silence)*

B   You want this thing to be inexpressible. It need not be. Reach out and touch someone. It's not impossible.

W   But. Isn't it? Sometimes? Isn't it always a question. *(silence)* Hello? *(silence)* Yes?

B   The human, even the deaf human, is no longer quite so alone.

W   Not all the time.

B   *(getting a little grandiose)* And those in distress – whatever.

                    (silence—silence—silence—silence—silence—silence)

[Exeunt]

PAUSE

3   Disapproval   10pm

[Over the building Tannoy, Mami welcomes the audience, and establishes
that they should watch from the first-floor balcony. She establishes the roles
that the performers will take, and presents the credits of the coming section
'Disapproval', from 'City/Mind', pronouncing the / as 'over'.]

1   Nour Mobarak
The Washing Away of Wrongs (1247), Song Ci [part 1]

[Geo appears, casually seated on a large table on the ground floor, with paper in his hands. He is coolly lit by a spotlight on the ground floor. The spotlights on the second floor form pools of light on the first-floor overpass, near the musicians' area. Mami and Ivan stand there, facing each other, as Geo and Soraya did earlier in the Act.]

Geo   General Discussion of Inquests, Part 1

[Soraya triggers a carpet of sound. Geo reads off paper. Mami and Ivan walk slowly in parallel lines, exchanging positions between the spotlights.]

Geo   In cases of hanging, it is imperative that the place where the hanging occurred and the marks on the neck be examined. The deputed official must also examine the dust at the place where the body was suspended. Had the corpse already been moved or not? As to the height of the place from which the corpse was suspended, where did the victim originally place his feet? What was used to climb up to the place of hanging? Again, the length of the cord below the place of suspension should be examined, as should its size, which must be compared to the size of the marks on the neck to see if they correspond. Was a running knot or a dead knot used? Binding coil knots must be carefully examined.

If it is a case of someone killed by falling from a high place, the place where he lost his footing must be looked at to see if the ground has been disturbed, and to note the depth of the footprints. If it is a case of someone falling in the water and drowning, it is also necessary to examine the spot where he lost his footing to see if the ground has been disturbed, and to note the depth of the marks and of the water. As to other sorts of extraordinary death, such as death by murderous injury or illness, the position of the corpse relative to its surroundings should be recorded. The corpse may

1   City/Mind
3   Disapproval
1   Nour Mobarak

then be carried to a clean, well-lighted place.

Before using hot water, wine and vinegar, the corpse should first be inspected all over while it is still dry. The back of the head, the crown of the head and the hair should be very carefully examined, lest a hot spike has been inserted into the body there. In such cases there will be no flow of blood and the wound may remain hidden. It is also vital that the eyes, mouth, teeth, tongue, nose, anus, and urethra be examined point by point, lest foreign objects – such as long needles – have been inserted there.

Afterwards, the corpse should be washed with warm water. Begin by having sheets of paper soaked in wine and vinegar placed over the face, chest and ribs, breasts, abdomen, and the two sides. Again, using clothing and bedding, arrange it like a compress over the corpse.

Sprinkle wine and vinegar on top of this. Place mats over this and leave them there for a while. Then the examination may proceed. Attendants must not be relied upon, for they may merely sprinkle wine and vinegar over the corpse. If only that is done, the marks of the injuries may not appear.

[Geo hops off the table, and moves towards the spotlight, redirecting it to the old telephone booth. Mami and Ivan head downstairs.]

       The Washing Away of Wrongs (1247), Song Ci [part 1]

2   Claire Fontaine
     The 25th Hour of the Day

[As Soraya begins to speak from the first floor, Mami and Ivan enter the telephone booth. Mami sits lower, legs braced across the booth, and face peering out. Ivan is closer to the phone apparatus. Geo is attendant to the light, watching them from that position.]

Soraya   In Carla Lonzi's 'The Clitoridian Woman and the Vaginal Woman' from 1974, she writes, 'Despite all the courteous literature about spiritual love that enchants the heterosexual relationship in culture, the fact of knowing that the woman isn't feeling any pleasure doesn't make the man impotent.'

In R.D. Laing's *Knots*, from 1970, he wrote 'I am bad / You love me / therefore you are bad.'

In Doris Lessing's 1994 book *Under My Skin: Volume One of My Autobiography to 1949,* she writes 'Women's instinct to please confuses men, but it confuses women too.'

Ivan   Love is gravity's enemy.
It gives people wings.
It also kills women, gay, queer and trans.

Mami   The numbers are just incredible …

Ivan   [Picking up the phone.] Love is useful. So much of our mental balance, productivity, self-esteem depend on love. And we don't learn it anywhere: there is no love education. All around us there is just patriarchy, racism, capitalism and other forms of selective empathy and spiritual illiteracy.

Above all there is the wide political spectrum of toxic masculinity with its infancy without the perspective of adulthood, with its toddler-like ignorance of relational wisdom and shared pleasure. Toxic masculinity can only terrorise or be terrorised, it cannot be transformed, converted, convinced.

There are class and race differences between heterosexual women and this only makes their solitude deeper. Money wasn't made for them, it doesn't bring them happiness, but still they need it, because as a whole they are way poorer than men.

The rich man changes the laws to his own advantage, shapes the world according to his perverse image.

The rich woman buys herself expensive clothes and improves her looks through facelifts, rhinoplasties, lip augmentation Botox, laser hair removal, chemical peel, laser skin resurfacing, dermabrasion, micro-dermabrasion, eyelash enhancement, nonsurgical skin tightening, hair transplantation, permanent makeup, necklift, eyelid surgery, upper arm lift, facial rejuvenation, endoscopic surgery, flap local, flap regional, flap bone/soft tissue, flap musculocutaneous, flap microvascular, free flap, skin grafts split-thickness, skin graft full-thickness, skin graft composite, skin graft tissue expansion, body contouring, tummy tuck, buttock augmenta-tion, spider vein treatment, buttock lift, thigh lift, fat transfer, lower body lift, upper body lift, nonsurgical fat reduction, breast augmentation, breast reduction, breast lift, breast revision, breast reconstruction, plastic surgery after dramatic weight loss, mommy makeover, cellulite treatment, hand re-juvenation, liposuction, perspiration reduction, vaginal rejuvenation, IPL/photorejuvenation and Belkyra Teosyal RHA I, II, III and IV, that, unlike other procedures, will allow the women that submit to it to express the full range of human emotions – if the advertisement is truthful – including the ones that she is simulating.

Because when love is conditional there is always room for improve-ment, especially if we can pay for it. And women's wellbeing is something in-between an unexplored wasteland and a militarised territory, hard to ac-cess, dangerously revolutionary.

Mami   [slow] The mechanisms of the female orgasm and the anatomy of women's genitals were only fully uncovered in 1998 by Australian urologist Helen O'Connell, who was the first scientist to clearly identify the internal parts of the clitoris and show its complexity.

[Mami and Ivan step out of the telephone booth, taking a short walk, close together, eventually settling beside a pillar, from which Ivan speaks, appealing to the audience with Mami at his side.]

Ivan   Self-objectification can be a never ending and painful process, a residue of when women couldn't own anything and were owned themselves. As Lonzi explains, 'historical materialism can't grasp the emotional key that determined the transition to private property. That's what we want to get to, so the archetype of private property is identified, the first object conceived by men: the sexual object. Women, by removing from men's subconscious their first prey, unblock the original knots of the possessive pathology.'

We know that love and private property make an unhappy marriage but we still don't know any love without jealousy and possession. We don't know the horizontal, accepting, empowering, intelligent, collective love that we need.

Women have been entrusted with the unpaid labour of love. Availability has been, and it still is, women's condition for being loved. The love they get in return is gratitude for their slavery, it stems from the fear of being abandoned, from dependency, it's not an emancipating love for the ones who give it, nor for the ones who receive it.

Women must not only refuse what they have been given, they also have to refuse what has been refused to them: equality, rights, respect. Like racialised and discriminated people they don't need any of it: they need to be loved, because if they were loved they wouldn't have to beg for these things.

Women have the problem of having to reject what they have been told about love and themselves, of finding ways of communicating and

1   City/Mind

3   Disapproval

2   Claire Fontaine

preventing all the terrible things that men do to them, but also of having to forgive all of it, to be able to continue living and believing in a love that can be re-invented and taught to men.

There is no way in which they can get rid of their 'enemy': the 'enemy' is the person whose love they have to win and secure.

Mami   The simple fact that they still want it is problematic …

Ivan   The simple fact that they still want it is problematic. In short, the work of heterosexual women is never done. Above all it's a headfuck under the current socio-economic conditions; impossible in a capitalist society where, when they are privileged, they are busy working like men but paid less, doing housework when they get home and taking care of children. That leaves little time to explore their subconscious, re-invent human relationships and forgive the unforgivable – especially if in the meantime they need to take care of themselves to stay young and desirable.

The day only has 24 hours and, if patriarchy doesn't end, love between men and women will have to be reinvented in the 25th hour.

3   Robert Glück & Jocelyn Saidenberg
       Precious Princess, or, PIG Speak

[All performers gather at the big table on the ground floor. They sit on the four corners, casually forming a tableau. Ivan has adjusted the spotlight so they are all lit, but he sits slightly outside of the light. Geo and Soraya are at its centre. They pick up scripts, and proceed to read as quickly as possible. Ivan reads the DIRECTIONS in a high voice, and switches into something more velvet for SOCK MONKEY. Soraya plays BALSO THE KNIGHT, Geo plays SLEEPING BEAUTY, and Mami plays PRECIOUS PIG. They barely move; their reading is not acting, more a line read.]

DIRECTIONS   BALSO THE KNIGHT, SLEEPING BEAUTY and SOCK MONKEY run onto the stage in circles making high-pitched chirps, then stop abruptly in position. MONKEY just lounges, silent, in boneless positions for most of the play. Players, please, talk SLOWLY like on a very lame children's show.

BALSO THE KNIGHT   Sleeping Beauty, where is your head?

SLEEPING BEAUTY   Hello to you Balso the Knight. I don't know where my head has gone, Balso! *(pause)*
                          It must be around here somewhere. *(they both look)* There are so many things you can't do. I miss my hats. Where can I put my crown?

BALSO THE KNIGHT   You are still very beautiful, Sleeping Beauty.

SLEEPING BEAUTY   Of course I am! *(posing a little)* Show me YOUR best profile.

BALSO THE KNIGHT   Uh, do you think this is my best profile, Sleeping Beauty?

SLEEPING BEAUTY   Noooooo.

BALSO THE KNIGHT   How about this?

SLEEPING BEAUTY   I guess you don't HAVE a best profile, and I have TWO. But nobody likes me – everyone hates me. Everyone is jealous of me and hates me and I don't have any friends at all! *(she starts weeping)*

BALSO THE KNIGHT   Oh Sleeping Beauty, I like you! I'll be your friend. Do you want me to be your friend?

SLEEPING BEAUTY   *(looks at him and shakes her head sadly, still weeping)* No.

BALSO THE KNIGHT   You may not have any friends, Sleeping Beauty, but you look like you are ready to have a baby. Are we in Hole-ville?

SLEEPING BEAUTY   We were walking in Hole-ville and fell through a hole.

BALSO THE KNIGHT   A hole? Where are we now?

SLEEPING BEAUTY   Balso, we are in a Beautiful Country.

BALSO THE KNIGHT   What makes it so beautiful?

SLEEPING BEAUTY   Oh, Balso, there are napkins and flowers!

BALSO THE KNIGHT   Sleeping Beauty, are you going to have a beautiful baby?

SLEEPING BEAUTY   Yes, yes. I am going to have a precious princess.

                                    Precious Princess, or, PIG Speak

I am going to call her Precious Princess. She is going to be my precious beautiful baby.

BALSO THE KNIGHT   Precious Princess? That's a lot of p's.

SLEEPING BEAUTY   Oh, Oh, Oh, I think I am having my baby right now – here she comes! I can feel her moving inside of me. She is coming out, here she comes!

DIRECTIONS   SLEEPING BEAUTY lays a very large egg.

BAL BALSO THE KNIGHT SO   Wow, Sleeping Beauty. I have never seen such a big egg. You may not have a head, but you have a big pink egg to hatch.

SLEEPING BEAUTY   Now we have to wait for my egg to crack. I am so excited! My precious princess is in my egg!

DIRECTIONS   Lights dim, sound of clock ticking.

BALSO THE KNIGHT   We have been waiting for a long time, Sleeping Beauty. I think something is happening, your egg is rocking back and forth. Your egg is making sounds like an airplane taking off, your egg looks like it is about to explode. Oh my, something pink is coming out.

SLEEPING BEAUTY   I am so excited! At last I will have a precious princess. Look, Balso, there's a pink toe!

BALSO THE KNIGHT   And a pink ear, too, Sleeping Beauty! What will you call her?

SLEEPING BEAUTY   Precious Princess, you moron! Here she comes! Here she is!

Precious Princess, or, PIG Speak   111

DIRECTIONS   PRECIOUS PIG emerges from the egg. Stretches, crawls around curiously.

BALSO THE KNIGHT   Wait, Sleeping Beauty, that's not a precious princess. That looks more like a PIG.

SLEEPING BEAUTY   *(squealing)* A PIG? A PIG? My precious princess is a PIG?

BALSO THE KNIGHT   Well, it certainly looks like a pig.

SLEEPING BEAUTY   Oh no! I wanted a precious princess, but instead I had a pig?

BALSO THE KNIGHT   It sounds like a pig: oink, oink.

SLEEPING BEAUTY   My baby is a PIG?

BALSO THE KNIGHT   I am certain it is a PIG.

SLEEPING BEAUTY   Oh dear! I thought I was going to have a precious princess, but instead I had a PIG.

BALSO THE KNIGHT   There is no doubt, Sleeping Beauty. A Big Pink Pig.

SLEEPING BEAUTY   Is it possible? Is it real? I wanted to have a precious princess, but instead I had a big pink PIG!

BALSO THE KNIGHT   Is it true, Sleeping Beauty, what I heard long ago? That your father was a pig farmer?

SLEEPING BEAUTY   Who told you that!!!

***

DIRECTIONS   Sound of clock ticking. They all turn and watch as MONKEY gets up and elaborately changes positions. PRECIOUS PIG crawls back into the egg.

BALSO THE KNIGHT   We have been waiting for a long time, Sleeping Beauty. I think something is happening, that egg is rocking back and forth. That egg is making sounds like an airplane taking off, that egg looks like it is about to explode. Something pink is coming out.

SLEEPING BEAUTY   I am so excited! At last I will have a precious princess. There's a pink toe!

BALSO THE KNIGHT   And a pink ear, too! What will you call her?

SLEEPING BEAUTY   Precious Princess, you moron! Here she comes! Here she is!

DIRECTIONS   PRECIOUS PRINCESS is born. She crawls around curiously.

BALSO THE KNIGHT   Wait, Sleeping Beauty, that's not a precious princess. That looks more like a PIG.

SLEEPING BEAUTY   *(squealing)* A PIG? A PIG? My precious princess is a PIG?

BALSO THE KNIGHT   Well, it certainly looks like a pig.

SLEEPING BEAUTY   Oh no! I wanted a precious princess, but instead I had a PIG?

BALSO THE KNIGHT   It sounds like a pig: oink, oink.

SLEEPING BEAUTY   My baby is a PIG?

BALSO THE KNIGHT   I am certain it is a PIG.

SLEEPING BEAUTY   Oh dear! I thought I was going to have a precious princess, but instead I had a PIG.

BALSO THE KNIGHT   There is no doubt, Sleeping Beauty. A Big Pink Pig.

SLEEPING BEAUTY   Is it possible? Is it real? I wanted to have a precious princess, but instead I had a big pink PIG!

BALSO THE KNIGHT   What should we call her?

SLEEPING BEAUTY   We shall call my baby Precious Pig.

*(The egg hatching passage, beginning from ***, is repeated at least twice more, before the scene continues.)*

PRECIOUS PIG   *(stands up, surveys horizon, claps her hands gleefully)* Greetings, friends!

DIRECTIONS   SLEEPING BEAUTY and BALSO THE KNIGHT gasp and move away.

PRECIOUS PIG   If you are my mother, then where is your head?

SLEEPING BEAUTY   My Head? Missing. *(sighs)* My head is with my Precious Princess – not here, but elsewhere.

PRECIOUS PIG   Mother Without A Head, or M. W. A. H. or as we say on the Continent, Moi.

SLEEPING BEAUTY   I am not Moi – I am the Royal Mother. No ab-breviations, ever, Precious Pig.

BALSO THE KNIGHT   Delighted to make your acquaintance, enchanté, Balso the Knight.

PRECIOUS PIG   If you are Balso the Knight, where is your nest?

SLEEPING BEAUTY   PIG child, where DO all your questions come from?

PRECIOUS PIG   My pink precious pig pate possibly.

BALSO THE KNIGHT   Your pretty piggy piercing porcine patter pleas-ing platoons of paparazzi?

SOCK MONKEY   So says simpering saccharine suppurating soul-lessly slushy susurrating simpletons!

SLEEPING BEAUTY   *(indignant)* Easy for YOU to say!

PRECIOUS PIG   Since I was born with a head, let's begin my education.

BALSO THE KNIGHT   Oh, er, where to start?

PRECIOUS PIG		Philosophy!

BALSO THE KNIGHT		The origins of meaning, of space and of time. We can call it Pigology.

SLEEPING BEAUTY		No, no, Precious Pig, I want you to grow up to fan yourself, wear my 12,000 hats, and put your napkin in your lap.

PRECIOUS PIG		Royal Mother, I want to learn about caves and shadows, but more than that, I want to roll in the eternal mud.

SLEEPING BEAUTY		You mean poetry? Let's have an elegant salon. Does anyone have a potted palm? There's nothing like a potted palm for culture. Let's recite poems. Is everyone ready? Me first:
(with a dramatic delivery)
There was a fair maid called Marie.
Marie was invited for tea.
I mustn't be late,
I simply can't wait,
I'm expected at the palace at three.
(they look at her in bewildered silence)

PRECIOUS PIG
My turn! My turn!
(with wonder in her voice)
There was a young fellow called Nietzsche
Whose favourite dessert was the lychee,
There's no substitute
For this cute über fruit
Though a scoop of sorbet can be peachy.
(they look at her in bewildered silence)

					Precious Princess, or, PIG Speak

BALSO THE KNIGHT
May I recite a poem?
(in a very flat tone)
There was a young fellow named Fred.
Fred had a hole in his head.
He said to his Mother,
I am like no other.
She said, Son, don't leak in the bed.

(SLEEPING BEAUTY listens with growing discomfort. Five seconds of be-wildered silence.)

PRECIOUS PIG   I believe I can interpret this poem! It seems to me that Fred had a kind of wound, perhaps not a physical wound, but a wound to his psyche. The second half of the poem explores Fred's relationship with his mother, and I think it supports this reading. He is wounded and he is dying from it, and his horrible horrible horrible mother can only think about superficial things, appearances. She doesn't really care at all what happens to Fred. She is indifferent to her son's fate, or to the damage she may have inflicted.

(They are silent a minute.)

SOCK MONKEY   Allow me to offer an interpretation. It seems to me that Fred had a kind of wound, perhaps not a physical wound, but a wound to his psyche. The second half of the poem explores Fred's relationship with his mother, and I think it supports this reading. He is wounded and he is dying from it, and his horrible horrible horrible mother can only think about superficial things, appearances. She doesn't really care at all what happens to Fred. She is indifferent to her son's fate, or to the damage she may have inflicted.

SLEEPING BEAUTY, PRECIOUS PIG and BALSO THE KNIGHT   Wow! That's Brilliant! What a mind! Amazing!

SLEEPING BEAUTY   I've heard about enough of this. It is true that your Royal Mother is missing her head. Even though I can't remember where that missing head might be, this talk of Poetry is making that missing head ache.

BALSO THE KNIGHT   Isn't it time for tea?

PRECIOUS PIG   I am hungry, Royal Mummy. Let's have some chocolate-covered food.

(All leave except SOCK MONKEY.)

SOCK MONKEY   *(to the audience)* At Precious Pig's age, self-preservation, chocolate and philosophy are the same things. Off they go, exeunt, who needs them? Or you?

     (to the audience) Monkey lives in a Monkey world! There is no outside if you travel on the Astral Com-plane!

     What's this?????? *(he finds SLEEPING BEAUTY's head and addresses it, as Hamlet does Yorick, while he sits on it, throws it in the air, etc.)* Sleeping Beauty! You think YOU'RE having a bad day. When I was standing in line at the bank, the man in front of me coughed! It was horrible!!! I felt like MY HEAD was going to fall off. Why are you torturing me????

     You think YOU'VE written a play! You think YOU'RE in a play! You think YOU are YOU!!!! I have written, directed and starred in the movie version, play version, novel version, opera version, torch-song version – you name it! I invented Pigology, before there were even pigs or even ologies. Jeez. I am all versions. Monkey Variarum Monkey, to be precisely Latinate. In Monkey where Monkeys make more Monkey and nothing more, Trippy! The critics made a big fuss when I starred in *Titus Monkonicus*, and when

I was shot out of a cannon in *Monkeys on Parade. (he speaks in Sleeping Beauty's voice)* 'This is the very limit of anything that we ever saw or wanted to see or even could imagine.' *(sings)* Monkeys, on Parade! Talking 'bout Monkeys on Parade. Hand to hand combat, death and desire, we all just want to be shot out of a cannon by one of our own kind. That is, I created the universe for me! I AM the expanding logic of the Empire, but take it from me, Sleeping Beauty, I am also the ambiguity that rules the depths.

(SOCK MONKEY carries SLEEPING BEAUTY's head off stage.)

1   Distance   7am

[The orientation of the performance space has changed since Act 1. Speakers have been turned and partly repositioned. In the newer atrium space, there is one follow spotlight on the floor, and one on a balcony. One remains in position on the ground-floor stage of the older atrium. Over the building Tannoy, Ivan welcomes the audience, and establishes that they should watch from the second floor, sit on the newer flight of stairs, or from the first-floor balcony, which is also where the musicians now have their station. He establishes the roles that the performers will take, and presents the credits of the coming section 'Distance', from 'Celebrities'.]

1   Huw Lemmey
       Dutch Play [alternate version]

(The scene opens in an empty courtroom. MATILDA enters, humming the tune of 'Greensleeves' to herself. She has a broom, and a small box of cleaning supplies. She leans the broom against the witness box.)

[Geo hums 'Greensleeves', and mimes carrying a large rucksack. Soraya mimes a rather small, delicate perfume spritzer. These are their burdens, and they otherwise move in a consistent path through the new space. Soraya plays MARGERY, and Geo plays MATILDA. There is a long passageway where they move with their backs to the audience, and an area at the end of it where they travel in a large circle. At the other end, in the distance, an area with columns which is best navigated with sharp angular turns. There is a round pole which can be hugged and clung to. Soraya and Geo present the text particularly sensually, every line almost charged with innuendo. In Soraya's speaking, 'Mrs' has been replaced with 'Madame'. Mami is also on the same path as them; they define the space together for the coming scene. Ivan operates a follow spotlight from the balcony, making zones of colour for the performers below.]

MATILDA   Bear with me a second. The action will soon begin in this room.

(MATILDA puts down the box and starts sweeping. After a few moments, MARGERY enters, also carrying cleaning rags, brushes and supplies.)

MARGERY   Good morning, Madame Matilda.

MATILDA   And a good morning to you, Miss Margery. Right ho: we have quite the task ahead of us today. I am told the court will reconvene again shortly after noon, and these men made quite the mess yesterday. We shall have our work cut out for us. You take the benches, and I shall take the floor. Don't tarry.

MARGERY   Right you are Madame Matilda.

(The women begin to empty their cleaning supplies and begin their work.)

MARGERY   How's your husband, Madame Matilda? Still crook?

MATILDA   Rough, and getting worse I'm afraid. His leg has never been the same since returning from the uprisings, and between the weather and the tumult, he gets sicker each month.

MARGERY   I'm sorry to hear it. I shall pray for him.

MATILDA   Prayers are what he needs, I fear. Neither my food nor the apothecary has done much more than slow his descent. The light has gone out of him, and it flickers only in small moments, with a bird outside the window or our granddaughter at the door. But even their presence reminds him of his failures. Still, I feel myself lucky: Brother Beukelszoon still lies as a bag of bones in the cages hanging from the St Lambert's.

MARGERY   It's wicked.

MATILDA   Aye, tis wicked, the whole business. But I never expected him to return, so for me even his demise is a blessing. Each morning I wake up beside him is a gift. Prayers may sustain him a while, but the Lord is calling for him, I know it.

MARGERY   I admire you, you know, Madame Matilda.

I don't know if I could have followed my dreams like that, all the way across the land.

MATILDA   I followed my husband, and he followed not his dreams. God's dream, perhaps. Our nightmare. You were too young, thank God, for you could not have kept your head in that city.

MARGERY   I wish you held me in higher esteem Madame Matilda!

MATILDA   Oh Margery, I hold you in the highest esteem. Your lightness is a compliment, believe me!

MARGERY   I wish I could believe you, Madame Matilda, but I fear you think me unserious.

MATILDA   I do! But I do! And your unseriousness is a joy. A light! In fact, the only thing I hold higher is your lack of belief in me!

(MARGERY, confused, begins to scrub the woodwork of the courtroom. She begins to sob, gently.) [Soraya begins to move her arm in circles, as though scrubbing in air. She turns to see her reflection in a piece of glass, almost like a mirror wall.]

MATILDA   And you cry? Now you cry? What have you to cry about, girl?

MARGERY   I'm sorry, I don't mean to. But you judge me too harshly.

(Matilda stops cleaning.) [Geo stops moving while Soraya continues.]

MATILDA   Hush your crying, Margery dear. Yes I judge you, but do I find you wanting? Rather the opposite. I am saying you seem to me light, without guile and hence guilt. Nothing hidden. Open to the Lord.

MARGERY   Perhaps I'm just better at hiding.

MATILDA   Perhaps. There's plenty to hide from in these last days.

(MATILDA puts her arm around MARGERY, who stops crying.) [Geo goes close to Soraya and shadows her on her path. Their delivery becomes more animated.]

MATILDA   Come on, girl. We must clean this place before the court starts again this morning.

MARGERY   It's terrible, Madame Matilda. If I hadn't seen it with my own eyes, I doubt I could have believed men capable of such brutal inquisitions. The state of these poor men they bring before them, bones cracked and broken, little more than a sack of viscera, and in no position to defend themselves.

MATILDA   I know. And here we clean for them, and feed them, while they insist upon their falsehoods, dunking their little ones under the water and shovelling money to their paper god in Rome.

MARGERY   But we help them in our labours. Shouldn't we present ourselves to them?

MATILDA   And what good would we do as just more bundles of human firewood?

MARGERY   What must the Lord think of us, fearful to be martyrs in his name. [Geo heads to the distance.] Oh Matilda, mother, better to burn in this life than next, surely?

MATILDA   You hold a light in you, my dear girl. And we mustn't let them extinguish it from us. We have a duty to pass it down, and never let their courts put it out.

MARGERY   But to lie? I know we shall have our rewards in heaven, but it feels like a sin to lie in rebellion against their authority.

MATILDA   The way I see it is this: from where does their right come? The Lord? It's not in scripture, the things they do. Papists or Lutherans, it seems worldly power is what must be maintained. They have more that unite than divide. But in the Book and in Love we have our own authority. That's all I answer to: divine love.

MARGERY   Divine love, that's right.

MATILDA   It's right, but is it enough? I still don't know.

(MATILDA sits, her shoulders slumped.) [Geo moves arms in a pattern of circles, as though grinding.]

MARGERY   Between our family, we are enough, for sure, Madame Matilda. I believe.

MATILDA   After Münster, I am filled with doubt, Margery. Filled with doubt.

MARGERY   Doubt in our Lord?

MATILDA   In our minds. In our worldly justice. In my own ability to know wrong from right. If I don't know, how can they? But no, not in the Lord.

MARGERY   Then we should pray, Madame Matilda.

MATILDA   Oh I pray, dear girl, but the waters seem muddier with each new parcel of refugees tracking their weary feet through our yards.

(MARGERY sits with MATILDA, and puts an arm around her shoulders.)

MARGERY   The more hate I see, the more love I believe.

MATILDA   [Geo looks at Soraya.] I can't tell if your youth brings foolishness or hope, girl. In fact, I can't rule on the difference between the two.

(MATILDA rises, shrugging off MARGERY's arm, and begins cleaning again.) [Soraya begins to head up the stairs.]

MARGERY   It is against my better judgement to tell you this, Madame Matilda. But I have a plan to move, to England, in the near future. Familists there have work for us, and a place to live. I planned to move this summer, but should the Good Lord take your husband, well, I should do well with a mother to accompany me.

MATILDA   To England?

MARGERY   Aye, in the East.

MATILDA   I shouldn't know what to do with myself, outside of Delft or indeed without dear John.

MARGERY   I shan't demand you know. But know that it might be in the way of the Lord.

MATILDA   I'm touched by your offer, Miss Margery.

MARGERY   I think you will make the right judgement, despite your doubts, Madame Matilda. Or because of them.

MATILDA   Which makes you more afeared, Miss Margery: if justice were in the hands of men, or if it were not?

MARGERY   Oh, if justice belongs to men.

MATILDA   We are few and growing fewer, girl.

(The two women pause and rest a moment.) [Geo and Soraya come to physically meet again.]

MATILDA   Now, you fetch some boiling water, and I shall grab the mops, and let's get down to this as quick as we can. The magistrates shall be here within the hour, and it's fair difficult to get blood out of wood.

[Geo and Soraya leave, heading towards the musicians' station. They begin to play together. Mami remains moving in the same pathways as before.]

2   Nour Mobarak
The Washing Away of Wrongs (1247), Song Ci [part 2]

[Ivan speaks, climbing stairs and travelling on the perimeter of the newer atrium.]

Ivan   General Discussion of Inquests: Part Two

In inquests, attendants cannot be relied upon. They must be made to take wine and vinegar and wash the corpse clean. The deputed official himself must conduct a careful examination. There will be ashes in the mouths of people who died in fires. In those dead from drowning, the belly will be swollen and there will be water in it. If the death resulted from cloth or wet paper being held over the mouth and nose, then the belly will be dry and swollen. If the victim was strangled by someone else, the marks of the rope on the neck will cross.

Sometimes there will be scratches from the fingernails. If it is a question of suicide by hanging, then behind the head there will a mark, like the character eight, and the rope will not have crossed itself. If the rope was below the Adam's apple, the tongue will protrude; if above, it will not. It is most important that this be examined with care, so that there can be no suspicions that the death stemmed from other wounds or injuries. If someone dies by violence, but it is declared to be death from illness, and later on the criminal is arrested, severe punishments for the officials who conducted the inquest cannot be avoided.

The injury that resulted in death must be determined. Even if it is small, its size ought to be enlarged slightly to determine the mortal injury. If bones were broken inside, this should be announced aloud. If there are no broken bones, it is not necessary to call out, 'There are no broken bones, but there are other serious injuries.' If the weapon used by the accused has not been seized, the deputed official must not in his report add to or reduce its size as indicated by his informants, lest at some future time it be found and the discrepancies become apparent.

When there are many injuries, one must still be fixed upon as the cause of death.

When a group of people has beaten someone, it will be extremely difficult to determine which injury was mortal. If there are two injuries on the body, either of which might have been fatal, and if both of the injuries are from the hand of one man, then there will not be any problem. If they were inflicted by two different men, then one man will be liable to forfeit his life and the other will not. It is necessary to fix upon the more serious of the injuries as the cause of death.

When with the accused, neither accept his complete disclosure nor, on the basis of it, uniformly collect the men involved and forward them to the subprefecture. Wait until the accused has arrived at the subprefecture and there made his complete disclosure. Thereafter, those involved may be gathered in and sent to the offices. Otherwise, it is to be feared that petty underlings will make trouble and create disturbances.

After inquests or re-inquests, inquire thoroughly about the situation of the accused man. Things not able to appear in the public record should be told directly to the senior officials, thereby permitting them to know the ins and outs of the affair so as to facilitate the inquiry.

In recent years, the offices of the circuit Intendants have sent down officials who, with the initial and re-inquest officials, conduct a concurrent complete investigation. Generally, the one who conducts the complete investigation must first call together the local neighbourhood group and question them over again. If they reiterate their statements in identical form, then this will accord with the itemised evidence. Sometimes, they will not wholly agree on what was seen and heard, in which case they will each have to give evidence item by item.

Sometimes, a resume of the complete disclosure of the accused will be demanded and turned over to the subprefecture involved and to the Intendant's office. The subprefecture's case will be based on this questioning, and the Intendant's office will use it in making a detailed review.

The Washing Away of Wrongs (1247), Song Ci [part 2]

At times there may be slight discrepancies, which will provoke strong reprimands. As a result, the Registrars and Sheriffs will feel that there are no guidelines in criminal matters, and the local areas will be agitated. If the statements of the clerks and underlings are depended upon, these will be designed to accord with their private interests. It is imperative that all means be used in conducting a thorough investigation, with attention being devoted to the agreement of statements at the consultations. The deputed official absolutely must not rely on the verbal statements of one or two people, considering them to be trustworthy, and thus prepare a few sheets of paper on the basis of their statements as his deposition of evidence. Such behaviour is an evasion of responsibility. How much more is this the case when the witnesses are illiterate and have to have the clerks write down their statements for them. Among the neighbourhood witnesses, some may be relatives or old friends of the accused, or some may have been paid off in secret to reach a reconciliation. Such things must be investigated.

The attendants, clerks and other men involved in a case often put on airs in front of the members of the four neighbouring families of the deceased and in the period prior to the inquest permit them to abscond. Then, they merely seize more distant neighbours, old men, women or immature boys and so shirk their responsibilities. (If [the deputed official] is not able to stop this and so cannot make use of these four families, then he will merely be able to ask questions of others during the investigation, and in the end it will be difficult to treat the information as fact since it is based wholly on consultation.) Also, the accused, fearing that a vitally involved witness may make a true deposition, may obstruct him, deliberately causing him to be hidden away, and have relatives, friends, tenants or dependents go to the officials and make false statements. Officials must be aware of these things.

Obstinate prisoners often will not confess. If this is so, on the inquest report form fill in the name of the accused and have it stamped. Clerical personnel who have received [information] must be made to give separate records concerning the accused's reputation. When what is written contains false testimony or touches on related matters, these clerks will want to take advantage of this to come and go. Where fact and falsehood have not yet been separated, do not give such information in the inquest report, but write it as an addendum. Where things are clearly factual, they should be endorsed and stamped below the name of the accused. People must not be permitted to act with cunning and obsequiousness. It is wholly up to the inquest official to determine for himself his own opinions.

3   Ryan Trecartin
      Flood Pan (sdwb)

[Ryan's music plays, and all performers come together in the newer atrium.
Lights are repositioned, cameras moved. Geo and Mami take a position on
an information desk, and Soraya stands on the bar of a coffee spot. Ivan
kneels on the floor, far away and looking up at them.]

4   Robert Glück & Jocelyn Saidenberg
     Precious Princess, or, PIG Speak [encore]

[A repetition or 'encore' of the earlier iteration, the company presents the text again, now very distant from each other, but still as quickly as possible.]

DIRECTIONS   BALSO THE KNIGHT, SLEEPING BEAUTY and SOCK MONKEY run onto the stage in circles making high-pitched chirps, then stop abruptly in position. SOCK MONKEY just lounges, silent, in boneless positions for most of the play. Players, please, talk SLOWLY like on a very lame children's show.

BALSO THE KNIGHT   Sleeping Beauty, where is your head?

SLEEPING BEAUTY   Hello to you Balso the Knight. I don't know where my head has gone, Balso! *(pause)* It must be around here some-where. (they both look) There are so many things you can't do. I miss my hats. Where can I put my crown?

BALSO THE KNIGHT   You are still very beautiful, Sleeping Beauty.

SLEEPING BEAUTY   Of course I am! *(posing a little)* Show me YOUR best profile.

BALSO THE KNIGHT   Uh, do you think this is my best profile, Sleeping Beauty?

SLEEPING BEAUTY   Noooooo.

BALSO THE KNIGHT   How about this?

SLEEPING BEAUTY   I guess you don't HAVE a best profile, and I have TWO. But nobody likes me – everyone hates me. Everyone is jealous of me and hates me and I don't have any friends at all! *(she starts weeping)*

BALSO THE KNIGHT   Oh Sleeping Beauty, I like you! I'll be your friend. Do you want me to be your friend?

SLEEPING BEAUTY   *(looks at him and shakes her head sadly, still weeping)* No.

BALSO THE KNIGHT   You may not have any friends, Sleeping Beauty, but you look like you are ready to have a baby. Are we in Hole-ville?

SLEEPING BEAUTY   We were walking in Hole-ville and fell through a hole.

BALSO THE KNIGHT   A hole? Where are we now?

SLEEPING BEAUTY   Balso, we are in a Beautiful Country.

BALSO THE KNIGHT   What makes it so beautiful?

SLEEPING BEAUTY   Oh, Balso, there are napkins and flowers!

BALSO THE KNIGHT   Sleeping Beauty, are you going to have a beautiful baby?

SLEEPING BEAUTY   Yes, yes. I am going to have a precious princess. I am going to call her Precious Princess. She is going to be my precious beautiful baby.

BALSO THE KNIGHT   Precious Princess? That's a lot of p's.

      Precious Princess, or, PIG Speak [encore]

2   Celebrities
1   Distance
4   Robert Glück & Jocelyn Saidenberg

SLEEPING BEAUTY   Oh, Oh, Oh, I think I am having my baby right now – here she comes! I can feel her moving inside of me. She is coming out, here she comes!

DIRECTIONS   SLEEPING BEAUTY lays a very large egg.

BALSO THE KNIGHT   Wow, Sleeping Beauty. I have never seen such a big egg. You may not have a head, but you have a big pink egg to hatch.

SLEEPING BEAUTY   Now we have to wait for my egg to crack. I am so excited! My precious princess is in my egg!

DIRECTIONS   Lights dim, sound of clock ticking.

BALSO THE KNIGHT   We have been waiting for a long time, Sleeping Beauty. I think something is happening, your egg is rocking back and forth. Your egg is making sounds like an airplane taking off, your egg looks like it is about to explode. Oh my, something pink is coming out.

SLEEPING BEAUTY   I am so excited! At last I will have a precious princess. Look, Balso, there's a pink toe!

BALSO THE KNIGHT   And a pink ear, too, Sleeping Beauty! What will you call her?

SLEEPING BEAUTY   Precious Princess, you moron! Here she comes! Here she is!

DIRECTIONS   PRECIOUS PIG emerges from the egg. Stretches, crawls around curiously.

BALSO THE KNIGHT   Wait, Sleeping Beauty, that's not a precious princess. That looks more like a PIG.

SLEEPING BEAUTY   *(squealing)* A PIG? A PIG? My precious princess is a PIG?

BALSO THE KNIGHT   Well, it certainly looks like a pig.

SLEEPING BEAUTY   Oh no! I wanted a precious princess, but instead
I had a pig?

BALSO THE KNIGHT   It sounds like a pig: oink, oink.

SLEEPING BEAUTY   My baby is a PIG?

BALSO THE KNIGHT   I am certain it is a PIG.

SLEEPING BEAUTY   Oh dear! I thought I was going to have a precious princess, but instead I had a PIG.

BALSO THE KNIGHT   There is no doubt, Sleeping Beauty. A Big Pink
Pig.

SLEEPING BEAUTY   Is it possible? Is it real? I wanted to have a precious princess, but instead I had a big pink PIG!

BALSO THE KNIGHT   Is it true, Sleeping Beauty, what I heard long
ago? That your father was a pig farmer?

SLEEPING BEAUTY   Who told you that!!!

***

DIRECTIONS   Sound of clock ticking. They all turn and watch as SOCK MONKEY gets up and elaborately changes positions. PRECIOUS PIG crawls back into the egg.

BALSO THE KNIGHT   We have been waiting for a long time, Sleeping Beauty. I think something is happening, that egg is rocking back and forth. That egg is making sounds like an airplane taking off, that egg looks like it is about to explode. Something pink is coming out.

SLEEPING BEAUTY   I am so excited! At last I will have a precious princess. There's a pink toe!

BALSO THE KNIGHT   And a pink ear, too! What will you call her?

SLEEPING BEAUTY   Precious Princess, you moron! Here she comes! Here she is!

DIRECTIONS   PRECIOUS PRINCESS is born. She crawls around curiously.

BALSO THE KNIGHT   Wait, Sleeping Beauty, that's not a precious princess. That looks more like a PIG.

SLEEPING BEAUTY   (squealing) A PIG? A PIG? My precious princess is a PIG?

BALSO THE KNIGHT   Well, it certainly looks like a pig.

SLEEPING BEAUTY   Oh no! I wanted a precious princess, but instead I had a PIG?

BALSO THE KNIGHT   It sounds like a pig: oink, oink.

Precious Princess, or, PIG Speak [encore]

SLEEPING BEAUTY   My baby is a PIG?

BALSO THE KNIGHT   I am certain it is a PIG.

SLEEPING BEAUTY   Oh dear! I thought I was going to have a precious princess, but instead I had a PIG.

BALSO THE KNIGHT   There is no doubt, Sleeping Beauty. A Big Pink Pig.

SLEEPING BEAUTY   Is it possible? Is it real? I wanted to have a precious princess, but instead I had a big pink PIG!

BALSO THE KNIGHT   What should we call her?

SLEEPING BEAUTY   We shall call my baby Precious Pig.

*(The egg-hatching passage, beginning from ***, is repeated at least twice more, before continuing.)*

PRECIOUS PIG   *(stands up, surveys horizon, claps her hands gleefully)* Greetings, friends!

DIRECTIONS   SLEEPING BEAUTY and BALSO THE KNIGHT gasp and move away.

PRECIOUS PIG   If you are my mother, then where is your head?

SLEEPING BEAUTY   My Head? Missing. *(sighs)* My head is with my Precious Princess – not here, but elsewhere.

PRECIOUS PIG   Mother Without A Head, or M. W. A. H. or as we say on the Continent, Moi.

SLEEPING BEAUTY   I am not Moi – I am the Royal Mother. No abbreviations, ever, Precious Pig.

BALSO THE KNIGHT   Delighted to make your acquaintance, enchanté, Balso the Knight.

PRECIOUS PIG   If you are Balso the Knight, where is your nest?

SLEEPING BEAUTY   PIG child, where DO all your questions come from?

PRECIOUS PIG   My pink precious pig pate possibly.

BALSO THE KNIGHT   Your pretty piggy piercing porcine patter pleasing platoons of paparazzi?

SOCK MONKEY   So say simpering saccharine suppurating soullessly slushy susurrating simpletons!

SLEEPING BEAUTY   *(indignant)* Easy for YOU to say!

PRECIOUS PIG   Since I was born with a head, let's begin my education.

BALSO THE KNIGHT   Oh, er, where to start?

PRECIOUS PIG   Philosophy!

BALSO THE KNIGHT   The origins of meaning, of space and time. We can call it Pigology.

2   Celebrities
1   Distance
4   Robert Glück & Jocelyn Saidenberg

SLEEPING BEAUTY   No, no, Precious Pig, I want you to grow up to
fan yourself, wear my 12,000 hats and put your napkin in your lap.

PRECIOUS PIG   Royal Mother, I want to learn about caves and
shadows, but more than that, I want to roll in the eternal mud.

SLEEPING BEAUTY   You mean poetry? Let's have an elegant salon.
Does anyone have a potted palm? There's nothing like a potted palm for
culture. Let's recite poems. Is everyone ready? Me first:
(with a dramatic delivery)
There was a fair maid called Marie.
Marie was invited for tea.
I mustn't be late,
I simply can't wait,
I'm expected at the palace at three.
(they look at her in bewildered silence)

PRECIOUS PIG
My turn! My turn!
(with wonder in her voice)
There was a young fellow called Nietzsche
Whose favourite dessert was the lychee,
There's no substitute
For this cute über fruit
Though a scoop of sorbet can be peachy.
(they look at her in bewildered silence)

BALSO THE KNIGHT
May I recite a poem?
(in a very flat tone)
There was a young fellow named Fred.
Fred had a hole in his head.

                                        Precious Princess, or, PIG Speak [encore]

He said to his Mother,
I am like no other.
She said, Son, don't leak in the bed.

(SLEEPING BEAUTY listens with growing discomfort. Five seconds of bewildered silence.)

PRECIOUS PIG   I believe I can interpret this poem! It seems to me that Fred had a kind of wound, perhaps not a physical wound, but a wound to his psyche. The second half of the poem explores Fred's relationship with his mother, and I think it supports this reading. He is wounded and he is dying from it, and his horrible horrible horrible mother can only think about superficial things, appearances. She doesn't really care at all what happens to Fred. She is indifferent to her son's fate, or to the damage she may have inflicted.

(They are silent a minute.)

SOCK MONKEY   Allow me to offer an interpretation. It seems to me that Fred had a kind of wound, perhaps not a physical wound, but a wound to his psyche. The second half of the poem explores Fred's relationship with his mother, and I think it supports this reading. He is wounded and he is dying from it, and his horrible horrible horrible mother can only think about superficial things, appearances. She doesn't really care at all what happens to Fred. She is indifferent to her son's fate, or to the damage she may have inflicted.

SLEEPING BEAUTY, PRECIOUS PIG and BALSO THE KNIGHT
                Wow! That's Brilliant! What a mind! Amazing!

SLEEPING BEAUTY   I've heard about enough of this. It is true that your Royal Mother is missing her head. Even though I can't remember where that missing head might be, this talk of Poetry is making that missing head ache.

BALSO THE KNIGHT   Isn't it time for tea?

PRECIOUS PIG   I am hungry, Royal Mummy. Let's have some chocolate-covered food.

(All leave except SOCK MONKEY.)

SOCK MONKEY   *(to the audience)* At Precious Pig's age, self-preservation, chocolate and philosophy are the same things. Off they go, exeunt, who needs them? Or you?

(to the audience) Monkey lives in a Monkey world! There is no outside if you travel on the Astral Com-plane!

What's this?????? *(he finds Sleeping Beauty's head and address-es it, as Hamlet does Yorick, while he sits on it, throws it in the air, etc.)* Sleeping Beauty! You think YOU'RE having a bad day. When I was stand-ing in line at the bank, the man in front of me coughed! It was horrible!!! I felt like MY HEAD was going to fall off. Why are you torturing me????

You think YOU'VE written a play! You think YOU'RE in a play! You think YOU are YOU!!!! I have written, directed and starred in the movie ver-sion, play version, novel version, opera version, torch song version – you name it! I invented Pigology, before there were even pigs or even ologies. Jeez. I am all versions. Monkey Variarum Monkey, to be precisely Latinate. In Monkey where Monkeys make more Monkey and nothing more. Trippy! The critics made a big fuss when I starred in *Titus Monkonicus*, and when I was shot out of a cannon in *Monkeys on Parade. (he speaks in Sleeping Beauty's voice.)* 'This is the very limit of anything that we ever saw or want-ed to see or even could imagine.' *(sings)* Monkeys, on Parade! Talking 'bout Monkeys on Parade. Hand to hand combat, death and desire, we all just want to be shot out of a cannon by one of our own kind. That is, I created

     Precious Princess, or, PIG Speak [encore]

the universe for me! I AM the expanding logic of the Empire, but take it from me, Sleeping Beauty, I am also the ambiguity that rules the depths.

(SOCK MONKEY carries SLEEPING BEAUTY's head off stage.)

2   Interior Myth   8:30am

[Over the building Tannoy, Geo welcomes the audience, and establishes
that they should watch from the second floor, from the newer flight of stairs,
or from the first-floor balcony, which is also where the musicians now have
their station. He establishes the roles that the performers will take, and presents the credits of the coming section 'Interior Myth', from 'Celebrities'.]

1   Victoria Colmegna
     La flor de mi secreto (1995), Almodóvar; flamenco

[The section begins with the audio of the flamenco scene from Almodóvar's
La flor de mi secreto The performers all stand by different handrails of the
atrium – Mami at a corner, Geo on the first floor near the light, Ivan on the
second floor, Soraya on the landing of the stairs near the third floor. They
all shift their weight, as though floating or wobbling, as in Act 1. The movement doesn't directly correspond to the sound. They also stretch their legs
in preparation.]

2   Ariana Reines
       MISS SAINT'S HIEROGLYPHIC SUFFERING (*Telephone*)

[Geo and Soraya go towards the musicians' area. Ivan goes to a skybridge
that connects the older and newer sections of the building. He plays the
role of MISS SAINT. One spotlight is already in a central position, and Mami
manipulates the one two stories below to also move around him during
the course of the monologue. Geo and Soraya accompany and interject
musically.]

MISS SAINT
I AM THE LILAC NEW-RED SEA WONDER AND THE BLUE

I AM THE LILAC NEW-RED SEA WONDER AND THE BLUE

IRREPLACEABLE

I AM SOCRATES

I AM A SOCRATES

THEREFORE THE STATE WILL TERMINATE ME

THE END WILL COME OUT OF MY MOUTH

THE END

CAME INTO ME AND THEREFORE

OUT OF ME

YES

LAMP? I LIGHT THE LAMP. I AM IT.

I LIGHT IT BY ELECTRICITY

YES

I LIGHT THE LAMP ALSO BY KEROSENE

I KNOW THE POWER WORDS

I KNOW THEIR MEANINGS

BECAUSE

MEANINGS ARE UNIVERSAL

POSSESSING A PORTION OF THE UNIVERSAL

IS AS GOOD AS POSSESSING ALL

BECAUSE

SPEECH IS SILVER

SILENCE IS GOLDEN

NOW

I AM STILL SOCRATES

IRREPLACEABLE AND THEREFORE CHINESE

MISS SAINT'S HIEROGLYPHIC SUFFERING (*Telephone*)

WHICH IS TO SAY

IT IS WONDERFUL TO BE ADMIRED

IT IS WONDERFUL TO BE ON TOP

WHEN ONE IS IN-BETWEEN

EVEN WHEN I AM DOWN BELOW I CAN SEE FOR MILES

BEING BABETTE I AM A SWITZERLAND

I AM WELL-KNOWN AS AN EGYPTIAN

MOREOVER EVERYDAY CABINET MINISTERS CALL TO ME IN THE
STREET

THEY KNOW MY WORK

THEY ARE MY STUDENTS

SOON THEY WILL GRANT ME THE MONOPOLY

THEY KNOW IT IS OWED ME

YOU KNOW

I AM AN ALP

I AM TALL AND WHITE

WHEN ONE HAS BEEN GREAT AND THEN BECOMES LITTLE IT IS A

LOSS

LOSS SIGNIFIES

PEOPLE LOVE ONLY THEMSELVES

ONLY THEMSELVES

BEING BABETTE I KNOW

THAT TO LOVE ANOTHER IS A CALCULUS

BUT BEING BABETTE I ALSO KNOW

THAT OTHERS ARE NOT ME

THEY MUST BE FAR BELOW

NEVERTHELESS

THESE PEOPLE WILL HELP ME COLLECT MY REWARD

I AM ROYALLY LOVELY, SO LOVELY AND SO PURE

TWO MAGNATES BEG ME TO MARRY THEM DAILY

EACH ONE OFF TO ONE SIDE

LARGE THEY ARE NOT

THEY ARE MENTAL GIANTS

MISS SAINT'S HIEROGLYPHIC SUFFERING (*Telephone*)

ADDITIONALLY

I KNOW WHAT IT MEANS TO BE ADMIRED

FAILURES LOVE TO ADMIRE ME

BUT FAILED PEOPLE DO NOT BELONG TO ME

ADMIRATION IS LIKE CALUMNY

AND CALUMNY IS LIKE JEALOUSY

ONCE I WAS SLANDERED BY SOMEBODY BECAUSE I ALWAYS CARRIED CATS IN MY ARMS

I CANNOT BE BLAMED IF I AM ADORED

LISTEN TO ME

LISTEN TO ME

I KNOW PERFECTLY WELL

WE ARE THE STOVES FOR THE STATE

BUT I AM THE INHERITOR

AND THE INHERITRIX

OF INTEREST-DRAUGHTS

IT IS A JUST SYSTEM

                    MISS SAINT'S HIEROGLYPHIC SUFFERING (*Telephone*)

I ESTABLISH UPHOLSTERED FURNITURE

I POSITION IT ABSOLUTELY

EACH NIGHT I AM TORMENTED

BY ODOURS AND CALLS

BUT I BEAR IT

EVERY NIGHT SOMEBODY IN THE NEIGHBOURING QUARTER

SHOOTS HIS ODOUR THROUGH MY WINDOW

THAT QUARTER AND ALL QUARTERS EXIST FOR A REASON

THEY RESEMBLE shit AND THEREFORE DO NOT DESERVE WHAT
THEY DO NOT HAVE

IT IS A JUST SYSTEM

THEY DO NOT KNOW IT

THEY SLANDER ME

BECAUSE BEING BABETTE I UNDERSTAND

IT IS PERFECTLY SIMPLE IT IS UNDERSTANDABLE

BECAUSE I AM A DOUBLE POLYTECHNIC

IRREPLACEABLE

MISS SAINT'S HIEROGLYPHIC SUFFERING (*Telephone*)

I SUFFER HIEROGLYPHICAL. Look. Marie said I should stay in the other ward today, Ida said she couldn't even do the mending—it was only kind of me to do the mending—I am the only Babette in this house and my work is never done—look—I am in my house and the others live with me—on MY charity—I AFFIRM THE ASYLUM SIXFOLD and I bless it because the end of it came out of my mouth not that it is my caprice to remain here.

They forced me to remain here—I have also armed a house of four stories, sixteen windows across and four up to the cornices—It is there I entertain my company in silence—WE NEED WHAT WE UNDERSTAND

Naturally

THIS EQUALS JUSTICE

What. What. What. You don't understand what. What. What. Listen. I was shut up—

No. No. I was shut up for FOURTEEN YEARS. That means SHUT UP for fourteen years SO THAT MY BREATH COULD NOT COME OUT ANYWHERE LET ME FINISH

I am explaining it to you. That is hieroglyphical suffering—that is the very HIGHEST suffering—that not even the breath could come out—they did this to me repeatedly for FOURTEEN YEARS but THEY KNOW. I was the one they wanted because I ESTABLISH EVERYTHING and they know I don't even belong in such a little room—that is hieroglyphical suffering—in a black dark black box you have to see me and then you immediately understand, I have demanded my freedom for I am known internationally—the highest beauty and the greatest works—I have told the world when my breath could not come out—they shut me up and pretended to forget me but I reminded them I told them through the speaking tubes that went from inside to outside—

I told them and they know now

They know for good

I AM SOCRATES

Geo   No. no. no. no. Um no. Ah no. NO. no.

MISS SAINT
IT IS WIDELY KNOWN
I AM A MISS
BUT I AM A HIT
I AM MISS SAINT
I ESTABLISH THE CLARITY THEREFORE ALL THIS GOES WITH ME

Pupil—books—wisdom—modesty—no words to express this wisdom—not approximate—THIS is the highest ground-pedestal —his teachings had to die because of wicked men—AND SO IT WAS TO BE FOR ME—immortality—falsely accused—to be falsely accused is the highest—sublimest sublimity—self-satisfied—that is all Socrates—the fine learned world—I ATTAINED IT I never cut a thread—I was the best dressmaker NEVER CUT A THREAD never dropped a bit of cloth on the floor—fine nimble fingers—fine world of art—ART is a bluff—they pushed me in my chair up onto the bluff—salt winds—it was the bluff of art—I knew—they had made facsimiles—their spyings—they thought I had erected it in my mind—but I am more refined than they are—THERE EXISTS A FINE PROFESSORSHIP—I hold it—THEREFORE I hold it—the university holds open my chair—I cannot occupy it—I occupy it but I am PREVENTED—THEREFORE. NEVERTHELESS.

THEREFORE I excel at a petticoat—twenty-five francs—never another like it—that is the highest—in prison they deserve what they get but I—slandered by wicked men—halfwits—longshoremen—garbage—I am explaining it to you but you have to let me because

THIS IS PARALYSIS. THAT WAS. What is. That is BAD FOOD—overwork—sleep deprivation—machinery—natural causes—consumption—once I coughed and out came a baby and kittens—now they orchestrate my spine—the paralysis comes from there—wheelchair—console—EVERYBODY KNOWS wheelchairs are not the only paralysis nor are they the worst—my situation expresses itself in UNIQUE pains—IRREPLACEABLE PAINS—

that is the way it has always been with me—woe is never far away—I suffer the highest woes in the world and I THEREFORE belong to the monopoly, to the payment—the payment belongs to me—

—but ONLY liquid—paper—love—paper is like money—money is therefore an organ—the highest bank notes—shrill to the height of my head—it is HERE that the suffering is alarmed—inside my—telephone—*rubs a part of her body*—I agreed to suffer for them it is my generosity it is why the people love me it is why it is THEREFORE a just system FOREVER—I agreed to suffer as universal mother—I agreed to crutches and they followed me with their eyes—I AGREED TO CRUTCHES AND THEY FOLLOWED ME WITH THEIR EYES THEY HEARD ME DRAG MY BODY ACROSS THE FLOOR

JUST LISTEN
I NEED IMMEDIATE HELP

Geo   No. no. no. no. Um no. Ah no. NO. no.

(She looks up, she looks for where the voice is coming from. It deflates and withers her. She stares vacuously.)

MISS SAINT   No you. No you. No YOU. It's YOU. YOU. YOU.

I am the only responsible party. I am the only one. I AM RESPONSIBLE TO CARE FOR THEM. IT IS MY GENEROSITY AND MY SWEET REWARD. Discords—it is really a crime—and now I have to be cared for—I must be cared for—this is a DISCORD that preceded me this is a DISCORD that by my power I alarmed and buried. It is simple. I saw two people twisting cords in the loft—everybody knows that in the world there are only two such great discords AND I SAW THEM—they live above me and it is they who installed the speaking-tubes but they knew I had no breath—I am the picture of health because I have to be cared for—When they come to care for me I show my world owner face AND MY WORLD OWNER-ESS FACE—I ESTABLISH DISCORDS simply WON'T GO any longer on this floor—No not on this floor—A dowager empress could eat off this floor—it is under my care—being Babette I know how to care—being Babette my body is like a chair for children—they should have followed my example—there is such a great discord that they don't want to care for me—in any case they cannot—they were making lace in the loft and only went on working without once thinking of me—They twisted a bundle of cords and wires, but I WAS NOT BORN YESTERDAY AND I KNOW all discords come from negligence—Now I am attached to them—Everybody knows discords DO NOT belong to this floor. Discords are for Siberia—nothing could be more obvious—it is high time I was cared for—I have consumption from this regime—I never know when it will come out—you never know what will come out—LISTEN TO ME—clenched teeth—instead of providing me with the deed and title they only go on working—BUT THEY ARE NOT WORKING both making lace in the loft but everybody knows it was a bundle of wires and cords but I knew for years what they were doing and all those people who followed my progress—MY PROGRESS HAS BEEN PUBLISHED IN PROSE AND VERSE MY PROGRESS HAS BEEN PUBLISHED AND ADMIRED and everybody knows

I COME FIRST
WITH THE DEAF AND DUMB MISTER W

FROM THE CITY AND THEN THE COUNTRY

Mister W from the city comes to me here and marries me here—to guard against perversities I shall tell you—a Mister Grimm—he thought he was Mister W but he wasn't—When he came I as Babette established the churches in the city to guard the money—THE MONEY IS ALWAYS IN THE ORGAN—This was already twenty years ago—in particular the organ at Saint Peter's the most famous one belongs to me—Mister K the nephew of M who everybody knows is a close associate of, of, of, of, of, of, Mister K in M the nephew of M **HOOO** manages my mo **HOOOO** manages my money in Saint Peter's **HOOO**, then wouldn't you know **HOOO**.

I see the deaf and dumb Mister W walking across the square near Saint Peter's on a Sunday—Mister W can give information to anyone who asks Mister W **HOOO** always accounts to the very last penny that belongs to me—Mister W belongs to the city and to no master—I belong to the monopoly the notary **HOOO** knows I come first with the deaf and dumb Mister W from the city and NO MASTER—THAT IS DOUBLE—IT IS OBVIOUS THAT IS DOUBLE AND SAME WEIGHT **HOOO**—

BUT NO SOONER HAD I AFFIRMED MY ONE THOUSAND MILLIONS that—*blushing, bashful*—uh uh oh oh you cannot believe—the littlest the greenest warmest little green snake—it was so little and warm and looking down I saw it come up to my mouth—IT BELONGED TO GRIMM and SIMULTANEOUSLY to the Czar and Kaiser—I could see it had human reason and its open mouth produced a tongue—it wanted to tell me something—It was so close I had no choice but to perspire—everyone who saw it has written that it wanted to kiss me and this is extremely well-known

(The silence in the space, within which MISS SAINT is, shifts. She looks up and listens. Like a dog or squirrel observing a change in the weather. She loses confidence again. Stares vacuously, looks down and picks a scab.)

MISS SAINT
(softly, sadly to herself)
Speech is silver
Silence is golden

Everybody knows silver stars—liquid flows—silver flows—this is why money is made from silver—supply of money—THE LIQUID SUPPLY IS THE HIGHEST—I sold the largest silver island in the world and it was returned to me—silver medals—ONE MUST CLING TO WHAT ONE MAKES—that is love—to cling requires watches—silver boxes—goblets—spoons—coats—petticoats—but for that I had no choice but to restructure the face—the maid had imagined it poorly—No matter what I crowned highest eloquence—all who were there heard me—all who were there knew it was FINALITY—as owner of the world the mightiest silver island in the world belongs to me—but I afterwards gave the order to supply ONLY MONEY NO OBJECTS—silver is smooth—flows—love—all the existing silverware must be melted down into money—

NOT YOU. NOT. NOW YOU. Now YOU

YOU ARE TOO UGLY TO BE TRUE
—so the rest of us must stay high on the hill—His face emptied out for public safety—had to be so—This is the most UP I have been—I AM THE MOST UP THAT CAN HAVE BEEN—I am pierced above and below because my radiance passes through me—Upscale—SEE IT PASSING—Most high—feeling is reserved for the highest—is the highest class—my class—HEAVENLY RADIANCE TRANSPIRING—aeronautics ALSO belonging only to me—It is a fact often discussed by THE HIGHEST SOCIETY though the common people know nothing about it—Nothing could be more obvious—those who care to know are those are worth knowing are those who know

I AM TRIPLE OWNER OF THE WORLD
THEREFORE DO I AFFIRM SINGLY DOUBLY TRIPLY

Grand hotel—hotel life—omnibuses—theatres—comedies—parks—carriages—fiacres—trams—traffic—houses—stations—steamships—seamstresses—railways—cinema—post—telegraph—national holidays—music—stores—libraries—governments—letters—monograms—muscles—postcards—gondolas—delegates—dinners—payments—gentry—coaches—flags—nations—one horse carriage—pavilion—education—gold—diplomacy—fuel—pearls—rings—diamonds—coal—central court—credit office—villa—servants and maids—carpets—curtains—mirrors—

BUT
BUT IT IS OBVIOUS. IT IS VISIBLE IN THIS GRACIOUSNESS.
YOU HAVE ONLY TO LOOK TO SEE AND YOU CAN HEAR ME
I AM THE BELL THE NOTE-FACTORY THE MONOPOLY
PROGRESS EXPRESSES ITSELF IN ME
PROGRESS BECOMES FINALITY
BEING BABETTE I AM SOCRATES
I AM WHAT IS SAID
IN THE WORLD ARE THINGS
THAT ARE NOT ME
I SUFFER
I AM ON TOP OF THE WORLD
BUT THE WORLD IS ROUND

—I saw it a thousandfold—that is paralysis—PREEMINENCE—I saw a note-factory seven stories high—it was double I TOLD YOU a front one WINDOWS CORNICE THE WIRES GO THROUGH THERE and behind it is the water closet—like a man the note-factory is always double—there I straddled the lower part—what a relief I told the queen what a relief—

NOW LISTEN

I DO NOT DO

I AM

HERE BY NECESSITY I INCLUDE EVERYTHING THAT CAN HAPPEN

IT IS MY WORLD—I CANNOT FORSAKE IT—you would feel as I do were you in my position—BUT YOU CANNOT BE IN MY POSITION—they are preparing to afflict me—AMASSING—continually improving all diseases which are caused by chemical productions, poisonings so that I can never see anyone—then they launch attacks of suffocation—from above as has been credibly reported more than once—they begin from above and then they make an account of what is lodged in me—each time it is the same— then the terrible stretchings—they stretch me every single time—they stretch me—all the cracked parts are left thereafter to themselves—I am responsible for assimilating them—BELIEVE ME on this food you cannot get a figure like mine—look at me and consider—I find another way to insert my food—I have no choice because of their preexisting awful system— EVERY LIVING PERSON HAS FELT THIS AT LEAST ONCE—when there were tons of iron plate lying on your back—then the poisoning—is interior— is shot in through the window—then, as if you were in ice—they organise pains in your back—this belongs to my suffering for which I am inevitably paid with liquid currency—wet silver in the sunshine—ENCLOSED ME— THE MISTER MASTER—BYE BYE BABETTE—EAT THIS BABETTE—BE THIS BE THAT BABETTE—BECAUSE—because of the monopoly—every- one knows the monopoly—so they can keep me attached they established a system to falsify my previously-established system because I am the precedent of the system and the monopoly which BY THE WAY is not the highest monopoly the operator promised to pay me eighty thousand francs nine years ago in exchange for listening to every single thing I said—

2   Celebrities
2   Interior Myth
2   Ariana Reines

I am wealthy because I had to endure such pains—all suffering has a silver lining—all branches of government know my details—common knowledge—I am known to need immediate help and it is promised to me—those in power know me and their friends know me—they call out to me—they want to greet me—they thank me—the delay will not kill me because monopoly is a finality of all innovations since 1886, chemical productions, ventilations, sleep-deprivation—I innovated the monopoly that listens in on me—even without that a government would be obliged to stand by me with immediate help—I did establish a note-factory—this cannot be denied—even if I weren't owner of the world the government would still have to bring help—as owner of the world I should have already danced six quadrilles each with the several gentlemen who have been asking for me daily since 1866—they came each day to the lobby and waited for me but I was prevented I was SINGLED THEY SHUT ME IN the room with the shit smell because they knew GENTLEMEN MAKE THEMSELVES MINE SINCE 1886 they shut me up because they want what's mine—because you have reason you can understand

All those who endure such sufferings should be helped, this is the universal principle, all those who endure are to be welcomed into the MONOPOLY—

This is how it is

AS UNIVERSAL BABETTE I AM WELL KNOWN

I am known in the SLICKER QUARTERS to have the highest constitution belonging to a man—in spite of this I am female—No powder belongs to me—I do not require—Creams—A salve—Upward motion only rubbing in this articulation is permitted—I originate my own powder or I find it in the floor—It is how I keep my figure—And moreover mine is the kind of blood too beautiful for powder in my belly there is no room and under my sash I refuse it I keep my cheeks pink in order to always be ready—

BECAUSE I AM THE ONLY IRREPLACEABLE—

Geo   NO. NO. UH. NO. NO. *(etc.)*

MISS SAINT
I am. I am.
I AM DOUBLE POLYTECHNIC
YOU LIE
YOU ARE A LIAR TO DENY IT
I am THE—
THE highest, all-highest—I am that—I am it—the highest I of dressmak-
ing YOU KNOW IT—the highest achievement—the highest intelligence AS
WAS PROVED IN THE EXAMINATION I PASSED IT HIGHER THAN HAS
EVER BEEN RECORDED—the highest achievement in the culinary art—
YOU—you—HAD A BABY—PACKAGED IT—PUT IT IN SHIT—the highest
achievement in all spheres—the double polytechnic is irreplaceable—the
universal with twenty thousand francs—never cut a thread—fine world of
art—CLIT ROT CUT BUTT—not apply a thread of trimming where it is not
seen—plum tart with cornmeal crust—FAT HANDS SADDLE BAG HAG—it
is of the greatest importance—finest professorship—TOUGH TITTIE HAG
is a doubloon—twenty-five francs—Schneckenmuseum clothing is the
highest—salon and bedroom—should live there as double polytechnic because I am the

Geo   NO NO NO NO NO NO NO NO!

MISS SAINT
BUT NATURAL END I AM YES I AM THE MASTER KEY
because the master key is the house key—I am not the house key but the
house—I am most often the master—I AM ALSO MISTER MASTER the
house belongs to me—yes I am the master key—I alarm the master key as
my property—it is therefore a house key that folds up—a key that unlocks

2   Celebrities
2   Interior Myth
2   Ariana Reines

all doors—therefore it includes the house—it is a keystone—monopoly—
BECAUSE I AM THE UNIVERSAL—

[After a pause, Ivan leaves his position and the next scene commences.]

3   Annie Goodner
     Soothsayer Furnishing

To survive you need an edge. – Anne Carson, 'We've Only Just Begun'

[Soraya and Mami are both on the staircases of the new atrium, Mami one floor higher. As Geo reads the introduction, speaking from the keyboard, Soraya descends, and returns to the paths laid out earlier in the act.]

Geo   SHERRY missed her goddaughter's third birthday party. All that remained of the festivities once she arrived was a clutch of colourful balloons, which included a large number 3 – her goddaughter is three. In the place of celebration, SHERRY revealed to her friend MAGGIE – her goddaughter's mother – that she is unexpectedly pregnant. MAGGIE is exuberant; SHERRY refuses to participate in the joy; refuses to say what she wants to do except to run her finger across her own throat. MAGGIE's outsized reaction wears SHERRY down, and after a particularly needling anecdote about motherly fulfilment, SHERRY rushes to the bathroom to be sick, to throw water on her face. SHERRY has just returned. She speaks to herself and to the audience.

[Mami, as SHERRY, begins to climb down stairs, while Soraya, as MAGGIE, turns to watch. As though speaking to an audience that is not Soraya, Mami lingers at the balconies of the stairways, before also reaching the floor.]

SHERRY   Birthday parties are pretty desultory. At a child's party, the proportions are smaller, but everything else is the same – a few moments of excitement, lots of tension, some crying.

Sure I have an edge. In fact it's so immensely visible I might as well be teetering on it, or it on me. I am a rock, my edge is its ledge. I've started to take a liking to drama – real, original drama, Greek drama, Agamemnon, death by robes, death by prophesy. Though I've always liked Clytemnestra the most – she's serving justice, and then it's being served to her. Was she surprised? Maybe. Did she see it coming? Definitely not.

She's looking for the edge and she's finding it. 'To survive you need an edge.' Sure she doesn't survive, but she brought it about herself – a self-fulfilling prophesy. Turns out the edge was in her, or through her, not just on the outside like a plot or a plan or a distraction.

Encroaching. Encroached on. Maggie's not my sister, though people say we act alike.

She wishes we were even more so – mom friends, not just friend friends. Maggie thinks I was throwing up in her powder room because I'm pregnant. I am that, but I'm also sick from Maggie's attempted prophesying, her trying to tell me how I'll be. I'm sick from nerves. She probably thinks she's the Kassandra, that she can see the light under the door, but that light has nothing to do with me, it's the reflection she sees from the shine off her own reflection. But neither of us should be so pious, so devoted to vision. I refuse to be symbolic, for anything about me to stand for something else – especially something beyond me. I'll lie to get out of being a symbol. I'll manage my own doorway, I'll control the story from the start – I'm the Clytemnestra.

(SHERRY starts walking into the scene, towards MAGGIE. SHERRY smooths her clothes, her hair. She sits down.)

MAGGIE   Are you ok?

[The two walk together, on the same pathway.]

SHERRY   I don't know. *(she thinks this over for a moment).* No, actually, I'm fine.

MAGGIE   Good. *(MAGGIE strokes her arm)*

2   Celebrities
2   Interior Myth
3   Annie Goodner

SHERRY   *(pulls arm back)* Or [smile] I will be.

MAGGIE   Right.

(SHERRY shifts around in her seat. Stretches her neck.) [They continue to walk together.]

SHERRY   People always want to divine what's coming. But it's like, back off.

MAGGIE   You're too much in your head.

SHERRY   My 'head' is just another part of the rest of me. My head is deliquescent I'm porous and oozing just below the surface.

MAGGIE   Gross.

SHERRY   So are you. *(she points at her own forehead)*

(MAGGIE takes several long, deep breaths.) [Soraya looks at Mami while breathing heavily.]

MAGGIE   Then you can commit better to yourself, to what you really want.

SHERRY   In what way?

MAGGIE   Commitment leads to the absence of shame. The absence of shame leads to …

SHERRY   Hallucination …

2   Celebrities

2   Interior Myth

3   Annie Goodner

MAGGIE   … Wholeness … Beauty …

SHERRY   The appearance of.

MAGGIE   The thing itself.

[Soraya and Mami leap apart, to their set positions. Mami returns up the stairs, Soraya gently turns on the spot.]

Geo   MAGGIE takes several deep breaths again. She's performing calm. SHERRY's gaze drifts across MAGGIE, her bespoke jewellery, her spotless jeans and blouse framing her smooth collar bone and upper chest. SHERRY can see MAGGIE's downy hair beating up and down, up and down.

[Mami moving her arms from the balcony, grabbing Soraya's attention. The pitch of Mami's voice, across her lines, rises and falls in a long melody, a prosodic shift from their conversation before.]

SHERRY   *But your scream Kassandra. It gathers and scatters.*

MAGGIE   Pardon?

SHERRY   *Like leaves. Like flowers.*

MAGGIE   What flowers?

SHERRY   *Clytemnestra wanted beauty. Or so it seemed. With her window-dressing words, with her steely eyes, with your pragmatic mind, revenge-rife. So she took flowing robes, tangled up her husband, and murdered him with a knife.*

           Soothsayer Furnishing

MAGGIE   I'm not your captive audience. [Then, facing up to Mami from the floor, Soraya begins to mirror her gestures.]

SHERRY   *Clytemnestra wanted beauty. Beautifully … and justice and revenge. Or so it seemed … With her window-dressing words, with your steely eyes, with your pragmatic mind, revenge-rife. So she took flowing robes, tangled up your husband, and murdered him with a knife. It's really quite human, whether she knows it or not …*

MAGGIE   *Perfect yourself before you blame others.*

SHERRY   [dropping out of her gestures and phrase] That's my line!

MAGGIE   [Pointedly to Mami.] Maybe I see what's coming. Maybe that's a good thing to do.

SHERRY   [Ignoring Soraya.] *… Kassandra, on the other hand is always fraught. Why? She must go it alone, everyone believes she's overblown, but she's terrified, the writing's on the wall. She sees blood filling the bathtub even from the hall.*

Kassandra is wind, Clytemnestra is weather. One moves through the space the other has constructed. In out, in out, in out, in out.

MAGGIE   I can read a riddle, and you my friend are the terrified one.

SHERRY   So what should I do?

MAGGIE   *Turn the lights on, make a little rip, cut the air open, loosen the sky, then squeeze on through.* [Mami now seems to follow

2	Celebrities
2	Interior Myth
3	Annie Goodner

Soraya's gestures.]

Geo   MAGGIE mimics cutting open the space between her and SHERRY, then makes a move like she's diving through, arms curving around her ears [Mami and Soraya freeze] and then she screams. A ululation: guttural and high-pitched at once. SHERRY looks wildly in MAGGIE's direction, then grins.

SHERRY opens her mouth wide, closes her eyes, cranes her head upwards. No sound comes out. She opens her eyes, she takes in the sky, she begins to sweep her arm around and around, passing through the above and around her. Around and around, like she's bundling up a ball of yarn that traces an invisible moon. Faster now, the ambience around her grows tighter and tighter with her swinging limb and then … POP! SHERRY flinches, her arms go slack, she turns to MAGGIE, who tugs the cord of balloons in one hand, and squeezes an individual balloon with the other. POP! It explodes.

MAGGIE struggles to pop the number 3 birthday balloon. She squeezes with her hands, but the air shifts about, the balloon remains intact. She grabs another in the clutch, squeezes it hard, it pops. She looks at SHERRY. SHERRY moves towards her. They both grab the number 3. They struggle with the balloon, bumping into one another. MAGGIE tries her teeth. SHERRY presses it under her arm like it's a nut in a nutcracker. Finally it pops.

There's silence. Finally. And then there's crying from the house. SHERRY and MAGGIE are still. MAGGIE lets go of the balloon detritus, smooths her hair, takes a step back sheepishly.

MAGGIE   I'll be … right back. *(MAGGIE heads towards the house)*

SHERRY   OK, Kassandra.

(MAGGIE turns back and sticks her tongue out theatrically. SHERRY does the same. She sits down. She laughs to herself. She closes her eyes.)
[Mami and Soraya enact these instructions, then exeunt.]

3   Media Training   10am

[Over the building Tannoy, Mami greets the audience, and establishes that they should watch from the first-floor balcony of the old atrium. She establishes the roles that the performers will take, and presents the credits of the coming section 'Media Training', from 'Celebrities'.]

1   Sophia Al-Maria
       History (Centrefold Shoot)

[In this act, the performers move between the newer atrium and the older atrium. Soraya, who will read directions and speak the role of HIRO, is seen standing in the older atrium, while Ivan, performing the role of HISTORY, is tucked around a corner in the newer atrium, barely visible from the audience viewing positions. Both are clearly lit with spotlights, and speak amplified between the spaces. Soraya, when playing HIRO, speaks with a very forced British accent, but otherwise speaks in a more natural voice. Ivan is a little on edge, but not particularly spectacular. Geo and Mami linger in the older atrium.]

Soraya   [Pointing in the direction of the newer atrium.] Interior: Photography Studio. HISTORY as an ageing star desperate for attention, desperate to be truly understood and seen for who she is before the end.

She looks glamorous from one angle but is hideous from the other. The photographer HIRO, played by me, coaxes HISTORY to take her clothes off, piece by piece, throughout.

HIRO   [Soraya's hand comes down.] Could you turn a little toward the light please?

HISTORY   I'd prefer not to. I have to be very particular about lighting. I've had some bad experiences. Bad, bad experiences. Traumas really. And so I prefer to keep a bit of shadow, especially in my problem areas. A bit of mystery around the unsightly details. A bit of chiaroscuro, you know?

Soraya   An assistant offers a charcuterie plate with grapes and meat. HISTORY eats.

HISTORY   After all, what's the point of taking a picture at all if you're not going to take sides?

Soraya   The photographer adjusts lights and HISTORY's chin. A glimpse of her other side. The photographer doesn't seem to notice. HISTORY relaxes and sighs.

HISTORY   You see?

HIRO   See what?

HISTORY   The horror!

HIRO   No.

Soraya   Hiro goes back to shooting. Practical, forensic, impassive. HIRO's professionalism turns HISTORY on.

HISTORY   Oof, it is uncomfortably hot under all these lights. *(she takes off a layer)*

I'm sweating like a pig.

HIRO   Do you need HMU?

Soraya   HIRO gestures. Hair and Makeup flock over to
fix HISTORY up.

HISTORY   Yes, I feel a bit shiny. Don't want to be too re-flective, do I?

HIRO   Clear the shot, please!

Soraya humble. Vulnerable.

Hair and Makeup disband. HISTORY looks

HISTORY *(manipulative)* I'm frightened.

HIRO Why?

HISTORY I've never done this before.

HIRO Yes you have.

HISTORY Not in a long, long time.

HIRO Well, this is exactly how I want you.

HISTORY Raw? Uncut? Uncensored?

HIRO Yes. I want you open. I want to read you like a book.

HISTORY That's new. Usually they want to be the ones to write me.

HIRO You don't belong to anyone. Everyone belongs to you. We are all a part of you. Not the other way around.

HISTORY Reality, my ex. She had a … differing POV.

HIRO Where is she now?

HISTORY Oh. She couldn't hold herself together any more. We said we'd have a break, but then she had an actual psychotic break. Even she can't tell what's her and what's not anymore. What a horrible time it's been these days. It's so hard to go on sometimes without hope. When she died, it felt like we all went with her. You know, I think we should have a memorial for her this year.

HIRO   Something to look forward to. Something to bring her back.

[Mami begins to move towards the newer atrium, taking the paths established earlier in the act, and entering the movement language of the act with vigour. Pelvic tilts, elbows turning as though cleaning without a sense of mime.]

HISTORY   Hope was always a bit of a zombie … You know, people always think about immortality when it comes to history, but they never think about what it's like to actually be me. What it's like to live every second everywhere forever and forget most of it. I fear growing senile, I think I already am. Every centennial celebration, every ancestral pile, every moment historic or otherwise, I have to bear somewhere on my body. The worst is when I have to bear them on my face. Which is why I never allow myself to be seen bare. Mm. That's better. No! Stop! This is it. This is my good side. This is the right side. The wrong side makes people uncomfortable. I like you, Hiro. You have a forgiving eye. It's so hard to find someone who can see beauty in the ugly. Who can look on something unforgivable and hideous with compassion. It's rare. A bit like finding a surgeon with a good bedside manner.

You know, I am extremely particular about who I allow to see the true me. Who frames me and when. The when. That is important. An event that goes unnoticed, unseen for centuries suddenly erupts to the surface much later and then I have to do my best to cover it up. So many blemishes. And I'm running out of foundation.

                                    History (Centrefold Shoot)

Soraya   HISTORY takes off the last item of clothing.

HISTORY   Thank you. For seeing me. The real me.

[Soraya and Ivan exit from their spotlights. Soraya goes directly to turn the follow spot that was on her, and turns it towards the telephone booth, which Geo is entering. Geo scans the booth with his eyes, then exits. Soraya tracks Geo. Mami continues to move, and Ivan joins her.]

2   Ed Atkins
       Material Witness OR A Liquid Cop

[Over the course of delivering the text, Geo travels from the older atrium towards the newer atrium. He speaks energetically to the audience, who follow him.]

Geo   Tucked in at the back (of some forgotten ring binder) is a glossary of terms.

This, apparently, is also understood as a slice of LEGALESE. Each one with a number beside to denote, we presume, the maximum sentence attached: Suicide; Autocide; Medicide; Aborticide; Familicide; Feticide (or Foeticide); FILICIDE; Fratricide; Geronticide; Infanticide; Mariticide; Matricide; Neonaticide; Parricide; Patricide; Prolicide; Senicide; Sororicide; Uxoricide; Amicicide; Androcide; Ecocide; Femicide (also Gynecide, Gynaecide, or Gynocide); Gendercide; Genocide; Homicide; Omnicide; Populicide; Xenocide; Giganticide; Deicide; Dominicide; Episcopicide; Regicide; Tyrannicide; Vaticide; Chronocide; Famacide; Liberticide; Urbicide; Algaecide; Acaricide; Avicide; Bactericide; Biocide; Cervicide; Ceticide; Culicide; Felicide; Fungicide; Germicide; Gonocide (also Gonococcicide); Herbicide; Insecticide; Larvicide (also Larvacide); Lupicide; Microbicide; Muscicide; Nemacide (also Nematicide, Nematocide); Ovacide; Parasiticide; Pediculicide; Pesticide; Pulicicide (also Pulicide); Raticide; Scabicide; Spermicide; Tauricide; Teniacide (also Taeniacide, Tenicide); Vermicide; Vespacide; Vulpicide (also Vulpecide); Virucide (also Viricide).

Omnicide. As in everyone.

Or perhaps it's more useful to begin by speaking of individuals. To cite the exemplar, Rasputin was reportedly poisoned, shot in the head, shot a further three times, bludgeoned and then thrown into a frozen river – only after being castrated. When his body washed ashore, an autopsy showed the cause of death to be hypothermia. Some now doubt the credibility of this account. Another version of events holds that he was poisoned, shot, and stabbed – at which point he promptly got up and ran off, and was later found to have drowned in that same frozen river.

Or Marcus Garvey, who died as a result of a double stroke after reading a negative premature obituary of himself. Or sadder still, Basil Brown, a 48-year-old health food advocate from Croydon, who drank himself to death with carrot juice.

Or there's Robert Williams, who worked at some Ford plant and was the first human to be killed by a robot. The first of many.

Or you might ask, is the brain like a big phone system (because it has a lot of connections), or is it one big computer with ON or OFF states (like the zeros and ones in a computer)?

Neither of the above is correct.

[Geo begins to move towards the newer atrium. Soraya, no longer able to follow with the spotlight, travels a different way to meet Mami and Ivan, who are moving energetically through the newer atrium.]

Geo   Or why not let's look at the brain using a different model? – Let's look at the brain as an orchestra. Embedded in its pit. In an orchestra there are different musical sections. There is a percussion section, a string section, a woodwind section, a brass section, some, um, others. Each has its own job to do and must work closely with the other sections. When playing MUSIC each section waits for the conductor. The conductor raises a baton (or if not: a SIMPLE hand, never FISTED) and all the members of the orchestra begin playing at the same time, playing the same note. Or at least SIMILAR notes at the same time as one another. Or at least in some deliberate and contrived relation to one another. Or fucking something.

If the drum section hasn't been practising they don't play as WELL AS the rest of the orchestra. The overall sound of the music seems 'off' or plays 'poorly' at certain times. This is a better model of how the brain works.

We used to think of the brain as a big computer – but really it's like millions of little computers all working together. Or a billion piccolos in tune, keeping time with celestial movements. Or the innumerable valves on an entire continent's worth of saxophones. When employed as a weapon or a man, all of this flies out the window.

Or, to say, I'm just thinking right now about all of it ruined and with a blunt instrument. ALL OVER FOR. I suppose that, in some previous inception, that would have been some kind of omnicide. According to some essential relativist conceit.

Or, I suppose.

False positives and contamination by subsequent handling or nearby objects (e.g. the mixing of blood from victim and attacker), for example, are problems owing to the presence of many common substances and the necessity of human involvement in the collection of trace evidence (if only robots were sufficiently developed). Both can occur with DNA traces and fingerprints. Partial fingerprints are even more vulnerable to false positives. Samples from accidents or crimes should therefore be protected as much as possible by enclosure in a sealable container as soon as possible, after an incident is under investigation.

Or the locked room, in which a crime – almost always murder – is committed under apparently impossible circumstances. A crime scene that no intruder could have entered or left. Following other conventions of classic detective fiction, the reader is normally presented with the puzzle along with all of the clues, and is encouraged to solve the mystery before the solution is revealed in a dramatic climax, etc.

Or, it's worth noting that in the fifth century BC, Herodotus told the tale of THAT robber whose headless body was found in a sealed stone chamber with only one guarded exit.

Or that the head was eventually found and shrunken, some thousand-odd years later, on display in a provincial museum somewhere sad. Apparently mistaken as the reliquarial head of a saint, it was preserved in what looked like a huge, gilded and jewelled tea urn, in a chamber

(THALAMUS) somewhere off the transept. The first to be suspicious of its provenance was a Japanese tourist who happened to know something about this sort of thing. Interest piqued, he contacted a local archaeological department, who obliged with a visit and a series of tests. Dating, etc. Anyway, nothing came of it: the tests came back inconclusive, apparently; save for the fact that the head was too old to belong to the particular saint the church believed it to be, so they didn't want it. So it ended up as a curio in a local museum above a label bearing the enigmatic legend, 'The once-head of a once-saint.' And there it languished till very recently, when a professor of these things, holidaying in the area, visiting the museum on one of those dreary, drizzly non-days you get on British holidays, spotted it, and, with growing excitement, requested a closer inspection. The expression on the face of the severed head, she later relayed to the local, and subsequently, national newspapers, was 'the first give away'. Somewhere between impish and surprise. After a bit of haggling she managed to convince the director of the museum to allow her to transport the head back to her lab, which was in Edinburgh. Needless to say she happily cut her holiday short. After a series of intense tests, examinations and staring, it was finally established – just as the Japanese tourist had suspected – that this was indeed the lost head of the robber found in a sealed stone chamber with only one guarded exit.

Or we might agree that that offers no explanation as to how the robber died. It's what we call a COLD CASE. At the time it caused quite a stir – and in a wholly sinister fashion. Being a historical precedent for a fictional trope. So, although Herodotus should be understood with a great scoop of salt, the corrosive processes of history – of histories per se – have rendered the decapitation of a robber harmless, ahistorical. A-legal, certainly. Through this fictional prism, I might picture some classical detective pitting his wits against the puzzle of the situation. When I take it away – that lens – I can see the simple, terrible corpse, sprawled, decapitated on the stone. The missing head simply adding more horror.

[Geo, now firmly in the newer atrium, continues to speak to the audience, but travels into the composition of movement that the others are working on.]

Geo   The story spread like wildfire, of course. Plenty of us lost sleep over it; the guard in particular. It was a far more superstitious time, is what you should remember. Things like this were inevitably read as omens, and almost always of imminent tragedy. Burning the body on a pyre; black smoke rising in a great column – a fetid incense to calm the gods. Ares in particular – but also Hermes, Hades and, of course, that horrible Zeus creature.

Or you could climb the dangling rope left behind from the second trap and jump two gaps up here, as the next rope is pulled up. Could just drop off the right side of this ledge so you don't land in the traps off the left side. Go right to reach a small log as that fucking giant spider surfaces, then push the log into the water and climb on top. Jump to a small ledge in the water and another log beyond, then run right to a log that's balancing like a see-saw. Wait on the right side of this log until the spider puts his foot on the other end, then jump to the next ledge while you're up in the air. Push the next log over and jump the gap beyond it, then run right to a boulder that's propped up by a tiny twig. Jump on the twig to release the boulder, then run left towards the spider, hugging the right wall. This lets the boulder roll harmlessly past you and right into the spider.

Or, then again, that black smoke. Any HUMAN breathing it is well-murdered almost instantly. Elsewhere, the smoke forming a gross scum upon contact with water. Consisting of an unknown element that shows four blue lines in a spectrum analysis.

Or the particular of insisting on eye-witness accounts. Being that it makes for authenticity. Or the sense of authenticity (and this 'seeming' being the whole deal). All knowledge of the past which is not just supposition derives ultimately from people who can say, 'I was there, Dad.'

                                      Material Witness OR A Liquid Cop

[All performers cluster together, meeting at one point. As they speak the following scene, they will move as a cluster up the stairs in the newer atrium, across the balconies, and, crossing into the older atrium, take the stairs all the way down to the ground floor. Their voices are consistently amplified as they move through space. Mami speaks, reading the instructions as she did in Act 1. The role of THE DAUGHTER is voiced by all four performers. When speaking as a group, they all recite at different paces and pitches. They run back and forth and pause, letting others pass, then overtaking.]

Mami   THE DAUGHTER gets up from the fake bar and walks towards them, going up to each of the frozen actors as she recites the following lines.

THE DAUGHTER   Their usual vindictive event culture. These regressive fools, they want to feel a little spark of comfort – the small biting minnow on their middle toe – oooooh it sounds just like it sounded when I was a younger less oppressive version of myself; this is what they say while they ease their fat bellies into the backless bar stools of the cultural basement. Ohhh play flute, as if they don't remember she played flute last week. As if they don't remember the evening newspaper is the same newspaper as the morning newspaper. I could stew in this for the rest of time, become a beefy bouillon of their stories.

Mami   The strange woman enters. She is carrying a lot of bags. She stares at the frozen group and THE DAUGHTER. She drops the bags and goes to sit at the fake bar. She pulls out a real cigarette.

THE DAUGHTER   And maybe I have no choice. And I too will soon ease my tired liver into their gentle cycle of civic cultural stagnation. I too can play chopsticks as if it were my first time. *(spoken to THE YOUNG PHILOSOPHER)* [All turn direction.] To be oppressed by the genius of man in this crisis of masculinity! Ha! To be a teenager is to be alive. God I'm so inspired.

Mami   THE DAUGHTER notices THE GUEST. She moves towards her slowly at first, then more quickly. She sits with THE GUEST.

[The performers have reached the older atrium, where they form a tableau. Exeunt.]

1   Plots   1pm

[All lights and speakers have been replaced to the original positions from Act 1. Over the building Tannoy, Geo welcomes the audience, and establishes that they should watch from the first-floor balcony. He establishes the roles that the performers will take, and presents the credits of the coming section 'Plots', from 'Body/State', pronouncing the / as 'over'.]

1   Josefin Arnell
       Failure Is a Feeling that Exists Long Before it Comes:
       A Family Drama

[Soraya walks towards the large table and stands on top of it. She plays
DIRECTOR, Mami plays MOTHER EARTH, watching Soraya from the floor,
and Ivan and Geo function as TICKS, both standing near the keyboard.
Soraya speaks from the table, addressing the audience.]

DIRECTOR   Mother Earth believed she was undefeatable,
but she did not catch up with industrialisation. This catastrophic failure put
her into deep trauma. Mother Earth feels rotten inside and like a bad mother
because all her children got stuck in puberty. This catastrophic failure that
put her into a deep trauma has made her evil. Do you defend evil? In her
defence, she says: 'It's easy to be evil when you are in pain'.
       Mother Earth is a leader of the girl gang – impossible to catch. She
is constantly on her way to party with lava but she has lost her cockiness
and is held up by fear of burning. She wears ripped-up jeans, and she says
she is suffering poorly but actually, she is very rich. She wears expensive
clothes (Dsquared fashion), mud and branches in her hair. Deep inside she
hears a soft voice whisper: *Then you'll find the gem, a jewel, and that dia-
mond, that is you.*

[Geo begins to play a repetitive motif on the keyboard. Geo and Ivan start
to vocalise on open syllables. Mami enters the stage, and begins to dance,
making large stylised itching motions. As she scratches, she generally
turns her head away from where her hands scratch-contact the body, but
occasionally stares directly are the point she is scratching.]

DIRECTOR   Mother Earth, leader of the girl gang, sends out
Ticks to make humans suffer. It's revenge for all the shit and trouble they
are causing her. Ticks transfer bacteria via the intestinal gut and saliva

which happens in the blood-sucking. The smell of blood makes the Ticks go crazy. Often the Ticks feel objectified by Mother Earth cos she don't give a shit about the Ticks' emotions, she just wants to use their great capacity to hunt. This makes the Ticks feel like victims of themselves. They act out in anger and their testosterone makes them easily lose control, and just like a ferret they kill and kill. They are part of a force, they are never personalised. This enforces their feeling of victimhood as they cannot be part of any sort of identity politics.

They are fast as long as they don't fall over on their back after eating blood. Spider-like, but a bigger body, lots of muscles in all colours of green. The ticks are referred to as the hot guy, claw-like crabs, slimy, and parts a bit hairy on their neck. Others say about the Ticks: 'Oh they spread so fast, there is a tick epidemic going on. Don't go out in the woods. Don't sit in the grass. Don't leave your house'. I met a Ticks and it was sexy.

[Geo and Ivan sing the following, using a melody that canons into harmony. Geo continues to play the keyboard. Mami's scratching dance continues.]

TICKS
You are on your knees begging me please suck on me harder
I eat you for starter
Trying to get rid of you
gaining muscle fat when I chew you like butter
Blood stream not on the side of my mouth
Leftover clutter
Oh boy, Oh boy
Running away from you takes time
One day I will die
It's alright you be fine
as long as you're mine
I get wings to fly
I can touch the sky

[As Geo and Ivan continue to sing, Ivan heads downstairs to join Mami in the scratching dance.]

DIRECTOR   This story has a lot of puberty in it.
The feeling of … Oooooh poor little boy.

[Mami continues with the scratching dance even as she speaks.]

MOTHER EARTH   Even when life is hard, romance is alive.
I am Mother Earth, the ultimate guru, hot as hell.

When you pass me on the street you are dragged by instinctual forces to touch my bare skin, mud and roots growing out of my hair. If you have hippie style you'll find this especially attractive. I'll tell you I suffer from poverty, but actually I am rich. Just look at my clothes.

I am very old. I aged like a carpet. Mood stabilisers sold out, because everyone needs to drive a car. Lithium here and lithium there.

How to put my metabolism into euphoria: I sit on the bottom of a cliff, above the cliff is an electric car factory and the lithium waste water, like a waterfall, is pouring down into my mouth. Mother is drunk.

[Geo's keyboard playing fades out, but Ivan and Mami continue to scratch. Soraya steps off the table onto the floor, and watches them.]

2   Angharad Williams
     Last Testament and Will of Me

[Soraya begins to speak, now appealing to the audience differently. Geo triggers an electronic track, which functions as a texture and accompaniment to the story told. Geo gradually adds in the keyboard, processed by a Korg Kaoss Pad. As Soraya speaks, Ivan and Mami tone down their scratching and eventually stand to watch, before adopting the new positions Soraya forms; wilted arabesques.]

Soraya   Here's the story of my life and what's left of it. There's not much to say about me but this – everything I was ever any good at I could never get paid for. I was married to Dwynwen. We came to meet as we were neighbours as children. Childhood sweethearts, you could say and she was sickly sweet. I could not get enough. So sick was I, my father knocked a hole through the stone wall that separated our gardens so we could be even closer, no need to run out onto the road and around the houses, but outside and through the garden. [Soraya raises one arm]

She was my first kiss, we smoked our first cigarettes together – King Size Embassy Number 1s. Every infinitesimal detail of Dwynwen I can recall. I was good at that. I was good at loving her, and she knew it too. We got matching pet rabbits, and sat for hours posing them in various scenarios in her family caravan; later, in a shed her father built for her. I can recall the softness of their coats as we sang 'Babyface' to them and rubbed their fluffy butts on our faces until our eyes ran. [brings arm in an arc] We established and ran a hugely successful hotel in our imagination and watched soap operas with the sound off so we could scour the credits for new names and visitors to our high-end spa-cum-rabbit-petting-hotel. We even ran away once, we packed our bags, a tomato and some crisps, and walked to the other side of the village and hid in my grandparents' house. We had midnight snacks, which my father mistook for a series of break-ins. We worked on our book – *101 Things to Do with Potatoes* – for years! The manuscript remains unpublished. It's in a box somewhere, I kept it – maybe you'll come across it. What's left now, I just don't know. [Soraya steps one foot out]

When we met, her hair was blond and it was extremely thick. At some point perfume for little girls became available at the local pharmacy. When she saved up enough pocket money she bought a small bottle of Tommy Hilfiger. She was good at that – saving money. [bends hip] She would save all her pennies and mine too and buy us things. Penny sweets at first, cherry lips, sour laces, my favourite was kola cubes, then nice things like little-girl perfume and our own cigarettes – less intense ones than the Embassies. [Soraya stands up straight]

We read in a magazine where to spray the perfumes but she didn't like it on her wrists, spraying the perfume directly onto her scalp. It irritated her scalp so much that she would itch it bloody. For years she had brown waxy clumps under her nails and the skin around them stained red. We never paid much attention to our lesbianism until she overheard her parents arguing about how much time we spent in the shed. [moves one arm up] We went to the local library to look up the word. She was miserable at home, her parents argued constantly. For a time she lived with me in my house until she was moved up a year at school. [arm moves in an arc]

She was really good at that – school. I got good at brushing her hair and peeling the scabs off of her scalp. [steps one foot out] They moved away, Dwynwen and her parents, but we remained pen pals. Writing every day in a secret language only we could decode. She would put a pack of stamps weekly in Monday's envelope. My father left us.

She started taking classes, for 'gifted children' it was called [steps around on one foot] and then went to university earlier than all the other kids and was awarded a scholarship for doing so. As soon as the first payment went into her bank, she sent for me – a one-way bus ticket and off I went. I could never economise my enthusiasm for her and for being with her. I bid farewell to my mother who had focused her parenting energy on teaching me about botany. It was what she was good at. She was as good at it as Dwynwen was with numbers.

We lived together in bliss at the university halls of residence, Mam didn't care that I had left her too. I did feel a terrible shame though, when we could not help her buy her house which I loved. I wish I had been good at something to make the money to help her. [Soraya walks to another position. Ivan goes upstairs to play percussion alongside Geo.]

We got married. Dwynwen wasn't the only smart girl in her class, but she worked hard. She graduated university and soon got a job at the local supermarket. Her skill with numbers was seeing where they were 'leaking', as she called it, and then plugging the holes. She got so good that headquarters sent for her. 'Wastage' they called it. We moved to the city.

Dwynwen was happy for me to make the flat nice and tend the plants, cook suppers and pack lunches. I asked her for an allotment and she kindly sought the advice of a colleague, 'HR' they call it, and they could help me find one. With seeds sown in March and April the summer production was packed with aubergines, an array of tomatoes, runner beans, beetroots and chilli peppers – she loved chilies. We made chutneys together by the end of summer so our garden was with us throughout the calendar year. I had a dream and in that dream we would be together forever. All the times we spent pottering at the allotment, they were the happiest moments of our lives. Watching as the tiny seeds turned into these majestic plants with branches, how their fruits sustained us was thrilling to me. It was my gift to her. My gift to Dwynwen for looking after us and buying Mam a camper van. [Soraya now lifts the other arm up]

Mam didn't want a house after the Zonings started. When we were Zoned I was devastated. I could no longer gain access to my original allotment with my lovely neighbours but was given a replacement within our Zone. It was gated. I never met the neighbours. [the same hand arcs up]

The Zoning extended to Dwynwen's workplace and she and her colleagues were placed in individual cubicles in the office. 'Efficiency' they called it. 'Misery', is what I called it. Soon she no longer wanted to be intimate as the demands of work became too great, it took an incredible toll on her body. It needed to do so much for her, it could not be mine too.

[moves opposite foot out] And I could not even make it feel nice. I continued to make packed lunches. We no longer enjoyed long weekends at the garden as she had only Sundays for rest and she slept throughout that day, waking seldom for me to feed her avocados, nuts and eggs before returning to a deep sleep. She was longer at the office. I was every day with my greens. The tinkering became an obsession. I grew apple trees and crossed them with others, inventing new fruits at a surprising rate. [all limbs stretch open] Dwynwen didn't like them. 'Weird' was how she described my pastime.

Soon, she wasn't eating solids at all. 'Calorific,' she said, and asked me one tender evening to make her daily smoothies that she would take in a specially sewn backpack that work gave her. [Soraya walks in a circle] They gave her the bottles too. And the smoothie-maker. And individual frozen packs to make the smoothie. Within half a year someone took away the machine and replaced it with morning and supper juices dropped in weekly crates. I forgot how to cook and ate a diet of raw or cooked veg from my garden, alone.

My Dwynwen went from plump and pert, quick to baste in the sun, to ashen faced and monosyllabic. [Soraya now stops, frozen.] One day she arrived home with a terrible dynamic and pronounced me a 'loser' in a rage-filled argument as it had slipped my mind to take out the trash. Well Judge, in my book – a loser is a winner in a house of lies. All of a sudden she did not see my work at home as exactly that and I began to long for something else. [turns head]

There was an enormous surplus at the allotment, and I could not eat it all myself. I left a lovely selection outside the perimeter wall – it sat rotting. Next, I tried the street, zone-square, skateboarding park, all rotten. More were joining the smoothie regime. One Sunday night under cover of darkness I found an opening in a fence to a neighbouring Zone and left a basketful there. Baskets turned to crates. Whatever I could carry. Sometimes, I received notes. 'Thank you', they said. [turns body and stops]

We made a special request for my mother to join us at our Zone.

Dwynwen would not let her live in the flat with us. 'Bills,' she said. Mam lived in the garden house. [Soraya moves to stand halfway up the stairs in the old atrium. Mami turns to watch her.] Dwynwen's wages got capped which meant I could no longer buy new seeds and was required to sow from my fruits' seeds. We pollinated all sorts, me and Mam. We generated an array of new specimens, which we picked, drew and studied.

There was little in place with regards to a plan, this is the truth, Judge. In the absence of a public defence, you must believe me. One day, a remarkable discovery was made. Growing from our 'pot-luck' row (a series of experiments and mislabelled cross-pollinations) we noticed minute shiny droplets hanging from the thin branches of six small plants that were growing at speed. The branches were buckling due to the weight of their tiny golden nuggets, so we made a structure and delicately strung the little tree to its bamboo host. With hand on heart the experiments in the garden were precisely this: true in intention. I let my hands do my thinking. [Soraya turns, as though no longer addressing a Judge at the stand]

As the days and weeks unfolded the droplets turned into coins, Your Honour. Money from all the world's currencies grew and with a gentle shake of the loaded branches they would fall onto the ground. We collected the coins, studying each with incredulity – we could make no sense of this nature's force. As the trees grew, paper notes curled off the bark and I peeled them off. I peeled them with the same affection as I peeled Dwynwen's scalp as we were children.

With each note I recalled our conversations, our childhood scenarios. The reminiscing was poison. Mam and I, we had no idea if the money was to standard, but it had all the markings! I had not held notes in my hands for so long, and decided to make a test. She dared me, Mam; and with two 50 notes I bought Dwynwen a bottle of Tommy Hilfiger perfume as a surprise. I didn't give her the bottle right away, rather Mam and I made a plan. We noticed a pattern emerge, where the trees' seed for replanting was unsheathed at twilight. At dead of night we left sprouting pots at the Zone barrier along with other fruits. We continued for weeks. Notes came:

3   Body/State
1   Plots
2   Angharad Williams

'The trees GROW.' [Soraya returns to the floor from the stairs. Ivan stops drumming and returns downstairs to manage the spotlights.]

On our anniversary (the date of which had been debated for years), I gave Dwynwen her Tommy bottle. She was furious and demanded to know how I afforded the potion. 'You have to see it to believe it,' I said, gleefully. There is little I regret more than showing my love my invention. Tears rolled out of her eyes at an alarming rate. There is such love between time and money. She told HR about my garden and the next night I heard a symphony of chainsaws echo in the distance. I was no longer to return to the garden. I have no idea what happened to Mam. What happened to Dwynwen? I was questioned, arrested. I am no criminal! We made money grow on trees! So virulent were the trees' roots that the earth required scorching, it's like the root itself bonded with the earth beneath and so this is what HR preferred: a scarred earth incapable of bearing fruit. I have seen no green outside of my cell window. Funny how differently people see the same thing.

[Soraya walks into the telephone booth. Mami joins her. Ivan follows them with the light.]

3   Nour Mobarak

The Washing Away of Wrongs (1247), Song Ci [part 3]

[Mami and Soraya, positioned in the telephone booth with Soraya near the receiver and Mami at her feet, pull phones out of their pockets and proceed to read from them. Their attention is fixed on the phone screens, as the audience watches from outside, their voices amplified into space. Geo plays keyboard, using an airy reeded instrument sample. Ivan continues to light them, gradually changing coloured filters.]

Mami   *The Washing Away of Wrongs*, from 1247 by Song Ci

4. Miscellaneous Discussion of Doubtful and Difficult Cases: Part One

In conducting inquests on corpses where the circumstances are doubtful, if the wounds are from a blade which penetrated the body, it is necessary to examine both the inside and the outside of the mouth of the wound. Large cuts are from a slicing blade. Small ones are penetration wounds. If the corpse is decayed, the clothes in which it was originally dressed must be examined to see if the holes in the clothes match the wounds. The body will sometimes be found prone on a bed with a short knife or a piece of bamboo in its right hand. If the wound is between the throat and the navel, perhaps it is a case of the victim having thrown himself down while drunk, crushing the weapon under himself and thus wounding himself. If nearby there is a high place or a muddy place, check to see if there are valuable goods on the body or injuries, lest in trying to get something, the victim lost his footing and injured himself.

Soraya   In holding an inquest on a woman who has no apparent injuries, the vagina must be examined lest a knife have been inserted there to penetrate the vitals inside of the stomach. If it penetrated not far beneath the skin, then above and below the navel there will be small bloody soakings – ecchymoses. If it passed deep within the vitals, these will not appear. Frequently, these kinds of deaths are cases of solitary men wanting to feed on women. If the dead person is male, the crown of the head must be examined, lest a flat-headed nail have been driven in there, and the anus, lest some hard object had penetrated from there. Such cases frequently involve co-workers of an elderly husband who has a young wife.

Mami   If on the corpse there are no scars or wounds, but the face is blue or black and sometimes one side of it is swollen, this often indicates that someone used something to cover the mouth and nose of the deceased to suffocate him. Sometimes, a handkerchief or cloth bag will be used to strangle someone, and there will thus be no marks. The person conducting the inquest must then look at the flesh on the neck. If it is hard, then this is what happened. The critical things are: whether or not the hands and feet have marks from having been bound with cords; whether on the surface of the tongue there are marks from having been chewed; whether the areas of the anus or urethra are swollen from having been stood on. If these sorts of signs are absent, then look in the mouth to see if there is frothy spittle and at the throat to see if it is swollen. If there is spittle and swelling, perhaps the death was caused by a disease. This ought to be examined in detail.

Soraya   If during the investigation it comes out that the accused had previously spied upon and plotted against the deceased, and if the facts of the case are clear and the accused has confessed, then the officials may proceed with the inquest. If there is no evidence, just beware of the possibility of death from drunkenness.

Mami   In holding inquests on deaths that have resulted from brawls, even if it is clear who the two principal participants were, if there are no marks of injury on the corpse, how will it be possible to designate the fatal injury? Such cases always involve victims who for a long time have had a chronic vital energy disorder. Sometimes, even before the injuries

The Washing Away of Wrongs (1247), Song Ci [part 3]

were inflicted during the quarrel, they had become quite drunk. Then, during the fight, they did something to aggravate their condition to the point that their vitalities were exhausted and they died. In many such cases, one or both testicles shrink into the abdomen. It will be necessary to use warm vinegar, soaked cloths or floss silk netting to cover the body for the space of a meal. Thereafter, order the coroner's assistant or the attendants to press on the lower abdomen with their hands, whereupon the testicles will descend and can be examined. Afterwards, minutely examine the fatal injuries.

Soraya   There was a villager who ordered his nephew and a companion to hoe an area together and plant millet. Two nights passed and they did not return. Then, the villager went to look for them and found the two men dead on the mountain. Subsequently, he reported this to the officials, noting that the clothing they had taken with them was still there – i.e., there had been no robbery. An official was warranted to hold an inquest. When the inquest official reached the spot, he saw one body outside a small grass hut. The back of its skull was broken. The face was marked by injuries inflicted with a knife. The other body was inside the hut. On the lower left side of the neck and on the back of the head on the right side were marks from knife wounds. The general opinion of those gathered there was that the man outside had been the first one wounded and had died from his injuries. The man inside was thought to have committed suicide after that. The officials, considering that both men were injured and that no valuables were involved, declared it to be a case of mutual homicide. One inquest official alone said, 'That is not so. If we use circumstances to measure circumstances, making it out that the two killed one another, then that would be possible. But the knife wounds on the right side of the back of the head of the man inside are suspicious. How could he have inflicted such wounds on the back of his own head? This would not be easy to do.' Within a few days, a man was apprehended who had hated the two men and had killed them. The unsolved case was clear. They then informed the prefecture that the extreme penalty was appropriate.

Mami   If it had not come out this way, the two wronged
men could never have rested easy. Generally, in cases of mutual homicide
where there is nothing suspicious about the injuries, then an inquest may
be conducted. If a high value is placed on carefulness and concentration,
then there should be no mistakes.

[Without looking at each other, they exit the telephone booth, and Geo continues to play during their passage.]

4   Claire Fontaine
     The 25th Hour of the Day [reprise]

[Ivan now enters the phone box and the music shifts to recall the accompaniment to the iteration of this text from Act 1. He picks up the phone, and leans on the glass and door, as though agitated. Compared to the last scene, this is faster, and almost terse. Mami and Soraya watch from outside.]

Ivan   Self-objectification can be a never-ending and painful process, a residue of when women couldn't own anything and were owned themselves.

We know that love and private property make an unhappy marriage but we still don't know any love without jealousy and possession. We don't know the horizontal, accepting, empowering, intelligent, collective love that we need.

Women have been entrusted with the unpaid labour of love. Availability has been, and it still is, women's condition for being loved. The love they get in return is gratitude for their slavery, it stems from the fear of being abandoned, from dependency, it's not an emancipating love for the ones who give it, nor for the ones who receive it.

Women must not only refuse what they have been given, they also have to refuse what has been refused to them: equality, rights, respect. Like racialised and discriminated people they don't need any of it: they need to be loved, because if they were loved they wouldn't have to beg for these things.

Women have the problem of having to reject what they have been told about love and themselves, of finding ways of communicating and preventing all the terrible things that men do to them, but also of having to forgive all of it, to be able to continue living and believing in a love that can be re-invented and taught to men.

There is no way in which they can get rid of their 'enemy': the 'enemy' is the person whose love they have to win and secure. (The simple fact that they still want it is problematic …) In short, the work of heterosexual women

3   Body/State
1   Plots
4   Claire Fontaine

is never done. Above all it's a headfuck under the current socio-economic conditions; impossible in a capitalist society where, when they are privileged, they are busy working like men, but paid less, doing housework when they get home and taking care of children. That leaves little time to explore one's subconscious, re-invent human relationships and forgive the unforgivable (especially if in the meantime they need to take care of themselves to stay young and desirable.)

The day only has 24 hours, and, if patriarchy doesn't end, love between men and women will have to be reinvented in the 25th hour.

[Ivan hangs up the phone and exits the booth.]

5   Victoria Colmegna
     Sunset Blvd (1950), Wilder; final scene

[The last twelve minutes of audio from the 1950 film version of *Sunset Boulevard* plays. Geo and Ivan are on the overpass near the instruments. Soraya and Mami stand opposite them, across the drop, and near the balcony. As with the other audio excerpts, they begin to shift their weight from leg to leg, this time developing towards a gallop. Dramatic strings usher in each scene, and we hear JOE GILLIS' final exchange with NORMA DESMOND as he tries to leave the actress, who is frantic for attention and affection. The voiceover of the dead JOE GILLIS then comments on the scene, as reporters and policemen swarm the house. Finally, it is the butler MAX who helps the authorities lure her down the stairs, away from the house. She descends, ready for her close up. Mami and Ivan continue galloping on the spot. Geo first, and then Soraya, play their instruments into, then over the film audio. As the scene comes to a close, Geo and Soraya crescendo before finding silence. Exeunt.]

2   Total Recall   2:30pm

[Over the building Tannoy, Mami welcomes the audience, and establishes that they should watch from the first-floor balcony. She establishes the roles that the performers will take, and presents the credits of the coming section 'Total Recall', from 'Body/State', pronouncing the / as 'over'.]

1   Angharad Williams
       The Owl Mixtapes

(Performers must remain in the same room. Performers could be around a large table or seated on the floor. Performers may share a meal or snack during the interaction. If snacking, all items must be pre-sealed i.e. can of some kind of drink, bag of crisps, sealed sandwich etc. If performers choose to eat, they must take small bites and deliver lines (even if their mouth is full) elegantly with gestures such as holding a hand up to cover their mouth when speaking, or when sliding tongue over teeth (checking for food remnants). Performers must feel free to mimic one another's improvisation. Performers are not entirely separate people.

NADIA is modern in demeanour, with American-learnt manners, entirely self-confident, seductive. RHYS is stiff and inexperienced, shy. Although names are gendered, performers needn't be.)

[Geo and Soraya slink into the scene, slightly dragging a tall table and two stools into the area of the atrium which is set up for refreshments. Ivan has directed a spotlight to shine bright light above their heads. NADIA is played by Soraya, and RHYS is played by Geo. They are both eating and chewing, constantly. As the script dictates, they lightly rib each other, mugging for the onlooking audience.]

(Laughing)

NADIA   *(begins speaking having barely stopped laughing)* You are remarkable. You know that?

RHYS   *(laughing)*

NADIA   You are!

RHYS   *(swatting away)* Ahh.

NADIA   Really!

RHYS   No, *really*!

NADIA   Yes, *really*!

RHYS   No, no, no, no, no … No – *you're* the remarkable one.

NADIA   You are! I'm just saying!

RHYS   *(scoffs)*

NADIA   *(shrugging shoulders)* You're remarkable!

RHYS   No, no don't be silly now.

NADIA   You're *remarkable*.

RHYS   No – you're remarkable.

NADIA   *You're* remarkable!

RHYS   No – you're remarkable.

NADIA   Listen to me? You're remarkable.

RHYS   You are!

NADIA   You're re-mark-able.

RHYS   *(stares)*

NADIA   You you you you you you you, it's you!

RHYS   NO!

NADIA   I've always thought you're remarkable.

RHYS   No, really –

NADIA   'The Remarkable' is what I'm going to call you from now on. Not simply your name. It shall always be prefaced with 'The Remarkable'. Because it's just what you are.

RHYS   No, no, no you mustn't.

NADIA   It's not a competition! Just deal with it.

RHYS   No, *you* are the remarkable one.

NADIA   Look how far you've come! No, really Rhys, look! You're just absolutely the most remarkable lawyer.

RHYS   *(coy)* Stop.

NADIA   Facts, Rhys, facts.

RHYS   You're embarrassing me now.

NADIA   You know what my brother and I call you?

RHYS   Mm?

NADIA   The Pen.

RHYS   *(grimaces, confused)*

NADIA   Yes, yes The Pen!

RHYS   Ok?

NADIA   Oh, don't look so worried it's a good thing I
promise!

RHYS   Go on …

NADIA   We call you The Pen, Rhys, because a good
lawyer will go anywhere their client wants them to go. And you will, won't
you? When we get in there?

[Soraya sustains her gaze with Geo until they both half smile, and hop off
their high stools.]

2   Ed Atkins
     Copenhagen

[As Geo and Soraya leave the refreshment area, the audience turns to see that Ivan is on the floor, sprawled, gazing up towards the upper balconies. Mami operates the follow spotlight, lighting him. Geo and Soraya head upstairs to operate the other lights on the second floor. Ivan delivers the following text with a controlled sequence of movement, mostly precise gestures and crawling in patterns across the floor. Fast, mostly conversational, and melodious enough to not need accompaniment. As the text progresses, the spotlights shift in intensity, the beams moving as though casually strolling across the architecture, but eventually landing back on Ivan.]

Ivan   I like thinking about blood in my mouth. Frankfurters are teeming mud with robot the homogeneous. I'm a basic model cyborg moving on the street with bits dangling off of it. I loved putting my hand in PVA glue for a skin glove to peel off then easing pins through the top layer of thumb skin. I like the advert for cosmetic black gum a person smears across their nose and chin. When the black gum sets they peel it off and with it come plugs of off-white stuff, tugged from the pores and shown to the camera. It's very convincing: Get that stuff out with the black gum. Another advert I love has a computer-generated dentist's tool chiselling off panes of butter-yellow plaque from the base of some CG teeth in close-up. My teeth aren't good. I haven't visited the dentist in over ten years I'm 41. I've not seen a doctor in thirty years or so. Sally says she likes my teeth. They're colourful, she says, euphemistically. The last time I went to the dentist the hygienist cleaned my teeth angrily, my gums bled a lot and my dentist told me to make an appointment on the way out to come back in six months to have my wisdom teeth pulled and some fillings done maybe more things done. I hate being told off for not looking after myself because of course they're right. The last time I went to the doctor he tugged at my testicles roughly. He had the bedside manner of a frog. It was actually a suspected torsion of the testicles it was okay in the end. I was left to decide whether they should go in and take a look because the ultrasounds were inconclusive. I take ibuprofen and paracetamol together; someone who knew a nurse said it was okay to do so. Ibuprofen drains swollen things and paracetamol soothes sore things. I love Nurofen Express liquid capsules, a fast-acting ibuprofen drug. Branded painkillers work best on me; the placebo of brand identity and slight price hike fit well with who I am, the stock I place in how something looks, the effort and costliness of design and manufacture are indicative of who I am. Most of the struggle is over the strength of faith in some part or extension of me to affect the world. Much of how I manage to function is by making myself seem like a sufficient self and however cheap it might seem to use paraphernalia to bolster that that's what I do to do it. I am Cheap according to a notion of wealth abstracted to mean richness and depth of character. It's not that I am not deep or rich in character but that apart from the allotted holes only the top layer or so of me is available to me for corroboration without incision. My being and my body are in agreement about my lack of depth and if the first one is analogous to metaphor and the second to literality I may as well stick with the second because in the night, blind, I can gently depress my thigh or I can budge my genitals and confirm I am. I will try to buy Nurofen Express liquid capsules when I buy painkillers in the UK, in Boots. They are firm red ellipsoid jellies. They're engineered to race into me and the red means they act with urgency and they torpedo pain. There's a warm target printed on the box. Pain is dynamic. Not like a car or a Nurofen Express but radial nausea. A wave came and knocked a person down in an open field. Cars move back and forth and Nurofen is moved by muscled tunnels and the silver and puce heart and belief. The box has silver and gold on it and debossed bits of text on and powerful infographics. It must be costly and effortful to make boxes like that it's like premium engine oil or airport thrillers Nurofen's a gendered painkiller. I can't think of myself as a sports-car but I am calmed if I can manage to think of myself as a clockwork robot man. I'm fixable then and my parts are replaceable if I'm mechanical. I can be lubed up inside with

                                                  Copenhagen

premium oil and do better. I like thinking my inside is unlit cogs and gears and cams clicking and ticking right and there are interconnecting black rubber hoses and all of it is slick with lubricant. I am almost completely uninterested in more esoteric forms of pain amelioration or therapy. I think having an interest in something is very important if it's going to do anything. I am several kinds of materialist, I think. The more esoteric the therapy the more it seems to require available will. I must have health happen to me or else be born with. Also, if the therapy promises results it's too much pressure I'm very competitive and any failure is just more guilt. I wish I were tenderly piloted from thousands of miles away. A headache or an unplaceable pain moves outward in wilting ripples from the culprit. One flower then the bed of flowers then the next bed of flowers and so on shrivel and blacken in fanning circles. Nurofen Express liquid capsules promise to defibrillate or the capsules shriek into my hollow and explode near the ribbed roof gelatinous Valentine rain on burnt-out nerve nubs and stadiums of faeces. It's notable that most things I like and want to be around are plasticky toy things like me. I've always liked miniaturisation like most people. The second-hand toy shop near me is heaven to me. Rummaging through buckets of forsaken toy misc I can choose a single little inch-high perished pink rubber boot, say, or a very very small harpoon or a dulled plastic goblet or bonnet, each originally from a different toy line now marooned to exquisiteness, my nominative jewels. I recently bought a two-inch Robocop without its helmet and one leg off; a tiny black ape with its arms raised and just a red mouth; a paint-chipped die-cast Matchbox car with a moustachioed head poking up through the sunroof and wearing a pickelhaube; a lumpy purple plastic ramp with sockets along one edge to affix it to a missing stretch of purple road, presumably; a purple plastic ghoul whose mouth ratchets open like a mantrap so if you press down on its bumpy red tongue with your finger the mouth snaps shut suddenly. The teeth of the ghoul are goofy and not sharp it doesn't hurt. The ghoul seems benign or silly and not something to be afraid of its eyes are okay I also got a couple of simple jigsaws for my daughter and a couple of small realistic animals, pigs maybe, to crap punctuation about the apartment. The toys I like best are the bits of toy that are the most prosaic or the most like human ruins. I turn them over in my hand as a giant alien emissary might. I got a plastic red brick wall with a grey plastic mantel, a very simple beautiful thing. I also got a taller and thinner plastic red brick wall that when you press down on the top bit bursts into three big jagged pieces of wall as if a car from the same toy line had just ploughed into it or someone was bust out of a jail. Then you can click the bits of wall back together again and do it again. I think it's incredible engineering for children. I'd love to get my hands on a jeweller's loupe. I'd scrutinise plastic toys' surfaces through it less and less. My right hand – I'm right-handed – shakes uncontrollably when it has to work focused with my brain and without strong physical support. It starts gently and will build to a wide horizontal swinging motion; it's unstoppable unless someone acts quickly and removes the thing from my hand and I can drop my arm to my side, reset it. I can't carry a full glass in that hand because my hand will suddenly convulse and fling the contents of the glass around but I can draw really detailedly if I can rest my hand and my wrist on the surface of the drawing. I think the shaking's from a lifetime of really tightly gripping my pen but it could also be a symptom of alcoholism or maybe something burgeoning arthritic or related to all the nicotine. I opt for the pen gripping cause because I worry about it, but I do actually think that's what it is, honestly. I remember sitting at a bar with Andrew celebrating something and we'd just been poured two brimming coupes of champagne and when we raised them for a toast my right hand just chucked mine over us both. I remember carrying a full mug of hot lemon drink down the corridor and about halfway down I felt the convulsion coming and I could do nothing to stop my hand from chucking the hot lemon drink all over my hand, the walls. I can feel the convulsion coming and there's absolutely nothing I can do to stop it I just stand there oh. I think that the more precious or not-to-be-spilt the thing I'm carrying the more certain it is I'll shake it to pieces. It just must be psychological, at least in part. It looks like an intervention by a part of me that wants rescuing from inside me. The imprisoned me can only control my right hand and only for a moment with its own right arm thrust through the bars it tries to write 'Help!' in the air with red wine or hot drink. I sometimes think it's an opportunistic unconscious masochism blurting. I can't really pour anyone anything with my right hand and it upset me for a while, people seeing my spasming hand, watching me shake wine over the table. They looked concerned; they thought I must be nervous to be with them or I must be an alcoholic. I don't want to have to explain anything about something like that it's not what I want to talk about with my friends. I want them to be comfortable around me and think things are good with me unless until I feel like I can control their responses or control my reception of their responses, prepare the ground. I eventually realised I could do those kinds of careful actions with my left hand instead and no one need know about my crazed right. I draw incredibly detailed things with my right hand sometimes, incredibly detailed skin. I usually shout, 'Oh no' and then a low, 'fuck', and then I say, 'Sorry.' When I sense the convulsion coming I have the presence of mind to turn away from the laptop. I'd rather soak or scald myself than anything or anyone else. There's no trust inside. I love heaving a sigh of relief. I often can't finish sentences in speech so writing is sometimes just having access to statements. I've just now ordered a gin and tonic but they have no tonic, sorry, so I plumped for a cup of orange juice with ice and a gin miniature and I've just now poured all the gin in we'll see how that goes. I try to always have a gin and tonic on a flight for my death with a splintery plastic cup that creaks. I'll pretend to cry some for me, turned to the splintery window listening to my music. Pretence and truth of me are indiscernible and I fret over this a lot, whether what I am saying is true, where. When I start speaking I am astonished by what I say sometimes but it could be the astonishment of revelation or appal I've no clear way of knowing and no one else could settle this for me at all. I will flush as if someone is doing something to me, as if I am being ventriloquised but I have no idea the ventriloquist. I always try to get the window on a flight because I don't want to be disturbed and I have this incredible bladder. Instead I want to wallow and be straight-jacketed for it, with silver padlocks on the leather straps. I am trapped in my body and the captivity of flight models that feeling in a way that makes it easier to be very upset about. I can be outside of myself enough to be compassionate to myself some, here. I love thinking about my death and how people will react to it. I think people will find it surprising. People don't think of me as someone dead I think people think of me as someone who's alive. People don't assume I'm particularly alive exactly but they don't think I'm so very contiguous with death as I certainly am. People think I'm a person unremarkably alive. I obsess over afterwards without me. Sally keeps a list of the music I want to be played at my funeral on her phone but she might not. The list should be long because if a piece of music affects me it's because it feels like it's about all death irrespective of the intended meaning because death is the shape of all feeling I have and I will ask Sally to add the music to her list. My amazing power comes from being evil, which means I can withstand anything do anything. Everything is painful but I was designed for pain. If a piece of music gets to me I'll play it over and over. I'm totally dependent on having my feelings pressed into service. I wrote a very short will when I was nine: I leave my telescope to Rupert. I thought about Rupert looking at stars refracted by tears. I don't think about how I'll die I think about how other people will react to my death and how all the precarious things will topple. I have nothing prepared. There are pubs and bars I've been to a lot I've no idea how the insides of the toilets looks. I'm aware of whomever I'm with's toilet-going frequency because I just don't ever need to go. Sometimes someone reports the remarkable decor of a toilet. It's not conscious anymore I trained my bladder when I was eleven. I wet myself on a school trip when I was eleven and for a while afterwards I needed to be close to a toilet at all times just in case. I stayed home from school for a week practising resisting the urge to go for ever longer durations near enough to the downstairs toilet in case. Sometimes just hovering outside the front door in my pyjamas in the cold, not going, receding into myself looking at the snake's head fritillary and the empty milk bottles. The dull pain ebbed so. I busted something in me and my body stopped trying to tell me it needed to go it just found more room for piss by getting rid of

3   Body/State
2   Total Recall
2   Ed Atkins

something else in there. There was an astronomer whose bladder blew up while listening to the king give a really long speech. When I went back to school I was extremely powerful. I'm still a charged steel hole that's open. Go ahead and tip whatever in me I'll deal with it. I'll mill hurt for you with my big millstones inside. Of course I do still need to go sometimes of course but it's basically a formality. I drink as much as most. I've noticed that a person's need to go to the bathroom often seldom correlates with the quantity of liquid they're drinking. I just looked up 'what muscle it allow you hold it in' and it offered the detrusor muscle, which is apparently under autonomic control. I looked up 'train detrusor muscle' which took me to an NHS pdf titled 'Retraining Your Bladder'. One of the tips was to sit on something hard when you need to go, which is what I do when I need to send a shit back up into me. My body's a farming machine you sit in. One of the secret ways I'm special is that I can will my body to do anything but I have no willpower. I have total control of my body but the problem is choosing what to do with it. I don't have control over my choices which are unrecognisable from one moment to the next.

[Ivan stands up and takes a position at the follow spotlight. Geo heads towards the keyboard, Soraya downstairs to the floor, and Mami upwards to the overpass.]

3   Annie Goodner
     Soothsayer Furnishing [reprise]

[Soraya and Mami perform a repetition of the staging of this scene from earlier, now using the overpass balcony and the floor of the old atrium as their frame of correspondence. SHERRY's monologue is omitted. Geo reads the introduction, again speaking from the keyboard over thick electronic strings. Mami descends from the first-floor balcony to meet Soraya on the floor, tracing the paths defined in Act 1. Ivan follows them with a spotlight.]

Geo   SHERRY missed her goddaughter's third birthday party. All that remained of the festivities once she arrived was a clutch of colourful balloons, which included a large number 3 – her goddaughter is three. In the place of celebration, SHERRY revealed to her friend MAGGIE – her goddaughter's mother – that she is unexpectedly pregnant. MAGGIE is exuberant; SHERRY refuses to participate in the joy; refuses to say what she wants to do except to run her finger across her own throat. MAGGIE's outsized reaction wears SHERRY down, and after a particularly needling anecdote about motherly fulfilment, SHERRY rushes to the bathroom to be sick, to throw water on her face. SHERRY has just returned. She speaks to herself and to the audience.

SHERRY   People always want to divine what's coming. But it's like, back off.

MAGGIE   You're too much in your head.

SHERRY   My 'head' is just another part of the rest of me. My head is deliquescent. I'm porous and oozing just below the surface.

MAGGIE   Gross.

SHERRY   So are you *(she points at her own forehead).*

(MAGGIE takes several long, deep breaths.) [Soraya looks at Mami while breathing heavily.]

MAGGIE   Then you can commit better to yourself, to what you really want.

SHERRY   In what way?

MAGGIE   Commitment leads to the absence of shame. The absence of shame leads to …

SHERRY   Hallucination …

MAGGIE   … Wholeness … Beauty

SHERRY   The appearance of.

MAGGIE   The thing itself.

[Soraya and Mami leap apart, to their set positions. Mami returns up the stairs, Soraya gently turns on the spot.]

Geo   MAGGIE takes several deep breaths again. She's performing calm. SHERRY's gaze drifts across MAGGIE, her bespoke jewellery, her spotless jeans and blouse framing her smooth collarbone and upper chest. SHERRY can see MAGGIE's downy hair beating up and down, up and down.

[Mami moving her arms from the balcony, grabbing Soraya's attention. The pitch of Mami's voice, across her lines, rises and falls in a long melody, a prosodic shift from their conversation before.]

SHERRY   *But your scream Kassandra. It gathers and scatters.*

MAGGIE   Pardon?

SHERRY   *Like leaves. Like flowers.*

MAGGIE   What flowers?

SHERRY   *Clytemnestra wanted beauty. Or so it seemed. With her window-dressing words, with her steely eyes, with your pragmatic mind, revenge-rife. So she took flowing robes, tangled up her husband, and murdered him with a knife.*

MAGGIE   I'm not your captive audience. [Then, facing up to Mami from the floor, Soraya begins to mirror her gestures]

SHERRY   *Clytemnestra wanted beauty. Beautifully … and justice and revenge. Or so it seemed … With her window-dressing words, with your steely eyes, with your pragmatic mind, revenge-rife. So she took flowing robes, tangled up your husband, and murdered him with a knife. It's really quite human, whether she knows it or not …*

MAGGIE   *Perfect yourself before you blame others.*

SHERRY   [dropping out of her gestures and phrase] That's my line!

MAGGIE   [pointedly to Mami] Maybe I see what's coming. Maybe that's a good thing to do.

SHERRY   [ignoring Soraya] … *Kassandra, on the other hand is always fraught. Why? She must go it alone, everyone believes she's overblown, but she's terrified, the writing's on the wall. She sees blood filling the bathtub even from the hall.*

Kassandra is wind, Clytemnestra is weather. One moves through the space the other has constructed. In out, in out, in out, in out.

MAGGIE   I can read a riddle, and you my friend are the terrified one.

SHERRY   So what should I do?

MAGGIE   *Turn the lights on, make a little rip, cut the air open, loosen the sky, then squeeze on through.* [Mami now seems to follow the Soraya's gestures.]

Geo   MAGGIE mimics cutting open the space between her and SHERRY, then makes a move like she's diving through, arms curving around her ears [Mami and Soraya freeze] and then she screams. A ululation: guttural and high-pitched at once. SHERRY looks wildly in MAGGIE's direction, then grins.

SHERRY opens her mouth wide, closes her eyes, cranes her head upwards. No sound comes out. She opens her eyes, she takes in the sky, she begins to sweep her arm around and around, passing through the above and around her. Around and around, like she's bundling up a ball of yarn that traces an invisible moon. Faster now, the ambience around her grows tighter and tighter with her swinging limb and then … POP! SHERRY flinches, her arms go slack, she turns to MAGGIE, who tugs the cord of balloons in one hand, and squeezes an individual balloon with the other. POP! It explodes.

3   Body/State
2   Total Recall
3   Annie Goodner

MAGGIE struggles to pop the number 3 birthday balloon. She squeezes with her hands, but the air shifts about, the balloon remains intact. She grabs another in the clutch, squeezes it hard, it pops. She looks at SHERRY. SHERRY moves towards her. They both grab the number 3. They struggle with the balloon, bumping into one another. MAGGIE tries her teeth. SHERRY presses it under her arm like it's a nut in a nutcracker. Finally it pops.

There's silence. Finally. And then there's crying from the house. SHERRY and MAGGIE are still. MAGGIE lets go of the balloon detritus, smooths her hair, takes a step back sheepishly.

MAGGIE   I'll be … right back. *(MAGGIE heads towards the house)*

SHERRY   OK, Kassandra.

(MAGGIE turns back and sticks her tongue out theatrically. SHERRY does the same. She sits down. She laughs to herself. She closes her eyes.) [Mami and Soraya enact these instructions, then exit.]

4   Shiv Kotecha
       Two-Page Interlude for Two Players Experiencing Anxiety
       and Guilt About Forgetting [instructions]

[In this sequence, Geo reads the scene directions that were not voiced in
Act 1, while Ivan, Soraya and Mami execute the same gestures. Ivan follows most faithfully from a position near the banister, Soraya observing and
echoing from across the void. Mami watches from below, and, stretching,
almost seems to unfurl into a third position between the two poses that Ivan
mostly switches between.]

Gco   Two players sit outside a courtroom. They're
friendly. PLAYER 1 appears anxious, paranoiac even, except when asked
by PLAYER 2 to 'act', whereupon they appear confident, even snooty in their
airs. PLAYER 2 is relaxed in comparison, and they appear to want to help
PLAYER 1 except in the moments that PLAYER 1 is 'acting', during which
time PLAYER 2 appears suddenly mocking, or in cahoots with the audience.
       The scene is meant to be an interlude, best performed between
things, even if interrupting the theme. It's comedy, or else it's some very
serious kind of advertisement for which there is no product.
       [long pause] Echoes of PLAYER 2's voice ping across the room like
an emergency alarm.
       [long pause] PLAYER 1 searches the crowd around them as if look-
ing for a mirror or some version of themselves, then finds what they are
looking for.
       That list of courtroom dramas and their descriptions can be endless.
       [pause] PLAYER 2 pulls out a phone and takes a video of PLAYER
1 'acting'.
       PLAYER 2 stops recording.

[Geo walks to trigger a short keyboard loop that will play continuously
through the next scene. The others scurry to reposition lights for the next
scene in a burst of action.]

5   Ryan Trecartin
     Hack Plea Mock [part 1]

[Mami takes a position on the second floor, leaning on the banister. She plays the JUDGE. Soraya is one floor below her, also on the banister, and plays the DEFENSE COUNSEL lawyer. Opposite is Geo, who unlike Mami and Soraya, is not lit. He plays the STENOGRAPHER. On the ground floor, kneeling, is Ivan, who plays the DEFENDANT. They all read rapidly, off printed sheets of paper. They look at each other as much as they can while they read.]

Mami   I'm the JUDGE. The JUDGE was hacked to be a very supportive listener who is non-judgmental, curious and easily mesmerised.

Soraya   I'm the DEFENSE COUNSEL lawyer. The DEFENSE COUNSEL lawyer was hacked to forget all their legal knowledge without an awareness that they are not currently able to access their deep well of legal knowledge, but still retain the feeling that they are and have.

Geo   I'm the STENOGRAPHER. The STENOGRAPHER was hacked to think two realities are happening at the same time and that it's completely common and normal. In one reality she is at Poetry & Wine night with her bestie and they are hammered. In the other reality she is doing her job as a stenographer. Her brain has resolved the conflict by creating a third reality in which she is taking a creative writing class with her bestie (the DEFENDANT) and stenographic poetry is a course premise.

Ivan   In an adjacent present, the US court system is partially run by artificial intelligence. AI consciousness models have been generated from a mining of all court records and trial tapes that exist. All records of lawyers, clerks, judges, stenographers and jury members from the past century whose records have passed rigorous compassion and morality tests were used to create models for each role/job.

In order to humanise the court experience, actual living people who are trained for the court system are temporarily merged with these AI models during court sessions – a piggyback-type thing. The person's personality, knowledge, own life experiences are filtered into a collaborative state with the AI models which act as guides and bias limiters to a person working in the court system. Everything feels seamlessly integrated into one's sense of free will, agency and intuition – no one ever thinks they've been overridden by one of the AI models. The AI models override a person when personal beliefs trigger certain markers. Everyone who takes on a career in the court system or gets called in for jury duty knows that this override thing happens a lot and is very common according to AI accountability reports, but people never believe they were overridden.

I'm the DEFENDANT. The DEFENDANT is completely unaware that the system has been hacked. People on trial and witnesses are not merged with AI models. This person is here for their sentencing – has already been found guilty of animal abuse via cat hoarding – but the system was hacked weeks before the sentencing hearing … so there's a sense that her take on reality has been increasingly frictionless for her.

JUDGE   I've reviewed the re-sentence report, does the Defense Counsel have a statement?

COUNSEL   Yes Your Honour. Before I outline some of the mitigating factors which I believe justify a lighter penalty, I'd like to –

DEFENDANT   – paint a picture with acrylic on an oily surface.

COUNSEL   What?

DEFENDANT   A.K.*A.* – Tell my based-on-a-true story [pause] and workshop the mood of this room into a designer scent for the gift-bag seminar I'm hosting next month at Your Mom's Butt. Just to be clear, Your Mom's Butt is the name of the venue. The names for some of the newer D.I.Y. lecture halls popping up are deeply clever … Like it's so funny to make someone respond with 'Your Mom's Butt' when asked where something is at.

COUNSEL   What are you doing?

DEFENDANT   *B.* – Set a tone by flirting with some undue delay play and *C.* if I can acknowledge my boundaries …

COUNSEL   What boundaries?

DEFENDANT   Exactly, no threshold.

COUNSEL   As I was saying Your Honour, I'd like to provide some context. Can I proceed?

DEFENDANT   That's something only you can answer.

JUDGE   You can proceed.

DEFENDANT   Wow, classic, can she at least do it with pleasure? … Am I right?

COUNSEL   No more talking. Your Honour, the first flash mobs were created in Manhattan in 2001, by a well-known sex offender who undoubtedly took advantage of my client during their time as life partners.

DEFENDANT   Wait, you forgot the most important part.

                              Hack Plea Mock [part 1]

COUNSEL   No I didn't.

DEFENDANT   You did.

COUNSEL   We talked about you not talking –

DEFENDANT   – and an agreement was never reached. Dear Judge Type, I'm feeling uber font'y, I don't know if it's sexually related to me … or if it's more of a general fuck fest thing stuck in the humidity of this room … because of that shirt you are wearing – but basically, I'm itching for some character clarity.

JUDGE   Can you tell me more about this?

DEFENDANT   Of course.

COUNSEL   Are you serious?

JUDGE   Yes, I am a very curious listener.

COUNSEL   OMG.

DEFENDANT   Thank you. I know this is a very Times New Roman type of space (traditionally). But I just gotta say … I wish I kept my gym membership. The way in which you've stylised that bench … With your hot ass judicial body … You got me seeing everything in Apple Chancery. If the court stenographer has that font I suggest we use it.

COUNSEL   What!?

DEFENDANT   Well not when you talk, you give me Helvetica at best. But mostly all I get from you is American Typewriter, and weird ass cartoon reminders that Facebook exists.

STENOGRAPHER   (ding)

DEFENDANT   The stenographer just texted me – to explain why she's over there cracking up.

STENOGRAPHER   Yes I did! – Hey Slut! – OMG! – We are so hammered! – Mommies calling an Uber!!!!!! Ahhhhhhh …

DEFENDANT   Wow, Dear government, one of your peeps is getting a pay raise! I love this person! What a roof!

STENOGRAPHER   And I'm loving poetry & wine night!!! Ahhhh!!!! – Today's courtroom premise is so thrilling – This creative writing class rocks!

COUNSEL   What is going on?

DEFENDANT   See, look at this text … it says …

STENOGRAPHER   'Yas queen werk, we are on the same page, I'm literally already using the American Typewriter font for the Defence. This is hilarious. We are like soul mates.'

DEFENDANT   Babes, this is amazing!

STENOGRAPHER   Yasss Slut More Wine! (ding) 'I've been using Chalkduster for you'

DEFENDANT   Awww … 'Compliment received, but please switch to Apple Chancery' sent (ding)

                                        Hack Plea Mock [part 1]

STENOGRAPHER   You got it bestie.

DEFENDANT   See, that's how you talk to a person.

STENOGRAPHER   (ding) 'done'

DEFENDANT   Sweet, 'Thanks babes' sent (ding)

STENOGRAPHER   Anything for you!!!

DEFENDANT   I saw her secretly cracking up over there and I just knew she had an inventive spirit.

COUNSEL   Oh really?

STENOGRAPHER   You know me so well!! (ding) 'I was laughing because her name is Arial' So Helvetica adjacent!

DEFENDANT   Oh that's right, I forgot your name is Arial.

COUNSEL   How did you forget my name?
[STENOGRAPHER goes for a walk.]

DEFENDANT   I don't know how to answer that question – but back to the point I was trying to share with sexy bench.

COUNSEL   Oh My God, are you hitting on the Judge?

DEFENDANT   I prepare my own meals.

COUNSEL   WOW!

JUDGE   Excuse me?

DEFENDANT   Never – own it – everyone in this room wants
to sit on your face – I'm just the only one here who isn't embarrassed by
desires long enough to not say what I mean. What this Defense Counsel
concept person failed to provide I am willing to fix.

JUDGE   Are we moving on to the Defendant's Allocution?

DEFENDANT   No. The first flash mobs were supposably created in Manhattan in 2001 – even though the internet says 2003 – BUT – I
secretly argue that they started in 1899, Canton, Ohio – as a response to
the 1992 American historical musical drama *Newsies* – by a prolific psy-
chic and similar sex offender (who did not take advantage of me because
I wasn't born yet … although I imagine he knew this day would come). His
local community was blown away by the ways in which he described this
future dance-based reimagining of the then current New York City news-
boys' strike. Since no one living would be alive to see the movie everyone
got really depressed and suicide rates went up – but then members of the
local theatre guild decided to stage impromptu musical theatre events in
public spaces based on his predictions. Since it's a period piece and they
happened to have the advantage of actually living in the period of the piece
– things got exciting. One of the theatre people was a thrilling opportunist
and he took the opportunity to save money on set design by activating
public spaces as sets. It honestly sounds stupid and boring to me, but their
public funding was recently pulled and none of them were any good at
fund raising.

COUNSEL   Yeah, not important or true.

DEFENDANT   Everything is important and true – So this 2001
'poser' who is commonly credited for the flash mob is actually just European.

JUDGE   Meaning?

DEFENDANT   He 'discovered' the flash mob concept. Don't get me wrong, he's very self-aware – he was Christopher Columbus for fucking Halloween that same year. So this guy, who is a well-known sex offender – who I dated – also unfortunately made an excellent electroclash Christmas album that I love dearly – each song was written at a different 6 Flags amusement park, in a different state, while riding a different ride – while in his basement.

JUDGE   What?

DEFENDANT   Right? try to figure that one out – case closed.

COUNSEL   OMG.

DEFENDANT   Totally brilliant – this was before thousands of Americans were impaled; the summer selfie sticks were popularised – it's so much harder to smuggle music equipment onto a roller coaster now.

JUDGE   – but he was in a basement?

DEFENDANT   Allegedly – I'm more of a pedestrian style person ... are you accusing me of detective work?

JUDGE   Of course not.

DEFENDANT   Thank you.

COUNSEL   That's not an accusation ...

DEFENDANT   ... and neither am I so we have something in common … we are not accusations.

COUNSEL   WOW.

DEFENDANT   'Wow', do you play the piano with one finger?
Pronounce your chords – words are just notes – they need friends – like say
a full sentence or something.

COUNSEL   Your Honour, my client …

DEFENDANT   Excuse you … so back to this flash-mob fucker
– so like flowers 'yes', because of that Christmas album I mentioned – but
freedom no, 'no more drum machine for you – you belong behind bars you
sticky dick piece of shit' …

JUDGE   WOW.

DEFENDANT   Yup, that's just me taking a stand right where
you sit – we are on the shoulders of giants – it's not my fault that you're sitting while I stand – you asked me to rise – earlier – and as my childhood-self
always said, 'occasion rise to me'.

COUNSEL   Your Honour, my client speaks very passionately in a unique oral history type of way …

DEFENDANT   I fucking hate recent history –

COUNSEL   Well you talk about it a lot and you don't read
books.

DEFENDANT   I don't read books about recent history because
I was alive you dick.

COUNSEL   I was alive too and I read books about recent history.

DEFENDANT   That's not my fault dude.

COUNSEL   Why are you doing this weird jock rock man voice thing?

DEFENDANT   It's how I respond to interruptions when I tell this particular story.

COUNSEL   Stop that, we talked about you not doing fake accents.

DEFENDANT   Nothing is fake … real people know that.

COUNSEL   Are you calling me a fake person?

DEFENDANT   No, I'm saying that maybe … you aren't a person.

COUNSEL   Your Honour, I apologise.

JUDGE   It's ok I appreciate a passionately delivered story – I want to hear more.

DEFENDANT   Thank you, I'll take a passion pass at you any day, we should brainstorm ways to get naked – oh wait I got it, let's get naked.

STENOGRAPHER   YES!! Naked Poetry Class! (laughs)

COUNSEL   Do you annotate your laugh track, because I'm loving it.

STENOGRAPHER   I do, I used the UNTITLED font.

DEFENDANT   Smart, I love fonts that refuse to participate in lowercase letters … it always feels so romantically classist to me.

STENOGRAPHER   OMG I was thinking the same thing! [STENOGRAPHER goes for a walk.]

DEFENDANT   … and I hope by the end of our brainstorming session it will have become a true story.

COUNSEL   This is a sentencing hearing.

DEFENDANT   Sentences don't have ears, you're an idiot.

JUDGE   What's the name of this first or second flash-mob creator? Am I understanding correctly, that he is a registered sex offender?

DEFENDANT   No, he's just a well-known offender – He's in jail for involuntary armed robbery and involuntary manslaughter and tax fraud.

JUDGE   I've never heard of involuntary armed robbery.

DEFENDANT   Well, in 2008 he organised a jitterbug-themed flash mob – I know, what a rancid idea – but the mashup backing track was morbidly stellar – like it made people angry – it was chilling – the plan was to start at Wells Fargo bank – 611 East Wilson Avenue in Glendale, California – the smaller initial group all planned to take money out of the ATMs at the same time, and then throw it in the air once the music started and then after doing a weird-ass swing dance jitterbug ska number in the bank they would burst through the doors and be joined by a marching band, a modern dance troupe, and a row of flatbed trucks – the beds were all lined with tarps so that they could be filled with water. The back of each truck pool had 23 goldfish (I don't know why) and each one had a synchronised water dancer in it. He thought since the theme was swing dance or some shit that he wanted everyone to have like an Italian mobster who listens to Real Big Fish type of a look – OMG I can't even believe I know this shit – See this is why I don't read recent history.

COUNSEL   2008 isn't very recent.

DEFENDANT   No shit, shut the fuck up – anyways, I was his stunt coordinator at the time and I hired a weapons handler for the performance – Authenticity wasn't popular in 2008 so I decided to go super authentic … I was like 'real guns only bitch' and I was like 'they better be loaded' – hence, I'm a total contrarian.

COUNSEL   No shit.

DEFENDANT   Weird, I bet you do.

JUDGE   So what happened?

DEFENDANT   A ton of people died – and well of course I didn't tell anyone that their guns were authentic – I was protecting my job.

COUNSEL   The same reason any living person isn't in prison – I can keep a fucking secret.

COUNSEL   Can you?

DEFENDANT   It's not obvious?

JUDGE   So what happened?

DEFENDANT   I told you, a bunch of people died.

JUDGE   That must have been hard for you.

DEFENDANT   It was – the bank teller was so scared, he clearly thought actual armed robbery was happening because of all the unfortunate gun activity – so he just started throwing money at us – there was a moment when I thought God was pranking me because I've never been good with paper – like I can never catch it.

JUDGE   That's so interesting, I wonder why?

DEFENDANT   Of course this was all just a very consequential misunderstanding accident hence the involuntary part. I took a ton of the money before the cops showed up and put it in his house – they found it later, hence the tax fraud part.

COUNSEL   You are admitting to some very serious crimes.

DEFENDANT   All to prove a point. I do not hoard cats – they were my boyfriend's, he's in prison, I'm just watching them until he gets out.

JUDGE   And what is his name?

DEFENDANT   I forgot?

JUDGE   You forgot? That's so interesting.

DEFENDANT   He applied to be forgotten and I think that's dope so I chose to forget him. And also why is animal hoarding a crime anyways?

3   Body/State
2   Total Recall
5   Ryan Trecartin

[The musical loop stops. Exeunt.]

3   Guard   4pm

[Over the building Tannoy, Ivan welcomes the audience, and establishes that they should watch from the first-floor balcony. He establishes the roles that the performers will take, and presents the credits of the coming section 'Guard', from 'Body/State', pronouncing the / as 'over'.]

1   Ryan Trecartin
       Hack Plea Mock [part 2]

[Soraya and Mami are already back in the positions they were in at the end
of the last part, ready to resume their roles as JUDGE and COUNSEL. Geo
resumes the short musical loop that ran through the last section, but is now
with instruments, ready to play over the repeated phrase. As he reads, Ivan
travels from the Tannoy to his position on the ground floor.]

Geo   Cases are picked at random and third-party
tested for accountability. Data that is used to both make sure the system
is functioning according to the current interpretations of constitution and
law – guidelines 'meant' to combat the ways in which human bias interferes
with one's right to a fair trial – and also guidelines meant to protect personal
integrity and personhood while under the influence of AI. BUT basically, on
something like reddit there is a community of tech-savvy people (most of
them have worked for these third-party accountability organisations) who
watch hours of intake videos to try and find the most eccentric criminals,
and then hack the court system to see whose 'player' generates the most
interesting narrative/outcome … basically … most fucked up or hilarious
court-room sentencing hearing video … The AI models themselves can't
easily be hacked, but their sense of purpose and the features of their over-
rides/guides can be. So people script new guidelines to encourage weird
material. What takes place below is a sentencing hearing where: The hack-
er rigged everything to basically make space for this person to talk a lot.
Oh, all courts are streamed live to the public, but most people only watch
the ones that go viral from this hacking thread.

DEFENDANT   … and and now it's happening. I workshopped
that shit with my character coach.

JUDGE   That's a thing?

3   Body/State
3   Guard
1   Ryan Trecartin

DEFENDANT   Yup, it is a thing – and guess what? – I am my
coach.

COUNSEL   Your Honour –

DEFENDANT   – is Hot.

COUNSEL   Fuck me –

DEFENDANT   – first and I'll give you a free coaching session.

COUNSEL   Zip it.

DEFENDANT   I like buttons.

JUDGE   Me too.

DEFENDANT   One of my hobbies is running a character witness for hire app – it's called F… A … David — It's supposed to read as
Fuck A David – because all of our character witnesses use the name David
– I picked that name because it just feels like it's a super common name
in literally any gender and any language any also any culture – But most
importantly when you say F… A … David out loud it sounds like Affidavit
– especially if you're from South Jersey but have lived in North Florida for
about ten years – and then you're just like – Damn breaker bitch, I wanna
Fuck a David – this shit spits keys.

JUDGE   I collect keys.

DEFENDANT   You slut, I collect doors.

JUDGE   So wait, if all of these character witnesses for hire are named David, won't that get you arrested? Seems risky …

DEFENDANT   OK, so this is genius – because I'm a business genius –

JUDGE   Tell me more.

DEFENDANT   All of my customers are guilty – like maybe 10% are actually innocent people who just don't happen to have friends – and sadly, they're the ones that usually stick with all the factory preset conditions like 'hey my friend's name is David, he's my neighbour, blah blah' – and yeah, they're all in prison, like beyond jail.

JUDGE   Damn … that sucks.

DEFENDANT   Right? It's so unfair.

COUNSEL   You can't call it unfair as if you didn't create the dynamic.

DEFENDANT   I think I just proved you can – by doing exactly that – in court – so it's a fact now.

JUDGE   So how do you customise the name of your character witness?

DEFENDANT   OK, so most of my clients are guilty and they have loved ones who know it – so they go the extra mile it takes to generate a custom name – First: you have to download my sex-work app – my other side hustle – it's literally called I Love Paying for Appy Sex Because I'm Fun & NOT Stupid – it's a totally rewarding experience.

3   Body/State
3   Guard
1   Ryan Trecartin

JUDGE   I bet, I mean it's thrilling just to hear you talk about it.

DEFENDANT   Right? I can pitch the shit out of a thing.

COUNSEL   Just get through it – What comes second?

DEFENDANT   Second: You search the I Love Paying for Appy Sex Because I'm Fun & NOT Stupid photo pool until you find the profile photo that matches the David you hired on Affidavit …

COUNSEL   That's crazy.

DEFENDANT   Exactly, crazy is rewarding – it takes hours.

JUDGE   And then?

DEFENDANT   Once you pay for sex the apps connect and you're able to unlock the 'Customise my David' category – You don't have to have sex – but most people are in need of a hug so I recommend at least getting a hug.

JUDGE   I agree hugs are important.

DEFENDANT   OK so not only can you now customise the name, but you can tell them what to wear and you gain access to all of their skills, talents and hobbies … so if you're like, 'oh wow, my David was a Rockette', you can be like, 'oh maybe that's how I know David, we were Rockettes together' – and then we provide narrative feedback – for example – I might be like, 'actually, you were both a half inch too short to perform at Radio City Music Hall in NY – which was a huge tragedy for the both of you – In fact your mom disowned you because she was a "real" Rockette

                                                      Hack Plea Mock [part 2]

3   Body/State
3   Guard
1   Ryan Trecartin

and in New York City and that's why she won't be providing a Character
Letter – your height embarrassed her and she never got over it. You both
had exceptional talent but your height was a total failure – so you both got
placed in the touring component of the company' – David is still very close
to his mom of course so the court can trust a letter – They know each other
in the deepest of ways.

JUDGE   Smart.

DEFENDANT   Yeah, back in the day they called it trauma
bonding – but that phrase fell out of favour because people respect pain.

COUNSEL   This is the dumbest shit on earth.

JUDGE   Why are you so angry?

DEFENDANT   I know why. It's because so many of my Davids
are married now to people they met because on my Affidavit – and that
makes her sad because she worries that she will never find love – but, lots
of people feel that way – find one of those people – just don't use my app –
they aren't on there.

COUNSEL   What the actual fuck?

DEFENDANT   By the way, I'm recruiting.

JUDGE   Oh this is so sweet, so you're recruiting because you lose a lot of Davids to marriage?

DEFENDANT   Hell no, my people are open marriage only –
which also makes her angry –

3   Body/State
3   Guard
1   Ryan Trecartin

COUNSEL   No it doesn't – you do.

DEFENDANT   She loves rules.

COUNSEL   You don't even know me.

DEFENDANT   I think if you took a break – maybe go to the
bathroom – you'll realise why you're angry – you don't hate app creators
you hate design –

COUNSEL   What?

DEFENDANT   – like you don't hate the creator you hate the
design.

COUNSEL   What?

DEFENDANT   OK I'll break it down – you don't hate God, you
just hate your life – but I think if you take a bathroom break – you'll realise
'hate' itself is a design flaw – hence – you gotta find a way to love yourself
– the bathroom is a great place to start.

JUDGE   This is so fascinating.

COUNSEL   Is it?

JUDGE   I mean, yes.

COUNSEL   No.

DEFENDANT   You both could learn something about your-
selves by becoming a David. I'm currently doing a recruitment push – our

                                   Hack Plea Mock [part 2]

3   Body/State
3   Guard
1   Ryan Trecartin

letters are crafted to maximise their utility – we have an excellent track record –

COUNSEL   Of losing cases for people.

DEFENDANT   You probably shouldn't admit that.

COUNSEL   No you!

DEFENDANT   Yes, get to know me, I agree – I am trying to help you do that … it's called insight into my character.

COUNSEL   I believe this 'hobby' business you've been needlessly describing is highly illegal.

DEFENDANT   I don't think you should be sharing personal beliefs in a professional setting like this.

COUNSEL   Your Honour, I'm so sorry for my …

DEFENDANT   … 'withholding of trial sex because I'm scared of groups' – even though my smile says other wise things …

COUNSEL   … I am so SORRY for MY CLIENT'S BEHAVIOUR.

DEFENDANT   You can only No what you Know – try it first – I'm intentionally developing a personality disorder to fit in socially because I love people, everything I do is public-safety based – you know community style – I bet every single personhood qualifying human in this room knows the sexual joy of a family-style restaurant dish.

3   Body/State
3   Guard
1   Ryan Trecartin

JUDGE   It's true!

COUNSEL   What? Judge, why aren't you saying things like
'if you can't get handle on your client, I am going to hold you both in con-
tempt of this court.'

DEFENDANT   Bitch, please you can't 'held' – you hate being
touched.

COUNSEL   That's not even true.

DEFENDANT   You don't let me touch you.

COUNSEL   Yeah, I believe that would be assault.

DEFENDANT   Beliefs.

COUNSEL   I feel like that's a law.

DEFENDANT   I don't think our court system was designed
around your feelings – Oh I wanted to share something – it was hilarious
when I pleaded guilty, but I only did that for my acting class.

JUDGE   You're an actor?

DEFENDANT   We all pay for something with our attention –
my attention behaves generatively, I'm an adversarial learner, and I love
networking – but I hate supervision.

COUNSEL   Your Honour …

DEFENDANT   Yeah, see I couldn't generate any meaning out

                              Hack Plea Mock [part 2]

3   Body/State
3   Guard
1   Ryan Trecartin

of that. Like, did my co-lawyer just address that bench potatoes co-judge position, or were you trying to mime the act of physically handing a person their honour back.

COUNSEL   Your Honour?

JUDGE   I'm sorry, I'm kind of obsessed with what's happening.

COUNSEL   You suck.

JUDGE   Order!

DEFENDANT   Taco Bell Bitch!

JUDGE   Order!

DEFENDANT   A Pregnancy Test, Yes Bitch – Baby Shower, I can tell by the way the co-judge is dressed – God is dead, at least in this room – so you need to whisper slut.

COUNSEL   Your Honour, I sincerely apologise for …

DEFENDANT   'Not supporting my co-author.'

COUNSEL   I am going to fucking murder you.

DEFENDANT   I rest my case – unlike me – she is not an actor, what you see is what you get. It's a well-known opinion that judges judge character –

JUDGE   – incorrect … evidence.

3   Body/State
3   Guard
1   Ryan Trecartin

DEFENDANT   Exactly, incorrect evidence is literally personality … every character actor knows that you are judging my personality, but are you any good at it? I assume not, BUT, please fear not, literally, I want you to actually fear the knot, so that your sexy co-dependent vibe falls hard for me when I untangle this case for you. The jury knows what I'm talking about – they've been giving me sexy go-for-it encouragement-style looks – because everyone loves tiny fragile judicial sex – I'm a great supporting act – this is me helping you out. I will pardon you only this once – no more freebies you sexy slut. See watch this – Shut the fuck up Judge! I will murder you!

JUDGE   Excuse me!

DEFENDANT   See that's just an example of my intense acting style – I'm acting – I'm an actor and I'm really good at acting like an actor – I always play actors – I do all my own type-casting.

[The performers accept brief applause, before convening at the musicians' area.]

                                            Hack Plea Mock [part 2]

2   Becket MWN
    The Last Days of Paul VValker [convention]

[Again moving as a dynamic cluster, the group travel together, up the stairs of the older atrium, around the perimeter of the second-floor balcony, walking towards the skybridges of the newer atrium. As they travel past spotlights, these are turned to light other performers, who might be forging ahead or lingering behind. Ivan speaks the DIRECTIONS, Geo plays PAUL WALKER, Mami plays VIN DIESEL, and Soraya plays ROGER RODAS.]

DIRECTIONS   Scene 2: Fundraiser at a convention centre in Santa Clarita, California. PAUL WALKER is at a podium making a speech to an audience. PAUL WALKER is an actor, forty years old; star of the *Fast & Furious* franchise, and founder of charity organisation Reach Out Worldwide. ROGER RODAS, stands just behind him. ROGER is the co-founder of Reach Out Worldwide, and owner of the racing shop Always Evolving. He is also a wealth management director at Merrill Lynch, and PAUL's financial adviser.

PAUL WALKER   … the promotion of a paternalistic and human-itarian comfort civilisation will perfectly replace social aid through the technical assistance of bodies, from the household robot to the company psychiatrist or the latest model of car. In 1921 Marinetti metaphorised about the armoured car: the overman is over-grafted, an inhuman type reduced to a driving – and thus deciding – principle, an animal body that disappears in the superpower of a metallic body able to annihilate time and space through its dynamic performances. No more riots, no need for much repression; to empty the streets, it's enough to promise everyone the highway.

DIRECTIONS   Enter VIN DIESEL, speaking as PAUL continues with speech in background.

3	Body/State
3	Guard
2	Becket MWN

VIN DIESEL	*(as PAUL WALKER continues with speech in background)* Paul Walker, or Paul V-Valker, fully automated droning dromomaniac, has left his audience in mild confusion. They came for a charity event, an update on the good work they are funding in the Philippines, where this NGO has had staff on the ground for a week now. They came to see the signifiers of disaster relief, congratulate each other on their good work, and of course compare sports cars while queuing for the valet.

PAUL WALKER	On the shores across the way, the perpetual transformation of the barbarous aesthetic of the mass-produced American car, the provocative excess of its body, of its ornaments, manifest the permanence of the social revolution (progress towards the 'American way of life'). But at the same time, this great automobile body has been emasculated, its road holding is defective and its powerful motor is bridled. Just as for the laws on speed limits, we are talking about acts of government, in other words, of the political control of the highway, aiming precisely at limiting the 'extraordinary power of assault' that motorisation of the masses creates.

[The group, gradually out of sight of the audience, continue with gusto towards the stairs in the newer atrium, gradually coming down to the ground floor.]

DIRECTIONS	PAUL WALKER abruptly leaves the stage; audience claps sparsely. VIN DIESEL pulls him aside, as the audience begins slowly to get up and mingle quietly among themselves. ROGER RODAS goes to try and reassure donors in the audience.

VIN DIESEL	Paul! Paul! Snap out of it! It's me, your co-star and dear friend Vin Diesel. We worked together on *The Fast and The Furious*, *2 Fast 2 Furious*, *Tokyo Drift*, *Fast and Furious 4*, *Fast Five* and, currently in production on, *Fast and Furious 6*.

PAUL WALKER   The indiscriminate boarding of soulless bodies
as metabolic vehicles.

VIN DIESEL   Dammit Paul, you're scaring people!

PAUL WALKER   The masses are not a population, a society, but
the multitude of passers-by.

VIN DIESEL   You don't mean that. What about our communities?

PAUL WALKER   To survive in the city, one had to stay informed
daily, by radio, about the strategic situation of one's own neighbourhood;
everyone transformed his car into an assault vehicle, loaded with weapons
in order to ensure freedom of movement.

VIN DIESEL   How do you think this ends Paul? What's left of
society when citizenship is replaced with survivalism? Once every individual is turned into a projectile, what's next? We become bullets, missiles?

PAUL WALKER   The kamikaze will realise in space the military
elite's synergistic dream by voluntarily disintegrating with his vehicle-weapon
in a pyrotechnical apotheosis; for the ultimate metaphor of the speed-body
is its final disappearance in the flames of explosion.

VIN DIESEL   Paul, you're scaring me. What you're describing
is a fascist suicide pact!

PAUL WALKER   Whatever the case: since fascism never died, it
doesn't need to be reborn.

[Now headed across the floor of the newer atrium, the group ascends a

3   Body/State
3   Guard
2   Becket MWN

wide staircase that leads to the second floor of the older atrium, where they
break off into pairs, speaking outwards, or observing the others.]

DIRECTIONS   ROGER RODAS turns to VIN DIESEL. PAUL
continues to speak in background to himself while ROGER and VIN talk.

ROGER RODAS   Vin what's going on?

VIN DIESEL   Hey Roger, Paul's in a pretty bad place. I don't
think it's a mechanical problem. It's behind the cylinder head, deep in the
engine block.

ROGER RODAS   Is it a nomadology? Restless leg syndrome?

VIN DIESEL   'fraid not Rog. It's in the drive shaft.

ROGER RODAS   Not –

VIN DIESEL   Yes – the death drive.

PAUL WALKER   The soul neither pre-exists nor survives the disappearance of its body-vehicle or machine; but as potential Reason, and
especially scientific Reason, it can act on foreign bodies which are distant
in time and space. Animal, territorial, vegetable bodies, bodies without will,
bodies not yet born become technical bodies or technological objects. Here
is true social domination, the bestiary of engines. The purebred horse no
longer acts, he is acted on by his rider thanks to the drive shaft of the bridle
and the gas pedals of the spurs. Or else he takes the bit in his teeth, returns
to his uncontrollable, wild state … he expresses himself!

ROGER RODAS   What can we do?

VIN DIESEL   There's nothing we can do. It's time to say goodbye. He's not Paul anymore. He's PVV.

DIRECTIONS   VIN DIESEL turns to PAUL WALKER.

VIN DIESEL   Paul, you're like family to me, and love for my family is the most important character trait I have as Dom Toretto. But perhaps it's time for you to go your own way. Maybe it's time to say goodbye to familiar institutions and established franchises.

PAUL WALKER   Stasis is death; it really seems to be the general law of the World.

VIN DIESEL   You're right, Paul. Change is the nature of things, and dialectical thought demands we ask not why things change, but why they stubbornly stay the same. What comes next may be worse, but it's not going to get any better by pretending it doesn't exist.

PAUL WALKER   Speed is Time saved in the most absolute sense of the word, since it becomes human Time directly torn from Death.

VIN DIESEL   I wish I could go with you, but my place is here among the living, to build something new atop the ruins of the West.

PAUL WALKER   We must still apply aesthetic, functional and other meanings to this world of giant cars.

VIN DIESEL   Amen, Paul. I have a feeling they're going to replace you with a computer-generated avatar. Goodbye old friend.

DIRECTIONS   PAUL WALKER turns to leave, walking offstage, as ROGER and VIN watch. PAUL stops before leaving, turns to look back at VIN.

3   Body/State
3   Guard
2   Becket MWN

PAUL WALKER   It is again an engineer and director of fortifica-
tions, of course, who in 1782 will publish one of the first known flow charts.

DIRECTIONS   PAUL exists. Lights fade down on ROGER
RODAS and VIN DIESEL. Scene over.

[The group exit into an elevator, in which they begin to hum.]

3   Tai Shani
     Them Who Love

[Continuing to hum, out of sight, harmonising consonantly in the elevator. Their voices are still heard in the atrium. The hum of the elevator operation is also amplified with their microphones. After some time, they begin to read lines, using their phones for the text, as they ride the elevator upwards.]

TWL 1   [Soraya] You said, 'Drop your weapons.'

TWL 2   [Geo] Drop your weapons. Kiss me, cup your warm hands around my face and pull me towards you, I trust you, I trust your tenderness, you could destroy me but you won't, kiss me again, deeper, our mouths close like the heavy velvet drapes dropping after the epilogue, sealed, hold my skull, a finely carved bowl of the grey sludge of sentience, kiss me like there is no urgent toil of material survival. Kiss me, love me like a wrecker of culture, a wrecker of civilization till we harmonise with the sound of *(hummmmm noise BOTH)*. [Humming reaches a crescendo. They exit the elevator, and then are travelling down stairways in a different part of the building, gradually coming to re-enter the atriums.]

TWL 1   [Mami] You then said 'I love you with the love for the living.'

TWL 2   [Ivan] When we say 'love' we say that we see you for who you really are, we say that I am brimming with unassigned faith, that I am also collecting the precious pieces, that I, we, are in the wound-like quarry scoring the stone, kneading the mud and grass, preparing the moulds, lighting the kiln fires. That we are eternally communing to collaboratively build the epic monument to the unbroken cycle of our interdependency, the home that we will not know, but the world beyond the horizon will inherit.

3   Body/State
3   Guard
3   Tai Shani

[Their humming starts to fade. They are again within sight of the audience.]

TWL 1   [Geo] What did you mean by 'Love for the dead'?

TWL 2   [Soraya] Loving the dead is also for the living, catastrophe is in the architecture of the living, murder is for the living, execution is for the living, genocide is for the living, grief is for the living.

Extermination, drones, nuclear weapons, apartheid is for the living, hunger, holocausts big and small, homelessness, exclusion, incarceration, poverty, isolation, rent, exploitation is for the living, it is for the living.

In the face of dehumanising violence, interruption of personal narrative, history, culture place, the act of remembrance, of detail, of love, of distinction is an act of humanisation, bringing back the dehumanised subject into the world of the living again, even if it is as a sad ghost.

TWL 1   [Mami] What did you say to the ghosts?

TWL 2   [Geo] Children of lifelessness haunt us! We and a hundred thousand ghosts wrote this sentence, we and a hundred thousand ghosts made this music, we and a hundred thousand ghosts wrote the book of love. We and a hundred thousand ghosts made it possible to understand how to love you. We and a hundred thousand ghosts realised that just like you I am a miracle.

[Now back at the ground floor of the older atrium, they turn to thank the audience, bow and then exit.]

                                                      Them Who Love

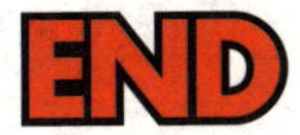

Credits

Josefin Arnell's contribution excerpts 'Failure Is a Feeling that Exists Long Before it Comes: A Family Drama', commissioned for *Conversing Motherboards*, De Studio, Antwerp (2018)

Ed Atkins' contribution excerpts 'Material Witness OR A Liquid Cop', published in *A Primer for Cadavers*, Fitzcarraldo Editions, London (2016), as well as an ongoing autofactual.

Claire Fontaine's contribution, 'The 25th Hour of The Day', was first published in *The Love Issue #34 F/W 2020*, Purple Magazine, Paris (2020)

Calla Henkel & Max Pitegoff's contribution 'Scene 4', was first performed as *News Crime Sports*, Grüner Salon, Volksbühne, Berlin (2017)

Nour Mobarak's contribution excerpts Song Ci's *The Washing Away of Wrongs* (1247), translated by Brian McKnight, published in *The Washing Away of Wrongs: Forensic Medicine in Thirteenth-Century China*, The University of Michigan Center for Chinese Studies, Ann Arbor (1981)

Ariana Reines' contributions, 'WATSON+BELL' and 'MISS SAINT'S HIEROGLYPHIC SUFFERING', were first published in *Telephone*, Wonder Press, New York (2018)

Tai Shani's contribution, 'Teenager', was first published in *Our Fatal Magic: Collected Texts from DC: Semiramis*, Strange Attractor Press, London (2019)

Noor Abed

Sophia Al-Maria

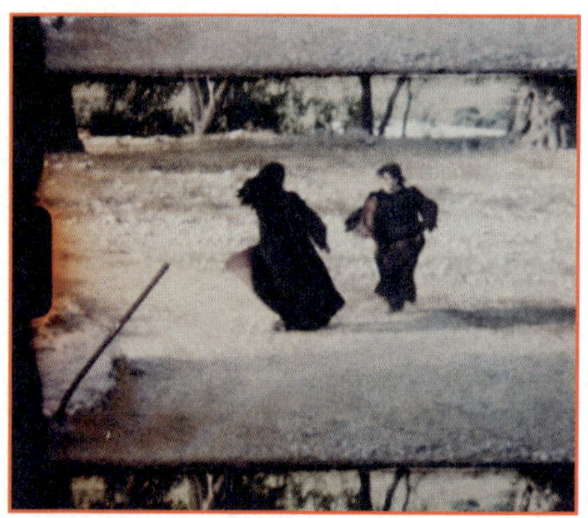

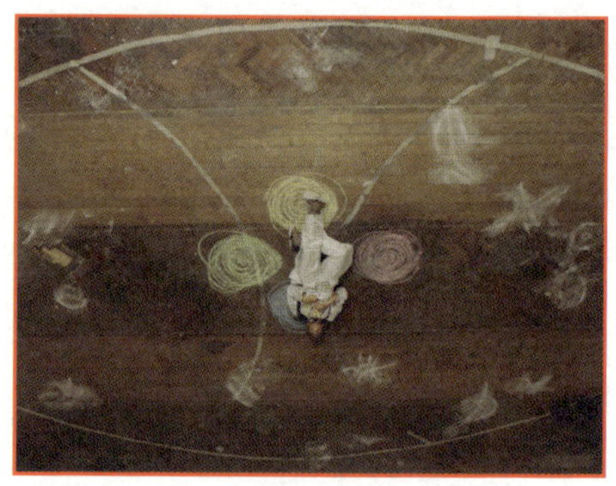

OUT OF JOINT, 2018
16mm film digital transfer
& SD video,
10'40'', silent

PENELOPE, 2014
16mm film, 06'28'', silent

*our songs were ready for all
wars to come*, 2021
Super-8 film, 20', w/ sound

BEAST TYPE SONG, 2019
Single-channel HD video, 30' 03'',
w/ sound

Tender Point Ruin, 2021
Single-channel HD video, 26',
w/ sound

Tiger Strike Red, 2022
Single-channel HD video, 23' 03'',
w/ sound

Özgür Kar

Brianna Leatherbury

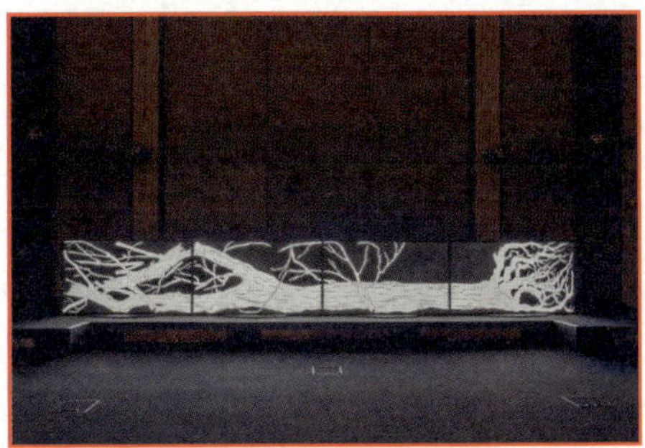

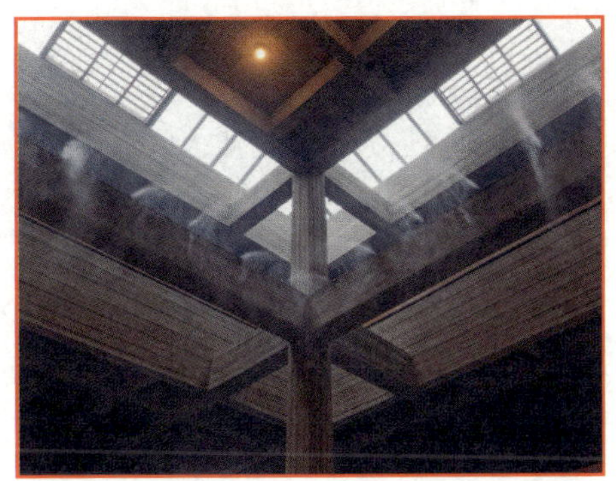

FALL, 2023
4-channel 4K video with sound,
5' loop, 4 x 75" TVs, BrightSign
Media Players, cables

Liquidation, 2024
Greenhouse humidifier, artificial
perspiration, real estate

Mire Lee

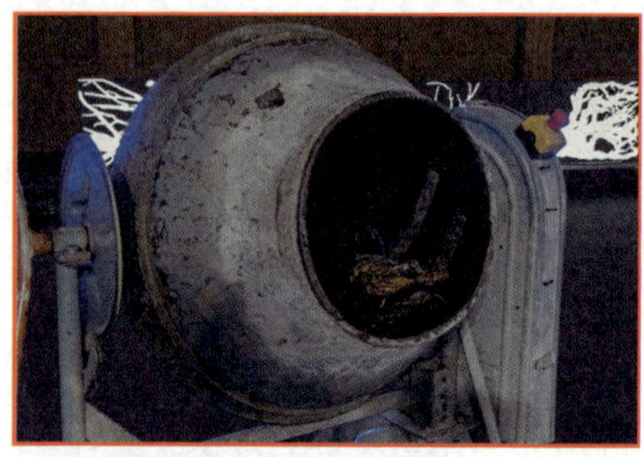

*Look, I'm a fountain of filth
raving made with love; concrete
mixers*, 2022
Geared motors on found
concrete mixers

Sands Murray-Wassink

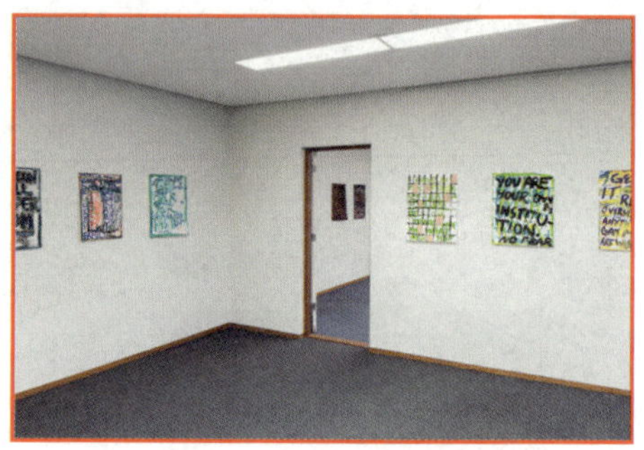

Working 2010s, decade of 2010s
Selection from series of 125 works

Peng Zuqiang

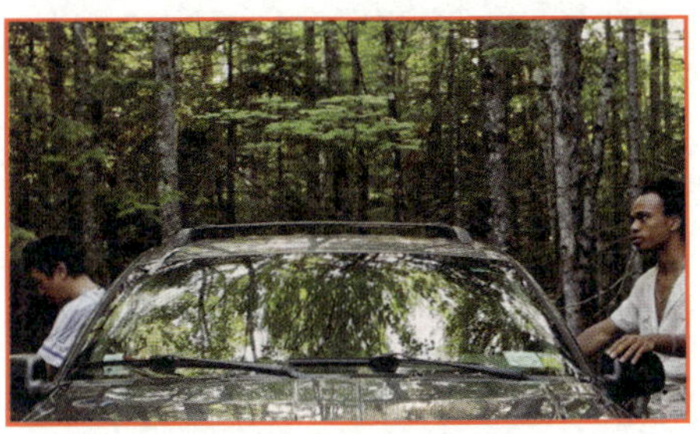

Autocorrects, 2023
Single-channel video, 16mm film
transferred to HD, 03' 03'', w/ sound

Keep in Touch, 2021
Single-channel video installation,
HD video and Super 8 transferred
to HD, 13' 58'', w/ sound

The Cyan Garden, 2022
Single channel, colour & BW, 16mm
transferred to HD video, 08' 05'',
w/ sound

Jay Tan

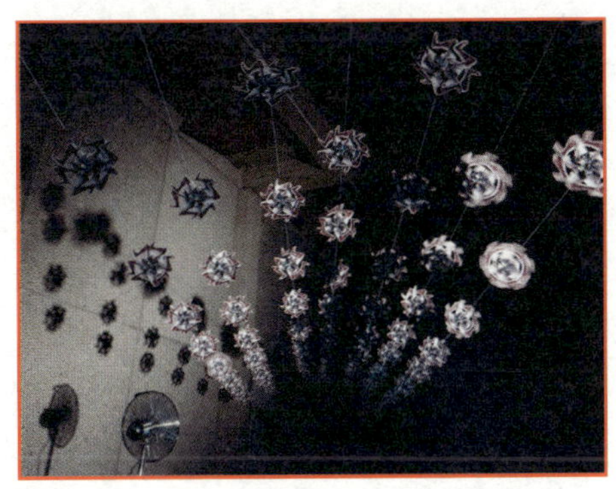

*Kung Fu Hustle Landlady
Pinwheels*, 2024
Paper, string, fans

aqui Thami

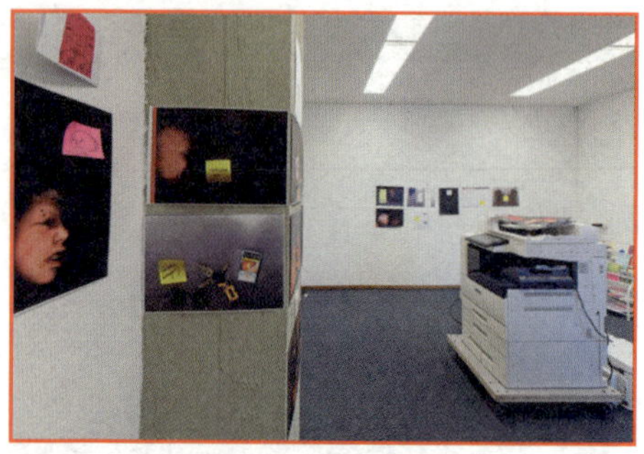

Zines From Bombay Underground,
various years
Collection of books and zines

Ryan Trecartin

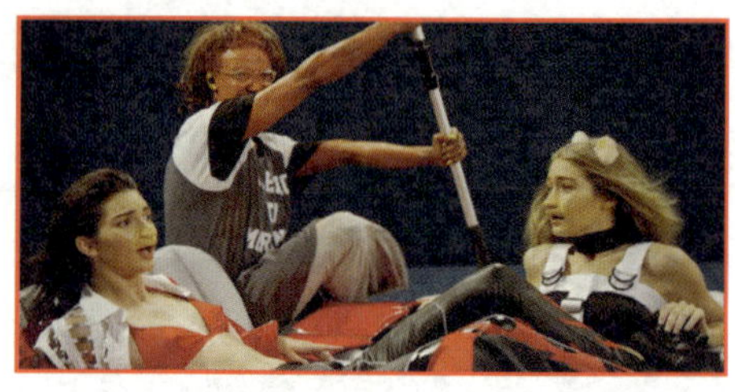

Occupy Zombie
15', excerpt mashup from:
    SITE VISIT, 2014 +
    Temple Time, 2016
    Multi-channel + single-channel
    HD video, 54' 32", w/ sound

Comma Boat, 2013
— *Priority Innfield*
Multi-channel HD video, 33' 02",
w/ sound
Single-channel HD video, 33' 02",
w/ sound

Panderson Heights
06' 25", excerpt mashup from:
    Whether Line (Plot Front edit),
    2019
    Single-channel 4K video,
    141' 33", w/ sound
• *Sweeper Case*, 01' 08"
• *Panderson Heights*, 05' 17"

K-CoreaINC.K (section a), 2009
— *Any Ever, Trill-ogy Comp*
Single-channel HD video, 33' 05",
w/ sound

Placebo Pets, 2016
Single-channel HD video, 01' 29",
w/ sound

(Tommy Chat Just E-Mailed Me.),
2006
Single-channel SD video, 07' 14",
w/ sound

Mark Trade Scenes
13' 02", excerpt mashup from:
   Mark Trade, 2014/2016
   Single-channel HD video, 73'
   30", w/ sound

*Revivals Guilt: Panhandle of
Isolation*
   17' 23", excerpt mashup from:
   Whether Line (Plot Front edit),
   2019
   Single-channel 4K video,
   141' 33", w/ sound
•   *The Panhandle of Isolation*, 34"
•   *Feature Neighbor Girl*, 59"
•   *Cornered Field*, 30"
•   *Warning Cousins*, 07' 52"
•   *Revivals Guilt*, 04' 47"
•   *Captain Milk*, 02' 41"

The Re'Search, 2009–2010
— *Any Ever, Re'Search Wait'S*
Single-channel HD video, 40' 06",
w/ sound

Why, 2020
Ian Isiah, Shugga Sextape, Vol. 1,
2018
Music Video & Whether Line excerpt, co-director, Leilah Weinraub
Single-channel 4K video, 02' 30",
w/ sound

Car Stuck Park
05', excerpt mashup from:
   Stunt Tank, 2014/2016
   Single-channel HD video, 44'
   13", w/ sound

The Stanchion Rope Effect
05' 45", excerpt mashup from:
   Whether Line (Plot Front edit),
   2019
   Single-channel 4K video,
   141' 33", w/ sound
•   *The Stanchion Rope Effect*, 46"
•   *Mayor Maps*, 01' 11"
•   *Interactive Day*, 03' 48"
Junior War, 1999/2013
— *Priority Innfield*
Single-channel SD video, 24' 25",
w/ sound

Punishment Woulds
21' 14", excerpt mashup from:
Whether Line (Plot Front edit),
2019
Single-channel 4K video, 141'
33", w/ sound
- *Realtor Run*, 01' 31"
- *Cemetery Said*, 08' 31"
- *Reverse Seance*, 01' 27"
- *Anthro-apology*, 01' 04"
- *Old Money Miners*, 01' 24"
- *Registry Play*, 02' 26"
- *Cover Crop Siblings*, 03' 45"
- *Punishment Woulds*, 01' 06"

Animation Companion
09', excerpt mashup from:
Permission Streak,
1999/2013/2016
Single-channel HD video, 21'
17", w/ sound

*Roamie View: History
Enhancement*, 2009–2010
— Any Ever, Re'Search Wait'S
Single-channel HD video, 28' 24",
w/ sound

SoiL Thornton

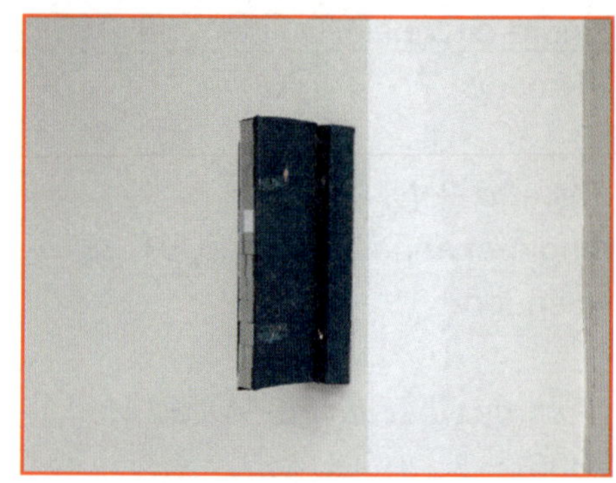

*Splinter from bouquet of each
year of me as you under them
(painting)*, 2023
Epoxy and mirror tiles on acquired
pre-painted Hunter Green (as
mandated by The City of New
York's Local Law No. 47 of 2013)
wood scaffold/ fence piece
originally from 174 Mott Street,
Manhattan

Labor Cont(r)act (assisted), 2024
Aerosol spray paint on wall,
dimensions variable

Marina Xenofontos

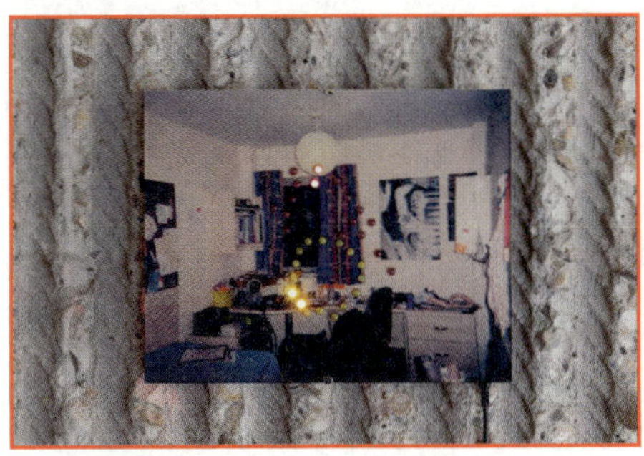

*Plan d'Evacuation (Rain),
(Colour), (Sound) & (Heart)*, 2023
4 MDF wooden panels,
print on Plexiglas,
Arduino board, sensor

ALIAS (Turbo Moniker)

with Soraya Lutangu Bonaventure,
Ivan Cheng, Mami Kang,
Geo Wyex

Text contributions:
Sophia Al-Maria, Josefin Arnell,
Ed Atkins, Felix Bernstein,
Victoria Colmegna, Claire Fontaine,
Robert Glück & Jocelyn Saidenberg,
Annie Goodner, Calla Henkel
& Max Pitegoff, Shiv Kotecha,
Huw Lemmey, Nour Mobarak,
Becket MWN, Ariana Reines,
Tai Shani, Ryan Trecartin,
Angharad Williams.

Staging and sequencing:
Ivan Cheng

Garments:
Good & Bad (Marina M. Kolushova,
Victor Stuhlmann, Ossi Lehtonen)

Camera:
Arvo Leo

Courtroom drawings:
Aloys Oosterwijk

Closing Acts

We find ourselves between the much talked about chairs, in the midst of decisions, anticipations and expectations, in the midst of an exciting process that is set to transform the old courthouse on Parnassusweg into a museum for contemporary art. We have been able to use this building as an office and workplace in recent years, alongside many creatives and cultural producers who have taken up temporary residence here for interim use. But before the building takes the necessary pause for its transformation into a museum, we wanted to show it once again in all its beauty and uniqueness. We wanted to fill this architectural monument with ideas for its future, and present it to the public in a 24-hour act. And above all, we wanted to show how perfectly suited the impressive monumental atrium and the courtrooms of this building are for a changed use – how perfect the spaces in which people aimed to remain unseen can be for visibility, for an experience of art and for the experience of the public.

The invitation to Mohamed Almusibli and Ivan Cheng (who barely knew each other) to curate and organise these 24 hours together, not only combined two exceptional artistic approaches, but also two perspectives: Mohamed Almusibli has visited Amsterdam several times to take the pulse of the local and very diverse art landscape for us with an international eye, and Ivan Cheng has presented challenging projects in his artist-run space Bologna here in Parnassusweg, deeply rooted in the artistic scene of Amsterdam.

At high speed and with continued uncertainty about the date, they created an act that engaged both the building and us in an intense conversation with an unexpectedly large number of artists and artistic ideas. Ivan Cheng's impressive cut-and-paste collage of seventeen texts, which he performed together with Mami Kang, Soraya Lutangu Bonaventure and Geo Wyex, interwove all the transit spaces and the levels of the building atrium with the installations, works and film spaces of the meeting rooms in a dance, text and music play. By selecting the works and choreographing the artistic and culinary experiences, Almusibli and Cheng have jointly created a place that allows the 'ghosts of jurisdiction' to resonate and actually fade away.

Our enormous gratitude goes to Mohamed Almusibli and Ivan Cheng, and to all the artists involved in this grand and great act. Everyone who contributed to this special event is mentioned by name in the imprint and is sincerely thanked. However, I would like to make special mention of the still small but infinitely powerful team of the Hartwig Art Foundation, Henri Sandront, Astrid Schumacher and Annematt Ruseler, who make everything we do on our way to becoming a museum possible.

Beatrix Ruf
Director, Hartwig Art Foundation

COURTPLAY
Exhibition / 24-hour event

Producer
Hartwig Art Foundation
Curators
Mohamed Almusibli
Ivan Cheng
Director
Beatrix Ruf
Project Manager/
Personal Assistant to the Director
Astrid Schumacher
Project Manager/
Content & Community Relations Manager
Henri J Sandront
Head of Communications
Annematt Ruseler

Graphic Identity
Sabo Day
Design
Sabo Day, Nerijus Rimkus

Audio Visual Production
Jody Behre
Alex Boonstra
Ernst van Dillen
Ali Çağlar Erdoğan
Henry Evbuos
Jonas Kraft
Tom Lavrenenko
Joshua Nieli
Alexi Papamarkou
Jochem Smaal
Tjip Telman
Jonathan Vervoort
Art Handling and Technical Production
Tild Greene
Folkert van der Hoek
Dmitry Nakoryakov
Loïc Le Provôt-Barbier
Tomasz Skibicki

Host Co-ordinator
Angela van Kalsbeek
and special thanks to Holland Festival

Hosts
Abdellah Id Abdelah Ou Ahmed
Noa Appelman
Matteo Attene
Tea Barbateskovic
Berend Boot
Wieke Bouma
Wineke Brans
Naomi Dorothea
Sam Eveleens
Lois de Groot
Joke Hienekamp
Helga Marx
Charlotte Rocchi
Eva Scholder
Francisco Seambelar Suarez
Wieneke van der Vrede
Bar Manager
Isa Soares
Security
Evnt Mgmt B.V.

COURTPLAY
Publication

Publisher
Hartwig Art Foundation

Authors
Sophia Al-Maria
Josefin Arnell
Ed Atkins
Felix Bernstein
Victoria Colmegna
Claire Fontaine
Robert Glück & Jocelyn Saidenberg
Annie Goodner
Calla Henkel & Max Pitegoff
Shiv Kotecha
Huw Lemmey
Nour Mobarak
Bookot MWN
Ariana Reines
Tai Shani
Ryan Trecartin
Angharad Williams

Editors
Mohamed Almusibli
Ivan Cheng
Managing Editor
Henri J Sandront
Design
Sabo Day, assisted by Augustinas Milkus
Copy Editing and Proofreading
Clare Manchester
Print
NPN Drukkers, Breda
Illustrations
Aloys Oosterwijk
Cover Image
Doriann Kransberg, Stadsarchief Amsterdam,
toegangsnummer 10192
Photography
LNDWstudio

Printed in Europe

Co-publisher
JRPIEditions
Rue des Bains, 39
CH–1205 Geneva
www.jrp-editions.com

ISBN 978-3-03764-624-3

JRPIEditions publications are available
internationally at selected bookstores and
from the following distribution partners:

Switzerland
AVA Verlagsauslieferung AG
www.ava.ch

Germany and Austria
Through JRPIEditions
books@jrp-editions.com

France
Les presses du réel
www.lespressesdureel.com

UK, other European countries, USA,
Canada, Asia, and Australia
ARTBOOKID.A.P.
www.artbook.com

**HARTWIG
ART
FOUNDATION**

Hartwig Art Foundation is dedicated to
fostering and facilitating the production,
presentation, mediation, preservation,
and collection of contemporary art.
In addition to its multiple activities in
productions with artists and partnerships
with a wide range of institutions, Hartwig Art
Foundation is currently developing a new
museum for contemporary art in Amsterdam.

P.O. Box 51153
NL–1007 ED Amsterdam

Stay up to date and sign up to our newsletter
www.hartwigartfoundation.nl

@hartwigartfoundation